Nick Bollettieri doesn't know anything about tennis.

—John McEnroe, 1978

Tennis coaches say that Nick doesn't know anything about tennis because he can't even play tennis.

—Jim Martz, *Tennis Magazine*, 1980

Nick will always be the greatest tennis coach in the world.

—Carling Bassett-Seguso

Nick Bollettieri is a national treasure. He has been one of the country's leading high performance coaches for decades. Nick was an early pioneer in creating a peer training model that became a standard for tennis academies all over the world, He's helped to develop and inspire some of the greatest players in our sport.

—Jon Vegosen, USTA Chairman and President, 2011-2012

Nick Bollettieri has always been a man with great vision and a charismatic personality that energizes everyone in his presence. I have watched Nick coach athletes of all abilities, from professional status such as Monica Seles, Andre Agassi and Jim Courier to junior high school beginners. His enthusiasm and ability to communicate to players of all levels is outstanding. His positive teachings, with his energetic approach, usually lead to the development of a successful tennis player.

—Dick Vitale, ABC/ESPN basketball analyst

CHANGING THE GAME

Nick Bollettieri
with Bob Davis
edited by Chris Angermann

Published by New Chapter Publisher

Bollettieri: Changing the Game

ISBN 978-1-938842-16-0

New Chapter Publisher
32 South Osprey Ave
Suite 102
Sarasota, FL 34236
tel. 941-954-4690
www.newchapterpublisher.com

Bollettieri: Changing the Game
is distributed by Midpoint Trade Books

Printed in the United States of America

Cover design and layout by Cathleen Shaw
www.shawcreativegroup.com

Photos credits:
Art Seitz: 146, 154
Amanda Ambrose Photography: 263, 271
Ashlie Fulmer Photography: 256, 266
Christine Lintz: 258
Soderquist Photography: 260

CHANGING THE GAME

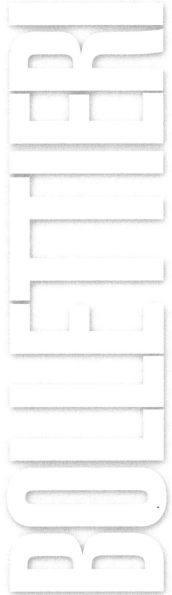

Nick Bollettieri
with Bob Davis
edited by Chris Angermann

CONTENTS

We make a living by what we get;
we make a life by what we give.

—attributed to Winston Churchill

DEDICATION

After six decades in the business of tennis (60 years filled with public accolades and harsh criticism), I thought I should take the dedication of my life's story very seriously. It would have been easy to choose an individual who altered the landscape of American tennis. Players with names like McEnroe, Connors, Lendl, Navratilova, Evert, Borg and Agassi came to mind. These players were dynamic role models who dominated the sport for a period of time. Their styles and personas were painstakingly imitated while they invoked images of greatness in the minds of children and adults alike. These and many others are worthy of mention when one speaks of great tennis players.

When I decided to name my book *Bollettieri: Changing the Game*, I felt compelled to dedicate my life story to the two people who not only changed American tennis, but also with poise and quiet confidence, elevated the sport of tennis to unprecedented levels worldwide. These two people "Changed the Game" across the planet and left an indelible mark on the human conscience.

I dedicate my life story to Arthur Ashe and Billie Jean King. Most people in life build foundations from the ground up. Arthur and Billie Jean tore down foundations. They did this to enable people to have a chance to survive in life. Without people like them, tennis wouldn't be where it is today.

Arthur could have been president—that's the way I feel about him. Very few people could endure the indignities that he encountered without succumbing to anger and despair. He turned the other cheek time and again while honing his skills to become a world champion against all odds. He then used his celebrity to advocate for diversity and changed the collective minds and practices of people

9

around the world. Arthur was a human rights activist who challenged us to reach inside and find our better selves.

Billie Jean is a pioneer who fought for women's rights. Don't think for one moment that her match against Bobby Riggs was simply a victory on the tennis court. That match was a defining moment in human evolution—a moment that allowed 3.5 billion women, about 50% of the world's population, to dream of equality. So, allowing another perspective, Bobby Riggs was not a combatant, he was a partner in an event that forever changed the landscape of human rights.

Billie Jean King and Arthur Ashe are much more than champions on the tennis court. They are both *"Champions of Humanity"* who were able to dream wonderful dreams, and each was willing to pay the price for those dreams to come true! I am proud to have known them and called each of them "Friend."

FOREWORD

by Jim Courier

Nick Bollettieri is a pioneer. He altered the tennis landscape when he started the Nick Bollettieri Tennis Academy (NBTA) in Bradenton, Florida in 1981. Until then, most top junior players practiced at their local tennis clubs or in public parks with whomever their parents or coach could find for them, a haphazard process at best. At NBTA, Nick created the first full-time boarding school where the best junior tennis players from around the world lived and practiced with (and against) each other in a highly disciplined, professional and competitive environment. He hired coaches, physical trainers and even a sports psychologist (Dr. Jim Loehr, himself a pioneer in *that* field) to give the students all of the tools they needed to pursue excellence. They were trained in the same fashion as the top professionals who also spent time at Nick's Academy. It was a remarkable new approach for those lucky enough to be there. I became one of the lucky ones starting in 1984 when I was 14 years old.

Nick has never been interested in conforming to the norm. One of the results of his tennis revolution was that he accelerated the path to the pros for male players. Teen girls like Chris Evert, Tracy Austin and Andrea Jaeger had already made the leap from juniors to pros with great success—made possible by the fact that in women's tennis, girls matured earlier physically and mentally. But before NBTA came along, all of the best American male players—Arthur Ashe, Stan Smith, Jimmy Connors, John McEnroe—went to college for at least one year to get more seasoning before they would turn pro.

Nick didn't believe in playing the waiting game. He wanted success, and he wanted it now. With Nick's vision being implemented at NBTA, the first male American teen prodigies, Jimmy Arias and Aaron Krickstein, who would be followed shortly by Andre Agassi, both made their marks on the pro game as teenagers without going to college. In fact, they turned pro and hit the road full-time before they turned 17.

Since then, Nick's innovations have become the norm. All of the top juniors skip college and go pro in their teens. It's rare for them to stay at home unless they live in cities like Los Angeles, Miami, Paris or Barcelona, which all have topflight coaching and training. It's a given that promising players have to move to where the best training is. I lived and trained at NBTA from 1985 to 1989. Those were incredibly formative years in my life and I look back on them fondly (even if Andre Agassi described it as being similar to *Lord of the Flies)*. Nick changed the course of my life, as he has with so many others, by offering me a scholarship to attend NBTA, which my family couldn't otherwise afford. Even though I was one of the best players in the U.S. for my age, I still knew I was at a disadvantage training-wise compared to the Academy kids, and I desperately wanted to be there to ensure I wouldn't get left behind.

The Academy was eye-opening for me. It was a proving ground where I received top-notch coaching from Nick and the many other capable members of his staff, and could test myself daily on (and off) the court against the best juniors in the world. Nick provided us the opportunity to push each other to greater heights. I'm not sure what course my tennis career would have taken had I not been given that opportunity. Little did I know I would end up being one of Nick's students who would reach the No. 1 ranking in the world.

One of the great things about Nick's experiment was that it was a true meritocracy. All of us there wanted to be the best tennis player on campus, and there was only one way to prove it—by winning on the court. We played matches daily to see which rung we occupied in our group ladders. I was in Group 1, which was the highest level on campus. At age 14, I was playing against boys as old as 18. Andre and I were the youngest in that group when I got there, and it was a big change having to battle on the back courts daily with players who were not only the best in their hometowns, as I was, but also bigger, stronger, and as hungry as I was. It made me tough in a hurry.

One of the rewards for playing well on the back courts in Group 1 and moving up in the pecking order was to get "called up" to Stadium Court, where Nick spent his days teaching a select few players. I remember my first time was nerve-racking. Nick was the guy who was footing the bill for me, investing in my future with no back-end participation clause. I desperately wanted to impress him and show him he had made the right decision, and I was going to be a great ambassador for the Bollettieri Academy—a star on his team. When I got to Stadium Court I could barely hit a ball on the strings.

He stopped the practice, pulled me aside and told me to forget where I was and to "just concentrate on hitting the damn ball." "It doesn't matter who's watching you," he said. "The ball doesn't care if I am here or not. Just do what you know how to do."

That seems like simple advice, right? For me it was like a door opened. Suddenly, I was freed up, swinging and playing my best tennis. I've carried that memory with me whenever I've gotten into situations where I'm under pressure and start to doubt myself. "Just do what you know how to do" can be transferred to many areas of life—pubic speaking, business meetings, etc. It's one of the great gifts Nick has given to me and countless others.

At the same time, Nick custom fits his advice to each player from a strategic and technical standpoint. Most other coaches operate with a cookie-cutter philosophy, insisting their players all play the same way. He's coached Monica Seles, Andre Agassi, Maria Sharapova, Serena Williams—the list goes on forever seemingly—and each of those players has a different grip, swing and style; yet they're all Bollettieri protégés. My own grips and swings will never be found in a textbook on tennis, and a few of my earlier coaches tried to correct them (although not successfully because I resisted). Nick saw what my limitations were (the extreme western grip of my forehand and my baseball swing backhand), and he built my game around maximizing my strengths (serve and forehand) and protecting my weakness (backhand) in order to give me the best chance for success.

Has Nick been proven right with this philosophy for his players? Just check the numbers. He's had 10 No. 1 ranked players in the world, and countless others who have been in the top 10 during his career. Case closed.

Nick is an incredibly generous man. Millions of Nick's dollars—and the dollars of several of his generous friends—made it possible for people like me to pursue our dream and come to the best place in the world to try and be a professional tennis player. He literally fed, housed, and coached many of us out of his own pocket, and for that I will forever be thankful.

In 1987 he raised about $200,000 to pay for a traveling team of eight young amateurs to get additional experience and test the waters in regards to our future. I was fortunate enough to be a part of that, to travel the world with his coaches (his son Jimmy was my primary coach on the team) and to see if we were good enough to turn pro or if we should go to college instead for more seasoning. After six months I had played well enough to turn pro, and Nick promptly assigned another coach to travel with me, at his cost, on the tour. He never asked for a penny in return.

There's a lot to admire about Nick. One of the things I admire most about him is his passion for everything he does. He loves what he does and that energy is infectious. Nick has used his passion and commitment to change the sport of tennis. But more importantly, he has changed thousands of lives for the better. I am lucky enough to be living proof of it. And to me, that is his real legacy.

Jim Courier is a former World No. 1 professional tennis player, holder of four Grand Slam singles titles, is a well respected tennis commentator and a leader on the Senior Tour.

INTRODUCTION

Quite often, articles and commentators talk about me as the greatest tennis coach ever, but I feel somewhat out of place being named the best when there are so many other coaches who have contributed greatly to the game of tennis, including Robert Lansdorp, Harry Hopman, Vic Braden, John Wilkeson, Dr. Robert Johnson, Richard Williams, Paul Annacone, Bob Brett, Rick Macci, Brad Gilbert, Niki Pilic, Dick Gould, Dennis Van Der Meer, Welby Van Horn and Steve Wilkinson, to name a few.

I would, however, accept being named the best-ever *crazy* tennis coach who went in a totally different direction in the development of players. I started the first stand-alone academy where youngsters received intense professional training. I encouraged them to turn pro earlier, in many cases before they graduated high school. I emphasized the power game in tennis with the Bollettieri killer forehand, the sonic serve and the ballistic backhand long before they became the norm.

Being something of a cowboy and pioneer has made me a controversial figure at times, and I have welcomed the occasional hullabaloo surrounding my approach. Yes, I am an entrepreneur and promoter, but if I had not done what I did, my chances of any success would have been much lower.

Writing this autobiography has allowed me to reflect not only on what I have achieved so far, but also brought to my attention the influence of others and the wisdom they implanted in me, notably my grandmother, my grandfather and my parents. Along with my stint in the Army, they taught me to have courage, believe in myself and that I could do what I set my mind to, and never think that failure along the way meant that I made a poor decision.

Many would say that I have lived an expansive, sprawling life, big as Mount Rushmore; and they may be right. Myself, I would say I've lived a heck of a life! I have had the opportunity to coach some of the best tennis players in the world and to introduce tennis to some of the neediest neighborhoods in America. I have met and worked with well-known, famous and wealthy people, and people from ordinary walks of life. Many of them have become good friends, have gone to bat for me in times of crisis and difficulties, and helped in any way they could.

Along the way, I have owned fancy cars and beautiful homes. And I have had several girlfriends and been married eight times, becoming the proud father of five children, two adopted children and grandfather of four.

There are plenty of other stories, too—some of them laced with life's lessons, others just crazy and fun. I will leave you to judge what they all add up to, although I can assure you I'm not finished yet. I'm just warming up!

One of the things I have learned on my journey is that I have been blessed with a unique gift for coaching, motivating and developing players and young people of all kinds of backgrounds and talent. I also know that without the help of numerous others—my friends, sponsors, supporters and my coaches and longtime staff at the Academy—I could not have accomplished all I did and would not be where I am today.

I am eternally grateful to them, and this book is a way of saying "Thank you, danke, merci, grazie, arigato, doh je, spasibo, gracias…"

If my example can help inspire others to pursue uncharted courses and crazy paths to realize their dreams, I have done my job. If my storied journey can help others to realize that everything is possible and that, despite occasional setbacks, life can be filled with fun, laughter, excitement and success for everyone, no one will be more pleased than me.

I know it can be done. I have lived it. So fasten your seatbelts and prepare for takeoff! This is a "we-can-do-it" story!

Nick Bollettieri
Bradenton 2014

Me at age three in front of our home
on the Fourth of July.

CHAPTER 1

My Beginnings

I was born in 1931 in my grandmother's house in a village about 30 minutes outside of New York City that was called North Pelham at the time. It was a natural birth, but I've been told that it wasn't an easy delivery. Guess I started out as a bit of a challenge, and I'm damn sure I'll go out the same way. My sister Rita told me that I was born early in the morning, and I think my natural habit of being an early riser is due to that delivery time. To this day, I am up at 5:45 a.m. I do my stretching and 50 sit-ups, work out with light weights at the gym or my "office" at IMG Academy—it used to be an old metal desk next to one of the courts at the indoor tennis center, but my staff recently surprised me with a new one—and begin my duties at 7. I don't eat breakfast, but I always seem to have energy to burn.

My grandmother's two-story house was large enough to accommodate both of our families. The DeFillipos, on my mother's side, lived on the ground floor and we, the Bollettieris—my father, mother, older sister, younger brother and I—lived upstairs. It was tight quarters on the top floor. We all shared three bedrooms—my brother and I doubled up—and one small bathroom. Imagine five people maneuvering around each other in the morning before school and work. By today's standards, it would seem impossible, but back then, families managed.

The DeFillipo house was situated on a large, two-acre lot, and every inch was covered with flowers, grapevines, a vegetable garden, a chicken house and fig trees. I was responsible for collecting eggs from the chicken coop each morning. Grandpa would make his homemade wine the old-fashioned way—in our basement. The entire family crushed the grapes by jumping up and down on them in bare feet.

Because of my diminutive size and because I was the youngest, I was allowed a little leeway growing up. No one ever told me to be quiet, and my friends will tell you I haven't stopped talking to this day.

We were one big happy family, both upstairs and downstairs, but make no mistake—the entire house, from the wine cellar to the attic, was ruled by Grandma DeFillipo. Every night, all 12 of us sat down to eat together at the table in her kitchen. Except Grandma; she never sat. She was busy serving the different pastas, meatballs, sausages, bread and salads. Grandma never asked us what we wanted; she simply made the selections for us. Salad always came with the main meal, never before.

Things would get going when Grandpa tipped a bottle of his homemade wine above his mouth and let the red liquid

The DeFillipo-Bollettieri house.

flow. At that point, we ate. And Grandma kept filling the plates. If any food dropped to the floor, she would point to it, pick it up, make the sign of the cross and put it back on our plate; and we ate it. No one in the household could smoke, though my mom and dad would sneak out to the open sun porch to get in a few puffs. Did I say no one could smoke? During dinner, Grandpa DeFillipo would always light up one of his five-inch guinea stinkers. The fumes would drift upstairs, downstairs and even to the cellar, but no one ever said a word about it.

When we were done, Grandma would take whatever was left over on the plates and the kitchen counter, and in the pots and pans, and pile it all into a huge pot. The next day, she would serve it as her most recent concoction, saying "mangia;" and we ate. No matter how it tasted, we would tell her it was good. Believe it or not, my grandma would keep feeding me and say, "Sonny, God is looking at you, keep eating." I'm told that when I was a baby I became so fat that I did very little walking until I was almost 18 months old!

My mother, Mary, was one of a long line of Marys in my family. She was a traditional Italian, stay-at-home mom who put all her time and energy into taking care of the family. She lived for others, worried a lot and never spent money on herself. She wore the same apron and dress all week long. After her death, we found birthday and Christmas presents she'd put away in the attic over the course of 20 years—all of them unopened! For as long as I can remember, she gave me three pieces of advice: "Save your money." "Eat." And, "Stay with the family." She repeated them to me often, even later on in life, probably because I only followed the second one.

Mom was a stickler for neatness. She didn't tolerate unmade beds, clothes on the floor or messy closets. She didn't get involved in our sports activities or schoolwork, leaving them to Dad. But she saw it as her personal responsibility to make sure all of us left the house in clothes that were clean and ironed.

In an effort to save money, she and my grandmother would wash the family clothes by hand and hang them in the backyard on the clothesline to dry. Not only was this economical, but Mom loved the way the clothes smelled when allowed to dry in the fresh, clean outdoor air. This was a common practice in suburban communities and was also a regular sight in apartment buildings in the big cities, until residents complained and the management companies no longer permitted it. But in our home, the practice continued. It made for a great place to play hide and seek, though Mom got annoyed if she caught us.

Of course, wintertime was another matter. Then Mom would dry the clothes on a line in the basement of our home. It took a bit longer, as there were no breezes, but it still saved the cost of buying and operating an electric dryer. At the time, we never imagined how that common, penny-wise practice would lead to a tremendous loss for the entire family.

In many ways, my dad and mom were polar opposites. He always looked on the bright side of things and knew how to enjoy himself. Handsome and flamboyant, he was meticulous about his clothes and his cars. He also was smart and had been an excellent student at New Rochelle High School. Somehow, Grandma and Grandpa Bollettieri saved enough money from their butcher shop to send him to Fordham University in New York City. He excelled there, too, and graduated at age 21 with a degree in chemistry and became a pharmacist. When he married my mom, they moved into Grandma DeFillipo's house, which is why he opened his own drugstore on 5th Avenue and Lincoln Avenue in North Pelham. It was directly across the street from the fire station.

The Bollettieri home.

A few years later, he became fire chief. He had political aspirations and ran for mayor, but lost by one vote.

Dad wrote and spoke his parents' native language fluently. I've been accused of speaking four languages—Italian, Spanish, English and with my hands—but I've never had difficulty getting my point across. At the tennis academy, my approach has helped me communicate with its many foreign students. In my dad's case, being bilingual allowed him to help many of our Italian neighbors who didn't speak English with their income tax filings—at no charge, of course. In fact, he helped everybody in whatever way he could. Everyone in our little town knew everyone else and many of the residents came to my dad's drugstore. It seems that most had charge accounts, and he didn't want to take legal steps to collect the money owed to him. It wasn't long before my dad went bankrupt. Unfortunately, I think his lack of smarts regarding finances rubbed off on me.

I certainly inherited his giving and trusting genes when it comes to being generous and seeing the best in others, as well as his ability to bounce back from failures and try again. He never stopped striving to improve himself. After he lost his pharmacy, he managed to achieve high positions with the Winthrop Chemical Company and later moved to Bala Cynwyd, north of Philadelphia, to become vice president of Baxter Laboratories, which manufactured medical devices and pharmaceuticals.

My sister Rita was a few years older than me and was an excellent student. Many thought she would become a doctor, but in the end she became an outstanding nurse. I really don't remember much about her until she was much older. She was married twice and had a son, Phillip, and a daughter, Mary Lou.

Rita and I didn't have much to do with one another because we lived far apart most of our lives, but we stayed in touch. My parents willed all their money to Rita—they feared my wife at the time would get her hands on it!—which was probably the right thing to do. By then, I had already experienced a few divorces. Actually, Rita played another important role in my life. Like my mom, she was a "glass-half-empty" type of person who worried about everything, and it was obvious to me that it affected the quality of her life. I vowed to take the opposite point of view, which was one of the best decisions I ever made and taught me early on the power of positive thinking.

My brother, James Thomas Bollettieri—Jimmy Boy, as we called him—was a kind and gentle soul. Although we shared the same room, we got along well. It didn't hurt that he idolized his older brother! He loved learning and spent all his free time with his nose in a book. While I was out playing sports, Jimmy Boy was reading. He was so bright that by the age of 14, he skipped two grades ahead in school! He wanted to be a doctor, and I'm sure he would have been a successful one—maybe a brain surgeon—but God had other plans for him.

When my grandparents came to the United States from Naples, Italy, they settled in two adjoining New York suburbs—the Bollettieris in New Rochelle, a mostly Italian community, and the DeFillipos in North Pelham, a middle-class town comprised mostly of African-Americans, Italians and Irish. The neighborhoods were all one happy family, a true melting pot. We met on the streets, mingled in school, played sports together and we all got along. The fire department and police force were integrated, too. Several of my uncles were cops. It made no difference what color, religion or ethnic background you were, and I grew up without prejudice toward anyone. Again, my father set the tone. When I spent time in his pharmacy, I'd see him treat all of his customers with equal respect.

In those days, parents never seemed to worry if their kids were safe. We walked everywhere, to grammar school about two miles away, and later on, to Pelham Memorial High School, an even farther distance on the rich side of town. We were seldom concerned with drugs, bullying or violence.

One time, though, I came home from grade school crying. My uncles asked me what happened. When I said that a big boy beat me up, they were furious. They told me exactly what to do the next day: "Walk up to the big boy and punch him right on his nose—and then run as fast as you can." I did! In fact, I'm still running.

The neighborhood was filled with kids and we were given our freedom. Every day when I got back from school, Grandma DeFillipo would look at my knickers. (For you youngsters, I don't mean Snickers. Knickers, short for knickerbockers, were baggy pants that fell just below the knees.) If mine were the slightest bit dirty at the knees, Grandma would smile because she knew I had been playing marbles on the side of the road. If there was no dirt, she knew I was wandering about—and that was a no-no. She would give me a smack and say, "Sonny, go and play and be a good boy." At dinnertime, Grandma would go to the front door and yell, "Sonny, come home!" If I didn't hear her, a few of my friends would find me and deliver the message. All my friends were terrified of Grandma.

Before my father opened his pharmacy, the Bollettieri family's popularity was due largely to my grandfather, who had a super-duper butcher shop in New Rochelle. He carried all the meats that Italian mothers would use to prepare the family meals. In addition to a variety of pastas, he also had a selection of meatballs, sausages and other delicacies. Directly across the street from the butcher shop was the original Bollettieri home. In later years, the family moved to North Pelham on 9th Avenue, right up the street from Grandma DeFillipo's house on 6th Street, and when my parents got married, they moved in upstairs.

Back in those days, family togetherness was everything. During the month of June, Dad would take vacation and Mom would prepare food, drinks and umbrellas for our weekend trips to Orchard Beach, only a few miles away. Sometimes we would brave the much longer journey to Jones Beach on Long Island, which had lots of crashing waves. This was always my favorite jaunt because I got a chance to surf, which is one of my most enjoyable pastimes. I turn 83 in 2014 and I still surf every chance I get, especially with my sons Jimmy Boy (named after my brother), nine-year-old Giovanni and six-year-old Giacomo.

Another of my fond recollections was our Saturday night visits to the amusement park in White Plains, which was about 10 miles away. I remember asking Grandpa to go on the roller coaster with us once. We assured him that it would go slow and when it reached the top of the track, he would be able to see the entire park. He had no idea what to expect. As the wagon climbed the long incline at the start, all our eyes were on him. At the very top, he enjoyed the panoramic view of the park for a split second before we raced down the other side at 60 miles per hour. I can still hear him yelling, "Rallenta! Rallenta!" (Slow down! Slow down!) We all thought this was hysterical, but let me tell you, at the end of the ride we ran like bandits. Mom finally calmed him down and by the weekend meal he proudly told the entire family about his ride.

Throughout my youth, I was something of a hustler. I would get candy and ice cream from my father's drugstore and give it to my friends. Sometimes, I'd sell it to them. I probably contributed to him going bankrupt. There was a black lady living nearby who had beautiful dahlias in her garden. I'd steal them and sell them back to her. She knew that I had taken them, but bought them anyway. I had a lemonade stand, too. Later on I caddied, washed cars and worked as a lifeguard. I loved being outdoors and getting a tan.

But all I ever really wanted to do was play sports. Touch football on a dead-end street, king of the mountain, ice skating on a nearby frozen lake or sledding down hilly streets—I lived for sports. My uncles on the DeFillipo side—Charlie, Tony, Joseph and Michael—were all big guys and outstanding football and basketball players (many of them received athletic scholarships to college), and they would often play tag football with me. I would be the quarterback and over a period of time developed confidence that I could deliver the ball to the receiver. When I entered high school, I was introduced to Coach Schilling, the football coach who was there when my uncles played for the team. I became captain of the team in my senior year.

There were actually three Pelhams back then: North Pelham, Pelham Heights and Pelham Manor, where the cream of the crop lived. When I got to high school, I found a way to spend time in Pelham Manor by dating girls from that part of town. One in particular, Bobbie, was my dancing partner at socials. She ended up marrying Alan Holton, who was on the football team with me and is a super-nice guy. They live in Boca Raton, Florida, now, and I always see them at the Sony Tennis Tournament. They subscribe to the philosophy that "marriage is a onetime deal—forever." My philosophy, as it turned out, was quite different!

During the summer months, I would spend a good deal of time at the Hampshire Country Club in Mamaroneck, New York, another upscale community. My cousin was the caddie master there, and that connection allowed me to make good money as a caddie and valet park attendant. I would also act as a server at the big parties that the club occasionally hosted.

Pelham Memorial High School.

My uncle, John Lightfoot, had married my Aunt Rose De-Fillipo; he was well-to-do and a member of a tennis club in New Rochelle. The Hampshire Country Club was closed on Mondays and one day he asked me to join him at his tennis club. He was one of the best players there and his opponent hadn't shown up, so he asked me to hit balls with him. I said, "Are you kidding? Tennis is a sissy sport!" But I obliged him, and I had no idea what I was doing; I chased the balls around, trying to hit them back any which way I could. I was almost too embarrassed to admit that I had had a great time and ask if I could play more often with him. That was my sophomore year in high school, and even though I didn't go out for high school tennis, I continued playing with my uncle from time to time. By senior year, he encouraged me to try out for the tennis team when I got to college, and I did!

I was a weak student, academically. This was not because I wasn't bright enough to master the subjects, but because I couldn't relate them to any plans for the future. I had no idea what I wanted to do, I just knew it had to be something big and exciting, so I couldn't get my heart into the schoolwork and was a persistent underachiever. As one of my teachers commented, "Nick's attention span is all over the place. When he applies himself, he ranks among the best of my students, but he falls short of his capacity." In biology class, for example, I didn't know one end of a frog from another, but I noticed that whenever the teacher—she stood 5' 1" on tiptoe—looked at someone and he or she looked away, she'd call on them. So when she looked at me, I always gave her a big smile, and she never called on me! That ability to observe habits and ways of behavior in others has served me well throughout my career coaching players, for whom a slight adjustment in grip or stance can make a huge difference in performance.

During my senior year in high school, my parents bought a new house on Lincoln Avenue and Young Avenue. It was a bit larger, but still in the same neighborhood, and we moved there to have more room to ourselves. My dad also bought himself a new car—a sleek, green Buick Riviera. Sixty-five years later, I can still see it in my mind, sitting proudly in our driveway.

One particular day is imprinted on my memory as if it were yesterday. There had been a morning snow, but by afternoon it had melted. My closest friend, Richie Daronco, came by to see me and, as we were talking, my dad surprised me by handing me the keys to his new Buick. "Take it for a spin and let me know what you think," he said.

Richie and I looked at each other and away we went. We drove to the next town where my girlfriend, Joanie Langbein, attended New Rochelle High School. I was excited to show off the new car, but as we arrived I spotted her getting into a four-door convertible with another girl and two boys. I said to Richie, "What the heck is going on?" and stepped on the accelerator to catch up to them. By then it was late in the afternoon and little did I know that the melted show had turned into slippery ice. When I took a turn too fast, I lost control and the car slid up on the lawn of a house that had huge rocks spread throughout the front yard. BANG!

I said, "Holy sh*t!" and we got out to assess the damage. We had smashed the passenger door. A lady came out of the house and waved at us, but we jumped back in the car, took off and just kept going. I quickly made up a tale about us watching a basketball game at the high school and when we came out, we saw the car all banged up. Richie looked at me with his eyes as big as snowballs. I told him not to worry, just stick to our story.

When we got home my dad was standing on the porch of our new house. He asked, "So, how do you like the new car?" I said, "Dad, I love the car, but you'll never believe what happened!" As I continued to talk, Dad moved closer to me, and Richie moved further away. When I had finished, Dad asked me to repeat my story. Before I could complete the first sentence—Pow!—he popped me for the first and last time in my life. Then he delivered a memorable message, "When you have to make up a story, at some point it'll catch up with you and the truth will come out. So no matter what—always tell the truth right off the bat and accept the consequences!"

I was as stunned by the unexpected blow as by the realization that he knew exactly what had happened. How could he have known? Well, I later learned that the lady who'd waved after us wrote down my license plate number and called the New Rochelle police, who tracked down the owner's name. She then called the North Pelham police station where three of my uncles were cops! They loved me, but had no choice but to tell my father.

Dad fixed the car; I decided not to continue my relationship with Joanie—and I didn't marry her! (Too bad I didn't follow that path throughout my life!) And I never let Richie forget that he set a world record in the long jump when he leapt down the six steps to our new house and took off!

He later was appointed by President Reagan as a federal judge in the U.S. District Court for the Southern District of New York. In 1988, two days after he dismissed a sex discrimination suit filed by a young woman, her father shot him to death at his house in Pelham. I was at the French Open at the time, so I couldn't attend his funeral. I was shocked and saddened by the news; Richie was only 56 years old.

Still, the Buick Riviera experience is a fond memory of better times with a good friend, and it delivered an important life lesson about telling the truth (well, maybe not always the whole truth). It also offers a revealing insight into my dad's character and values, which I have built on, hoping that I would one day possess the same characteristics and be admired by my own children.

I know that he's smiling down on me as I follow in his footsteps.

*On the steps of the DeFillipo-Bollettieri house
during a recent visit.*

I went to college with Nick and graduated with him in 1953. During that time we became close friends and have remained so for over 50 years...I would not be alive today but for Nick's intervention and salesmanship.

It was my freshman year and the Korean War was just starting up. I had Father John O'Keefe as my professor in the first philosophy course I took in college. I flunked the final exam and won my way out of college, so I decided to go back to Milwaukee and join the Marine Corps.

Nick said, "Baloney. Let me talk to Father O'Keefe." He went to his office, told him that he and many of his classmates were interested in keeping me in school, and that it would require Father O'Keefe to lose the exam and give me a passing grade. Well, I wound up with an 83 on my report card and stayed in school.

Two of my high school classmates joined the Marines. One came back from Korea with a steel plate in his head and had to learn to speak all over again, and the other came home in a box and I was one of his pallbearers. So there is no doubt in my mind that I would not have lived past 1950 without Nick's intervention. He saved my life and that allowed me to finish college, do my time in the service, get married and have three kids and eight grandchildren and live a wonderful life.

—Jerry P. O'Leary, Sr., Potomac, Maryland

CHAPTER 2

College and the Army

Even though I was a pretty darn good quarterback and might have played on a few small college teams, my dad had other ideas. At Fordham University, his professors were Jesuit priests who valued learning, and he wanted me to have a good Catholic education, too. He became good friends with Father Colkin who, among other duties, was in charge of intramural sports. In one of their conversations, Father Colkin mentioned that he was being transferred to Spring Hill College in Mobile, Alabama, a small school of only 1,500 students. He was going to be the athletic director there and promised my dad that if he sent me to Spring Hill, he would make sure I took part in the sports activities, although they only had intramural football. Dad thought that would be perfect for me.

I was surprised that he insisted on driving me himself from New York to Mobile—I figured he would just put me on a plane. I didn't know what to expect, but when we arrived and drove down the long entrance road lined with beautiful azalea bushes to the administration building, I noticed that the men there were all dressed in black with white collars. When I asked my father who they were, it finally became clear why he'd driven me there himself. They were priests and lay brothers, and they would be my teachers. Jesuits—what a surprise! I didn't say much, but as time passed I found out how to sway them, and most of the time, I got things my way.

I majored in Spanish. Mr. Cuen, my language teacher, wasn't a priest and had a large family whose health he worried about. By then, my dad was working for the pharmaceutical company, and so I had him send down some special vitamins to give to Mr. Cuen, which he appreciated. When the time came for the final, I told him I wasn't prepared for it. I asked if I could just put down what I knew, and he could grade me on that? He agreed and I managed to squeak by. The philosophy teacher, Father O'Keefe, liked to tipple, and taking him out for a glass of wine from time to time did wonders for my grades!

By the time I was an upperclassman, I basically ran the whole college. Every important student activity went through me. I organized everyone's social lives, setting my friends up with dates, pulling off pranks and hazing freshmen who were too full of themselves. As in high school, I made no big academic splash, managing to get by in my classes while concentrating on ROTC and sports. I participated in intramural football and, following my Uncle John's advice, went out for the tennis team and played both singles and doubles for the next four years. Although I had fun, I knew I had no special talent for the sport and had no plans to do anything with it in the future. Wow! What a turnabout!

I include this photo (me, lower right) to prove to John McEnroe and Jim Martz that I did play tennis before opening my cademy. In fact, this photo of my collegiate tennis team was taken about five years before John was born.

I don't know if I could have stayed in one place for four years if we didn't have a lot of fun along the way. One weekend a buddy of mine and I drove his car to Miami. Coming back, we loaded up with bags of grapefruit and oranges. It was foggy and when we reached a place where the road diverged, we drove straight on, right through the billboard in the middle of the fork. Luckily, we were okay, just a little banged up. My friend's insurance company made a settlement, and everyone at school loved both the story and eating the tropical fruit, bruises and all.

My college years would have made for a happy-go-lucky, all-American experience if it hadn't been for a tragic event that befell my family. You always hear about terrible accidents that happen to others, but you never think it will happen to you, and then one day, it hits home with a vengeance. In my case, it occurred when I was 19, the winter of my sophomore year. I was making one of my rare visits to the campus library—I considered it sort of out of bounds and preferred to spend my time with my "underbosses" planning social activities. I can still remember looking up from my textbook to see Father O'Keefe walking towards me. He had such a serious expression I figured I must be in big trouble. But then he sat down next to me, sighed and told me that my younger brother was dead.

Remember the clothes my mom would hang up to dry in the basement? Apparently, Jimmy Boy was on his way down there and tripped, fell down the stairs and hung himself in the clothesline. He had just had breakfast, and as the line cut across his throat, he vomited and choked on his food.

I was stunned. I hardly heard Father O'Keefe assuring me that it was all part of God's divine wisdom and that God had big plans for my brother. On my flight from Mobile to New York, I was in a daze. I went directly to the funeral home. When I saw my brother lying in the coffin with nothing but kindness written across his innocent face, a wave of hopeless sadness washed over me, and I sobbed uncontrollably. It still happens sometimes, even today, almost 65 years later.

It was by far the most traumatic event that I've ever experienced. Sure, parents we love pass on and we miss them. But parents are supposed to die *before* their children. It's the "way" of things. So many people say that time will heal everything, but whenever I think of Jimmy Boy today, tears come to my eyes and I wish that he could be here as part of my life and career. I think about what magnificent feats he might have accomplished, had he survived. My parents never got over his loss either. Even now, I can't figure out why he was taken so soon. My only hope is that Jimmy Boy can look down, smile and say, "Big Brother Nick, I'm still proud of you!"

I returned to Spring Hill with a heavy heart, vowing to make something of myself, to make my life matter. By my senior year, I

My college yearbook picture.

decided that I wanted to become a Navy fighter pilot. So in May of 1953, I traveled to New Orleans to take the exam for the Naval Air Corps. I passed the physical part of the test, but didn't do so well on the written part. I was deeply disappointed not to be able to pursue my dream. I haven't had many regrets in life, but for more than 40 years I couldn't look up at a plane flying overhead without wishing I was the pilot. But life goes on, and upon my college graduation, I received a second lieutenant commission from the ROTC and was assigned to the Army's Transportation Corps at Fort Story near Norfolk, Virginia.

On weekends off, I would travel to Virginia Beach, Virginia for fun and relaxation and to have a few drinks. It was on the Fourth of July in 1953 that I met a girl named Phyllis Johnson. She and her sister Shirley were at a club called The Casino on the board-walk. They were originally from Roanoke and had come east for greater opportunities than a small, sleepy town in the foothills of the Appalachian Mountains offered. Phyllis worked as a lab technician for an orthodontist and loved to dance. We both did. That night, we boogied with each other for more than two hours. It got late and as

they were leaving, I asked where they normally went to go swimming. Phyllis said at the beach by the Coast Guard building. From then on, whenever I had time off and on weekends, Phyllis and I would go surfing there on rented boogie boards.

Because I was not happy in the Transportation Corps, I volunteered to become a paratrooper

Second lieutenant, Nick Bollettieri.

and began my jump training in Fort Benning, Georgia. Some of my friends kidded me that I only did it for the dough—we got an extra $150 per jump, a lot of money at the time. But there was more to it. Many of my buddies dropped out when they weren't able to keep up with the mental and physical demands, and the total commitment required to succeed in an elite unit. Each member of the team had to be exceptional. Excuses were not tolerated and being content with second place, even if you did the best you could, wasn't acceptable.

I can still remember when our drill sergeant said "give me 10," meaning 10 push-ups, and we had to take a two-second pause between each rep. This made it increasingly difficult to perform the exercise and ridiculously difficult to handle the next 10 push-ups that he would be demanding. About 50 yards away from the regular training ground was a muddy stretch of territory, and that's where the sergeant had us do *our* push-ups. He knew that most of us would not succeed and end up face-first in the mud. His mission was to find out who among us would throw in the towel and quit, and who could deal with the adversity!

Before going further, let me explain my attitude about the paratroopers. I volunteered because I thought the training would allow me to be with others who aspired to be exceptional—gung-ho individuals who had the same outlook that I had. Yes, the training was insanely difficult, and many participants decided that they had made a poor choice and quit. As for me, sometime during the six-week training program, I realized that we were being pushed to be leaders and to accomplish what others felt couldn't be done. This was another important life lesson for me: Only a few, determined individuals possess the resolve and focus to become the best at anything; and I wanted to be one of them. Sure, we worked our butts off every day, 24-7, but it was fulfilling our dreams of becoming paratroopers, to achieve something special. That kind of determination and pride of accomplishment motivates me to this day.

I made it through the six weeks of rigorous training (and would later employ similar tactics at my tennis academy), graduated jump school and earned my paratrooper wings. I was now Second Lieutenant Nicholas J. Bollettieri 04003116 in the 187th Airborne at Fort Campbell in Hopkinsville, Kentucky.

Besides our military duties, we also played football. Our team was a highly competitive outfit as we competed against teams from other bases. Having been the quarterback in high school and college, I felt that I was fairly good at leading the team. It was a lot of fun, especially when the cheerleaders and pretty girls came to watch us play. Unfortunately, the good times didn't last very long.

One afternoon, I was late returning from off base for a football practice. I had a beautiful, souped up, yellow and green Ford convertible that my dad had given me when I graduated from college. You guessed it: In my rush to get back on time, I sped along and was stopped by a state trooper who clocked me doing over 100 mph. I guess I wanted to be a fighter pilot so badly that going that fast in a car was as close as I could get to flying. The incident was turned over to the military police and because I was an officer, referred to the commanding general, General Smith. He reamed me out for being so reckless (as if jumping out of a plane at 10,000 feet were a common, rational act) and said that I was guilty of conduct unbecoming an officer. For punishment, he gave me an Article 15 citing, ordering me to be reassigned to Japan.

Fortunately, one of my innate gifts is to extract the positive out of difficult circumstances. I actually looked forward to spending the remainder of my military career in Japan. The Korean War was over. How bad could it be? So I drove my car to my parents' home, which at this point was in Bala Cynwyd, Pennsylvania. My dad asked if there was anything he could do for me before I left for San Francisco, my port of departure. I didn't think so. All the while, we had never told Mom that I had been jumping out of airplanes for the past several months. We knew her nerves would have gone haywire at the thought. We also spared her the news that I had been reassigned as a punishment. We led her to believe that the government was providing me with the opportunity to travel and see exotic parts of the world.

As I traveled to the west coast to get ready for my departure to Japan, I began thinking about Phyllis. I called her up and we talked for a few minutes. Finally, I asked if she would visit with me before I left for Asia. She laughed and said, "Nicky, you're as crazy as a bed bug!" Not being a guy who takes no for an answer, I asked again a few more times and got the same response. Finally, I gave up and we parted on good terms.

On the day before my departure, an announcement came over the speaker system at the base in San Francisco: *Will Second Lieutenant*

Nicholas Bollettieri please report to the orderly room? I thought for sure that I had managed to get into trouble again and spent the time on my way to the orderly room trying to figure out what rule I might have violated. When I finally got there, imagine my surprise to find Phyllis waiting for me. She had apparently changed her mind about traveling across the country for a visit. I proposed to her on the spot, and we were married in the base chapel a few hours before I left for Asia on September 15, 1954. Fortunately for us, Phyllis had thought to pack a wedding gown in her suitcase and we went before a newly appointed judge who waived the typical three-day waiting period.

Phyllis returned to Roanoke and I shipped out on the *General Mitchell* to Japan, where I was stationed in the city of Beppu on the island of Kyushu. With Mount Tsurumi and the Pacific Ocean as backdrops and warm weather, it was a tropical paradise, but a lonely place for a newlywed. Fortunately, Mom and Dad decided to send Phyllis over to spend time with me as a honeymoon and Christmas present to both of us.

It was a wonderful time. We lived in a cottage off base, in a three-house compound owned by a Japanese family. We even had a maid who would shine my boots to the point where I could see myself in them. Phyllis and I took in the famous hot springs in Beppu—hot steam rising from incredibly cobalt blue water—and went to Tokyo on weekends. We'd go shopping and to nightclubs where we put on dance shows to American big band jazz music, which was all the rage then. During that time, my son Jimmy Boy was conceived.

The rest of my tour was uneventful, and we left Japan to return to the United States in the summer of the following year. We ended up at Fort Bragg in Fayetteville, where Jimmy Boy was born in a private doctor's suite in June of 1955.

*Phyllis visiting me and Jimmy Boy, who was taking
a break from kitchen duty, at NBTA.*

I've always been proud of the fact that I was one of Nick's first students. As a junior I won many titles under Nick, including Junior Nationals, Orange Bowl and Sugar Bowl. The lessons taught me so many years ago have stayed with me throughout my life. Thanks to Nick I've enjoyed a life in tennis through teaching, coaching college, playing league tennis and having a wonderful social life...[and] he has remained a good friend through the years. When I was fighting stage 4 cancer, he made arrangements for me to go to the U.S. Open as his guest, something he knew I had always wanted to do. When I was in remission, he sent me a new tennis racquet as inspiration to get back on the tennis court. His friendship has meant a lot to me. I've been fortunate to see the real side of Nick, the softer side.

—Sheryl Smith Craig, Saint Augustine, Florida

I was falling into a rough crowd of guys that hung out in the late 50s around North Miami Beach, smoking, riding around in cars, causing trouble. I was also playing tennis at the time, and one night outside of the two old cement courts, Nick pulled me aside and pretty sternly said, "Either come here and continue with tennis, or go hang out with those thugs and don't come back." Well, I took his advice and it led to a pretty fortunate life that I have had through tennis and friendships with some great people.

—Joe Szucs, Miami, Florida

CHAPTER 3

Learning the Ropes at Victory Park

When I finished my military service, my dad called me to ask about my future plans. I didn't really know what I wanted to do, so he suggested I become a lawyer. Throughout my early life, I always loved warm weather and being outdoors—going to the beach, riding the waves. So I asked if it was okay to enter the University of Miami law school in Coral Gables, Florida. I knew that Dad would be pleased because one of my mom's brothers, Tony DeFillipo, lived in nearby North Miami Beach and could "keep an eye" on us. I had a wife, a nine-month-old son and a 1949 Plymouth; and with the cash from having sold my previous car and our personal belongings, we headed to Florida. Dad provided the additional money I needed and we bought the house right next door to my uncle Tony DeFillipo for $17,000.

We got settled in, and I started law school in the fall of 1956. Although the G.I. Bill paid for my tuition, I needed to earn some money to take care of my family. Uncle Tony, besides owning the largest gas station and the biggest sanitation company in North Miami Beach, was very well connected politically in the community. One of his good friends was Frank Sepedi, the director of the city's water department. My uncle knew I had played tennis in college, so he suggested that I offer tennis lessons at the two courts across the street from the city administration building and next to park administration, where the mayor and other politicians spent most of their time. Back then, it was a broken-down facility not much in use. Actually, "broken-down" is an understatement—the place was a wreck. The courts were best described as hard-grass-dirt: Hard, because they were made of concrete; grass, because lots of greenery was poking through the cracks in the playing surface; and dirt, because there was dirt everywhere. The nets, which were iron mesh to prevent theft, had holes in them. The facility had three amenities—an umbrella, a shell-and-brick wall and a Pepsi-Cola machine.

Until then, my only experience with tennis had been batting the ball around in high school and playing in college, but I applied for the position of head pro and was awarded the contract at Victory Park in 1957. My "sponsors," the local mafia, also made sure that I received a decent salary and a benefits package. Let me put my cards on the table: The only reason I got the job, knowing less than zero about teaching the game, was the influence wielded by Uncle Tony and Frank Sepedi.

I would get up early, drive to law school for my classes, come home at 2:30 in the afternoon and teach tennis until 8 or 9 at night.

My early coaching days.

The law professors expected the students to dress properly—at least slacks and a collared shirt. I was going from school directly to the tennis courts and had other ideas. I had moved to Florida to wear shorts and a t-shirt, and so that is what I did. After a semester of listening to their constant complaints about my attire, I told the professors where they could put their books and quit law school for good.

By then, I had decided to make a go of it as a tennis instructor. I sent Phyllis to "spy" on other programs in the Miami area and report back to me what the instructors there were doing. When I went out to visit some of them myself, I was amazed at how easy it was to earn money teaching this sport. Most of the coaches used what seemed to me mindless, robotic techniques with their beginner students. The advice I heard repeatedly and most often was, "Put your palm on the face of the racquet and slide it down on the grip; shake hands with the racquet forming a "V" between your thumb and index finger on top of the racquet; ready position, racquet back early, step to the ball, hit the ball, catch the racquet with your non-hitting hand and back to the ready position."

I figured if they could do this and make $3.00 an hour, why couldn't I? You didn't need to be a good player, because to a beginner, perception is everything. If you look the part and speak with authority, they can't tell the difference between a novice and a world-class instructor. Even if I was on a downward spiral from my earlier dreams of becoming a fighter pilot and my brief stints as a paratrooper and law school student, I was going to make the most of it.

When I heard that Fred Perry lived in the area, I decided to pay him a visit. He was a tennis legend who won eight Grand Slam titles in the 1930s, including three consecutive Wimbledon championships—the last British player to win that tournament until Andy Murray did it again in 2013. I drove up in my yellow-green convertible to the Diplomat Hotel in Hollywood, Florida, where he was director of tennis, and introduced myself. He approved of my taste in cars, and we met several times after that socially, although we never talked about tennis. Fred Perry was a very flamboyant man and he always smiled when I arrived. His favorite piece of advice to me was, "Make sure you always have a good-looking woman with you."

I decided to use the experience at Victory Park to hone my teaching skills. I discovered that I had the innate ability and the compassion to genuinely help my students improve their tennis. For a while, I learned a lot from watching the best tennis coach in the area, Slim Harbett.

The grips, backswing, follow-through and other components were pretty uncomplicated, so I mimicked his techniques and language. But unknowingly, I began to add my own concepts and found that I was creating my own style. I began to evaluate technique and strategy and provide meaningful recommendations for improvement. No more teaching by the numbers. I wasn't going to have my students look like soldiers parading at Buckingham Palace.

Frank Sepedi and my uncle noticed the increase in activity at the tennis courts. When I mentioned that the facility needed to be upgraded to accommodate the growing numbers, Uncle Tony said, "Don't worry about it, we'll take care of it." They hosted a picnic at Victory Park to impress the town administrators and offered free food and drink to whomever wanted to come. Believe me, the place was packed. As things got going, Uncle Tony and Frank came up to me and said, "Nick, when everything settles down, take the microphone and this is what you say, 'Ladies and gentlemen, this is a big day in North Miami Beach. Mayor Diefenbach wants to announce the resurfacing of the two existing courts, construction of four additional courts, the installation of lighting and a new pro shop.'"

I did as they told me, and the mayor was taken completely by surprise. When they joined him on the podium with a shovel, he shot them a look that would have turned lesser men to stone. A brief, quiet discussion ensued, and then the mayor announced that ground was being broken for the upgrading of the facility. He stuck the shovel in the dirt as a symbolic gesture to save face. I now had a six-court facility and my local reputation was spreading. I hope you all get the message. Italian names end in A, E, I, O and U. The "mafia" had done its work. Need I say more?

I spent a lot of time and energy building up the programs at Victory Park. But like many hard-working young men, I also partied hard. Most evenings and weekends I hung out with my cousin Ken DeFillipo, who lived at my uncle's next door, and his friends. We all had a lot of fun carousing. To give you an idea of the kind of trouble we got into, one night in a lounge, we happened to see two guys and an attractive woman. The next night at our hotel, we saw them again. As they walked past, I glanced at her appreciatively, and one of the guys said, "What are you looking at?" Well, one word led to another, and we got into a fight. It didn't last long. Kenny was 6' 4", played football for the University of Miami, had a brown belt in karate and took care of things. That's how things went: I'd start the arguments and he would finish them!

Later that evening when we returned to our hotel, as we entered the lobby, one of the guys came down the stairs. He pulled out a gun and said he would kill us both. I was mortified. While the night manager called the cops, Kenny walked up to the guy, said "You don't have the balls," and broke his nose. When the cops came, Kenny gave them Frank Sepedi's number to call. They did, wished us "good night," and we went on our way unscathed.

Getting ready to work on my tan.

I had a good time, but in the process, I did neglect my family too much. One night when I came home at 2 a.m., I found my packed bags sitting on the front porch with a note from Phyllis that read, "Nicky, I love you, but I can't take this life any longer. I'll miss you!" And that was the end of my first marriage.

Phyllis was a kind soul, but she had taken about all she could handle from me, staying out at all hours of the night. She wanted to make sure I stayed in touch with my son as much as possible, and Jimmy Boy spent the summers with me when I ran tennis camps up north. In the meantime, Phyllis kept the house and I moved into an apartment at the Sun City Motel on Collins Avenue by the beach, sharing two bedrooms with five other guys. I resumed my life as a hard-working, hard-playing bachelor.

By 1960, the city of North Miami Beach began getting recognition from the United States Tennis Association (USTA). I was starting to develop some darn good players who were making waves on the national tennis scene. Sheryl Smith (now Sheryl Craig), one of my first four students, was the 14-and-under National Champion. Other outstanding players were George Shuert, Joe Szucs, Margie and Herb Cooper, and members of the Kantrovick family.

From left: Lionel Standerd, guest, me, Sheryl Smith, Herb Lewis, my uncle Tony DeFillipo (in back), guest, unknown, Judge Balaban and Colonel Bannister. Abe Rebman, stooping, later replaced me at Victory Park.

The best player to come out of Victory Park was Brian Gottfried. He arrived at age 11 or so with huge ears and an even bigger champion's heart. He did very well. In 1962, he won the national 12-and-under singles title. Before long, Brian came to train with me and travel with me during the summers. With only about five years separating them, he and Jimmy Boy became close friends, almost like brothers.

Brian was an extremely talented young man with determination, focus and a world-class volley. (And they said I couldn't teach the volley.) He had an outstanding professional career, winning 25 singles and 54 doubles titles, reaching No. 3 in the world at some point and becoming the runner-up at the 1977 French Open.

Brian Gottfried and me at Beaver Dam.

With the success of some of my young players, I began to gain some name recognition for myself in other parts of the country, too. In Springfield, Ohio, Dr. Howard Dredge, a dentist with a thriving practice and considerable influence in the community, was nuts about tennis and loved children. He wanted to help the kids in the city and directed a tennis program at two of Springfield's tennis centers, Snyder and Reid Parks, free of charge. Somehow he heard about me and arranged for me to be interviewed to become tennis director for those parks from mid-April through September. I was delighted to get the job, because it was much too hot in Miami in the summer to spend any time on the tennis courts.

Every Wednesday and Saturday during the summer, 1,500 children would use public transportation and make their way to Snyder Park. We made special arrangements with the bus company to provide them with 25¢ fares. The best young players in the community (some were college students) helped me give lessons to these kids. We called them the "Leaders Club." As a reward, the "leaders" received free winter instruction at the YMCA's indoor gymnasium. My staff joined in and, with the assistance of local pro Gunnar Polte, ran the program for two years in 1961 and 1962.

"Free Clinic Day!" in Springfield, Ohio.

I did not stay there in the winter, but went back to Florida. When my marriage ended and I had wanted to move on, I became the tennis director at the Sahara Beach Hotel in Miami Beach. There were two Har-Tru courts across the street on Collins Avenue. Har-Tru is often called green or "American" clay, but it's actually composed of crushed stones, which make it a little harder and faster than the red clay courts popular in Europe.

The problem was that these courts had very little Har-Tru left on them. The hotel wasn't ready to spend the money, and I didn't have any extra after alimony and child support. Enter my cousin Kenny, who was already following in my uncle's footsteps, solving problems in a "creative" manner. He borrowed a pickup truck and late one night we cruised by another resort, the Hollywood Beach Hotel in the adjoining town. There were a number of 100-pound bags of Har-Tru lying by the sidewalk next to the tennis center—we thought they were garbage. Somehow, as if by magic—don't ask me how—a few of them ended up in the bed of our truck, and the next day I had brand-new courts at the Sahara. Kenny, by the way, later became vice mayor of North Miami Beach!

I can't take credit for coaching Harold Solomon to success, but I did get him started at the Sahara Beach Hotel. One day, his father, Lenny, brought his young son "Solly" to meet me and get a tennis lesson. When we started, I noticed that Harold had his hands more under the racquet in a strong, semi-western grip. Although common today, it was odd at the time, but I didn't change it at all, and it worked very well for him. He had a terrific professional career, winning 22 singles titles and ranking among the top 10 players in the world for five consecutive years. In 1976, he reached the finals of the French Open. Harold was a handsome kid, and in 1980, when he won 64 matches, *Playgirl* named him one of the 10 sexiest men of the year.

That first and only lesson paid unexpected dividends. Lenny Solomon was a kind man who loved tennis. Years later, his daughter Shelly attended NBTA in Florida. At the time, we didn't have a lot of extra room and needed a library, so Lenny had one built for us. Today, it houses the executive office and my Hall of Fame room at IMG Academy.

Meanwhile, several notable juniors emerged from Springfield, Ohio, including Robin and Marmee Fry, Chuck Parsons and Ginger Pfeiffer, who was ranked No. 2 in the Western Tennis Association's Girls' 14 Division in 1962. The following year, she won the singles title of the American Tennis Association, the black version of the U.S. Tennis Association (USTA). Previous title holders included the great Althea Gibson, the first African-American tennis player to win Wimbledon and the French Open (she had 11 Grand Slam victories altogether).

Springfield also hosted the Boys' 16 and 18 Western Conference Championships as a warm-up to the National Championships in Kalamazoo, Michigan. I coordinated the tournament and met a number of the best American teenage players there, including Bob Lutz, Marty Riessen, Stan Smith, Charlie Pasarell and Arthur Ashe. The latter two were to have important roles in my life and career.

When Jimmy Boy first started spending his summers with me, he was only eight years old. He would climb on the seat in the red and silver public phone booth by the pro shop and call his mom every day, reversing the charges (which I would pay for later). In those days, calls still went through switchboards and telephone operators would make the connection by hand (you can see them plug in lines in movies from the 40s and 50s). On one occasion, when I made the call for Jimmy Boy, the operator, Nancy, started a conversation with me. She said that she often made the connection for us and knew I was the tennis director at Snyder Park. I thanked her for being so kind to my son and mentioned that we might meet one day and share a drink. She said that would be a good idea. We got together sooner rather than later and found that we enjoyed each other's company… you can see where this is headed.

The next winter, Nancy visited Miami on vacation. Nancy was a kind and generous person. She played tennis every day and we got along very well with one another. By the end of her stay, we decided to get married when I returned to Springfield in April. In the meantime, she went back there ahead of me, determined to make all the necessary arrangements for our wedding.

A few weeks later, another attractive young lady from up north stopped in to play some tennis at the Sahara Beach Hotel. Her name was Shirley Phillips and we got along just fine. We danced the night away and I told her all about my seasonal travel. She invited me to visit her in Franklin, a small town just south of Indianapolis, on my way to Springfield, and I did. We had a good time and she said she'd love to marry me. I said, "Okay," and told her that I'd return in a week and we'd work out the details then. But when I got to Springfield, Nancy had all her wedding arrangements ready. So I married her the weekend I was scheduled to return to Franklin. Having stood Shirley up, I was almost afraid to travel to Indianapolis for years after!

It all started some 50 years ago when I decided to seriously pursue the game of tennis at the highest level. I flew to Dorado Beach, Puerto Rico, in the early 70s where Nick was teaching. The minute I stepped on the court to take up the game, I felt like I was in seventh heaven. Nick practiced feisty, combative, unparalleled motivation to make you better; psychology par excellence; cutting-edge strategy and had the wisdom of a sage. I was treated to a clinic that dazzled my inner thoughts. And guess what? Over these past 50 years—including 35 years of state and regional competition—I delivered my two daughters and now four grandchildren to his tennis camps for personal instruction. Nick Bollettieri always delivers more than he promises.

—Harvey Mackay, author and entrepreneur

Nick, a crazy Italian? You bet. But he is a generous person with a big heart and talent to match. He was extremely influential in helping to guide my three children, Harolyn, David and Michael in their early developing years. To me, he has always been a friend that was as true and loyal as a friend can be.

—Nate Landow, longtime friend

Nick is not only my friend, he is part of the Marx family. I have supported his crazy ideas because he made the ideas come true and has taken tennis to another level of excellence. We all LOVE him.

—Louis Marx, longtime friend

CHAPTER 4

My Big Break

One day at the Western Conference Championships in Springfield, a woman came into my pro shop and asked to borrow some tennis balls so that her son could practice his serve. When she brought them back, I refused to take payment for their use.

A few weeks later, I received a call from RockResorts, the management company for the Dorado Beach Resort in Puerto Rico, which was owned by Laurance Rockefeller and his family. My name had been submitted on a long list of applicants for the head tennis pro position. Would I be interested in applying for the job? I was stunned. Of course I would! I didn't have much of a name in tennis yet, so I didn't think my chances were very good, but what did I have to lose? A few weeks later, to my surprise, I received a call telling me that I was among the final three applicants.

At the U.S. Open, which in those days was held in Forest Hills, New York, I went into the pro shop and had a conversation with Eddie Moylan, the director of tennis, and a friend of mine, his assistant Bill Parks. They told me, "We just landed a plum job for next year—at Dorado. I didn't know what to say. I was on pins and needles, not knowing whether or not to believe them. So I called my dad on the telephone and told him about it. He said, "Stand tall. Don't worry." And he was right.

Three days later, I got a call from RockResorts notifying me that I had been selected for the job. I was thrilled, of course, but also amazed. How had it happened? It turned out that the woman who had borrowed the practice balls was Dora Pasarell, the mother of

Charlie Pasarell, who at the time was one of the best junior players in the country. She and her husband, Charles Sr., were well respected business leaders and athletes in Puerto Rico—he held the distributorship for Philip Morris for all the Caribbean. They belonged to Dorado Beach and were good friends with Laurance Rockefeller. Dora had proposed me for the job and offered a strong recommendation in my favor.

Nancy and I packed our bags—no more Sahara!—and flew to San Juan where we were met by a car and chauffeur from the hotel. I was so excited, I still remember the 90-minute drive to the resort past the Bacardi Rum headquarters and through a series of small, scenic towns. But nothing compared with the beauty of the resort itself. It was located on a section of pristine coast. As we entered we could see the private airport, which allowed wealthy clients to fly in from San Juan. There were individual, two-story cottages along the beach, nestled among lush trees, a main hotel and a house called "Su Casa," where Amelia Earhart spent time before her fateful flight. It still stands on the premises to this day and commands a big price tag: $25,000 for one night's stay!

Naturally, Nancy and I were impressed. Then I got even better news! When I met with the manager, he told me I would earn $3,500 for the winter season, November through March, plus all the money from lessons I taught and the proceeds from the pro shop. We were given a beautifully furnished condo with maid service and offered free meals. As a director I had dining privileges to eat with the guests of the hotel. To say I was in paradise would be an understatement. This was the big time!

I quickly realized, though, that the people who stayed at Dorado Beach came mostly for the golf. The two 18-hole courses hosted the famous Dorado Cup, which attracted all the top 1960s golfers, including Arnold Palmer, Jack Nicklaus and Gary Player (his daughter later attended my tennis academy for a year). The assistant golf pro there was Chi Chi Rodriguez, a promising "local boy" on the cusp of realizing his extraordinary talent. He and his beautiful wife lived in another condo on the grounds, and he and I became good friends.

Fortunately for me, hotel guests had to pass by my three front tennis courts on their way to the golf shop and golf course. When Nancy and I saw them heading our way, we'd race out on a court and start hitting balls back and forth to give the impression that tennis was a fun, lively activity at the resort.

As the tennis program grew, I used some of my street hustling skills to augment my income. We had five courts at the main tennis center close to the golf shop, two of them behind the main three show courts. This was where all of the action took place. My biggest spenders would be assigned to play on "my court." There were also two courts on the west side of the complex near the 13th hole of the golf course, right next to the ocean. We called them "The Wind Tunnel" because the constant breezes and heavy gusts often blew both tennis and golf balls into the sea. That's where we "banished"

Me demonstrating good form.

those guests who would not come into the pro shop and purchase our merchandise or sign up for lessons.

Most of our guests left their racquets with us overnight. Many of these racquets were strung with gut, a resilient fiber made from cow's intestines, favored by professional players. During the evening, a sprinkler system would come through the window of the pro shop—

ha, ha—and wet the strings. The next day in the heat and humidity, they would begin to pop and the guests would wonder why their strings were breaking, as they often had them newly strung before coming to Dorado Beach. We would tell them to put talcum powder in their racquet covers to absorb the moisture from the tropical climate. They would use so much of it that it often looked like a snow shower when they pulled their racquets out of the sleeves. Naturally, we gave them a great deal on restringing.

The tropical climate did have its drawbacks. Whenever it rained, it cost me money; brief downpours would halt our lessons for half an hour at a time. To get back in business quickly we'd take the white hotel towels and use them as squeegees. It was quite a sight when we dragged 30 towels across a court at one time. Unfortunately, some of the green paint came off in the process, and the hotel administration went crazy and stopped the practice.

Jimmy Boy and me on vacation in Fort Myers, Florida.

About the only thing that could get me off the court in those days was when the surf got big. I've always been crazy about surfing, and while the other side of the island had the big waves, there was a small point on the golf course, surrounded by rocks and jutting into the ocean, that made a great local spot for us. I'd phone Jimmy Boy at the condo to alert him that the conditions were ripe, and we'd have fun together body and boogie board surfing.

I met a number of interesting people at Dorado Beach, including Robert Kraft, the owner of the New England Patriots, whose son Jonathan later attended one of my summer camps. Another was

A.C. Nielsen, Jr., then president of the famous market research and television ratings company.

One day when I was giving a tennis clinic for the children of some local club members, a solidly built, middle-aged gentleman stopped on his way to the golf course and watched me teach for a while. Then he commented, "Young man, you belong with children!" I didn't know who he was at the time, but soon found out: Vince Lombardi, the coach of the Green Bay Packers, who had recently been named the most successful coach in the history of the National Football League, winning five NFL championships in seven years and the first two Super Bowls. After football season ended, he came to Puerto Rico to play golf and relax. He stopped by the tennis courts nearly every day, and we became friends. I loved football and would send bags of golf balls up to Green Bay for Vince and his friends. Later on, he helped me start an important summer camp.

The old adage, "It's not what you know—it's who you know," again proved incredibly accurate! You never know whom you are talking to and what might happen as a result of that friendly conversation! My grandmother would always say, "Thank you," to people who helped her and did things for her, and I learned early on to follow her example. Nowadays the buzz word for what she did is "networking," and I have no doubt that it is one of the most important practices that has made me and my career so successful.

In a very real way, Vince Lombardi and Dora Pasarell played key roles in my early development and ultimately, all that followed. I will be forever grateful to them. Vince died in 1970, and Dora's son Charlie went on to represent the United States in the Davis Cup, and excelled especially in doubles, sometimes with Arthur Ashe as his partner. After his retirement from playing, Charlie was instrumental in the creation of the BNP Paribas Open in Indian Wells, California, a Masters tennis event with one of the largest audiences after the four Grand Slam tournaments. He and I have remained close friends over the years.

In the meantime, the tennis program at Dorado kept growing and our courts were often completely booked. One day, a guest telephoned the pro shop to reserve a court at 9 a.m. the next day, and Nancy told him we were booked up until 3 in the afternoon. She had no idea what it meant that she had just turned down Jay Rockefeller! When I found out about it, I just about had a hernia and quickly called him back to tell him that a court had opened up for him at the time he had requested. This was before he became governor of West Virginia and later on, a U.S. senator, but I knew the Rockefeller name carried plenty of clout.

I later had the privilege of teaching the Rockefeller family at Pocantico Hills, their 4,000-acre estate and family compound in Tarrytown, New York. It was an amazing place. The first thing you saw when you arrived was a three-story greenhouse so big you could have parked a 747 in it! The Har-Tru tennis courts, surrounded by ivy, were beautifully decorated in an Egyptian motif. For me it was almost a surreal experience, coming as I did from the streets of North Pelham, to be welcomed to the governor's place!

The Rockefeller brothers—David, John D., Laurance and Nelson, who was governor of New York at the time—each had a mansion at the estate, all except Winthrop, who had a house in Arkansas. The brothers all got along exceedingly well and were always pleasant. Chi Chi Rodriguez would give golf lessons and I taught tennis to the family. All of the Rockefellers, including Happy, the second wife of the governor, overwhelmed us with kindness and affection and made us feel like a part of the family. We played together, swam together and had lunch together. But when we were summoned to come up to the "big house" on the top of the hill, where the governor had his own tennis court, it was all business. Even I got a little nervous. Everybody was intimidated by him.

Brian Gottfried and Jimmy Boy traveled with me a lot in those days. Brian was only 13 and played singles and doubles. I remember one match when he and Jay Rockefeller, who was the best tennis player in the family, were paired against Laurance's son-in-law and Bones Spencer, the husband of John Rockefeller's daughter and later the dean of Deerfield Academy. The spectators were the wives of Laurance and John, among others. It was a very competitive contest, and you wouldn't believe the colorful language the players used throughout the match, which showed how down-to-earth they all were, even though they had unimaginable wealth.

Along with my son, they also invited my mother and father to come up from nearby North Pelham. Jimmy's favorite place was the Playhouse, a big building on the golf course that had two bowling lanes,

My father, Jimmy Boy and me on the golf course in 1969.

an indoor swimming pool and a gym with all kinds of gymnastic equipment. There was also a family ice cream parlor. The first time Jimmy Boy came along, his eyes were as big as saucers. Then he said, sadly, "Daddy, I don't have any money," until I assured him, "No, no, it's for free!"

In the meantime, my marriage to Nancy came to an end rather abruptly. I'm not sure what went wrong. I was too busy with tennis lessons, schmoozing with guests and running tennis camps during the summer—which all may have contributed to our breakup. I think that maybe coming from a quiet Midwestern town, it was too hard for her to fit into my wild, erratic life, and she decided to move on. The end came in the fall of 1964 when she went to Mexico and got a divorce.

I didn't remain a bachelor long, though. Chi Chi Rodriguez was planning to play an exhibition golf event in Des Moines, Iowa, and then head to Las Vegas afterward, and he invited me to join him. I drove to Des Moines, and directly across the street from the airport was a restaurant/hotel called "Johnny and Kay's." Working there was a cute waitress whose name was Jeri Sylvester. She was a senior at Drake University, liked music and had a fun personality. Her sister Jeannie was the maître d', and as I was leaving, I mentioned to her that I would like to take Jeri with me to Las Vegas. She assured me that her sister would not be interested; she didn't even know me! I left my car near the airport and following the golf exhibition, Chi Chi and I flew to Las Vegas. After a few days there, I called the restaurant and invited Jeri to join me. She refused, but asked me to come back to Des Moines for a Dave Brubeck concert. So I returned and we had a good time both at the concert and afterward.

A day or so later I drove back to Miami and flew to my winter gig at the Dorado Beach resort. Before long, I called Jeri and invited her to come down to Puerto Rico, and she accepted. Soon after she arrived, we were married by a judge in his office in Old San Juan.

Our two daughters Danielle and Angel were born in 1967 and 1969, and we had a lot of fun at the resort. I can still remember Angelas a little girl walking into the pro shop with live lizards for "earrings." She'd have them bite her earlobes and they dangled by her head as she came in to show them off! Danielle, Angel and Jimmy Boy, who visited during the winters, all later told me that the times at Dorado were some of the happiest in their young lives, because I was always there. During the summers, when I continued to conduct tennis camps, I couldn't always take them along.

At some point in Springfield, Dr. Dredge and I no longer saw eye to eye, and after co-managing the Snyder Park program for two years, we parted amicably. By then, I had other job offers, and spent time at a variety of tennis clubs on the East Coast and in the Midwest, including the Woodmont Country Club in Rockville, Maryland and the Nassau Country Club in Glen Cove, Long Island. In the summer of 1963, my staff and I began teaching at the Lake Bluff Racquet Club in Lake Forest, Illinois, on

Me, Angel, Danielle and Jeri at Dorado.

the north shore of Chicago. It was a very upscale club that had Har-Tru courts that needed constant attention.

After about five winters at Dorado, Bland Hoke, the general manager of RockResorts, called me into his office. He told me that I was doing a great job and he wanted me to stay at the resort year-round. When I said to him that I couldn't do that because of my summer camp commitments—I wasn't about to give those lucrative jobs up— he informed me that it would be my last year at Dorado. Some days later, Laurance Rockefeller and his wife Mary stopped by to say hello. They were kind, soft-spoken people and they told me how much they loved having me there. When they asked me if everything was okay, I said, "Yes, but I won't be here much longer," and told them about the manager's ultimatum. Two hours after they left, I received a call from Bland Hoke and he told me I could do as I pleased.

One day I met a kindly gentleman with horn-rimmed glasses who just sat courtside for a number of days and watched me teach tennis.

He finally got up the courage to take a lesson, and during our session, he told me that he loved the sport, but was really a squash player. Hy Zausner chipped this, chopped that and kept spinning the ball until I had to tell him to stick with squash! He had a good sense of humor about it. He was a successful businessman, one of the largest importers of foreign cheeses. At some point he asked me where I would be going for my summer job. When I explained that I would be at the Nassau Country Club in Long Island and would spend some time at Pocantico Hills with the Rockefellers, he offered me the use of his guesthouse located in Sands Point, a wealthy Long Island community. His home had its own tennis court, and Brian Gottfried and I would hit with his two older sons from his first marriage, Marty and Dick. He also had two younger children, Susan and Michael, with his current wife, Annabell, a kind and beautiful lady. When word got out that I was in the area, three little girls came over for lessons—the Gengler sisters, Nancy, Louise and Margie. Louise later became the ladies' tennis coach at Princeton University, and Margie married Stan Smith, a former No. 1 tennis player and two-time Grand Slam tournament singles champion.

The next summer, Hy invited me to return, but this time he had a surprise for me. He had purchased several acres in the town adjoining Sands Point. He was going to build the Port Washington Tennis Academy and invited me to become its director. I was speechless, but decided to go for it. Brian Gottfried, Jimmy Boy and I helped spread the Har-Tru as the first clay courts were built. Most people think Harry Hopman, the legendary Australian Davis Cup team tennis coach, was the first director, but those people would be wrong. After Hy and I had a falling out, Bill Weisbach replaced me, and then Harry Hopman replaced Bill some time later. The academy has some illustrious graduates, notably John McEnroe and Mary Carillo. Today, the Port Washington Tennis Academy is run by Hy's sons and continues to be a very successful enterprise.

Jeri and me in 1966.

Beaver Dam, Wisconsin, 1970 to 1971—we would go to Wayland Academy, where Nick had one of his summer camps. We would play tennis and train six and a half days a week. There was a group of eight of us on scholarship. Our payment for all of this was to wash Nick's yellow Corvette "thoroughly," and he would inspect it. Some of the best times a kid could ever hope for we spent there. Lessons I still carry on in my life even now, I realize I learned during those summers with Nick.

—Larry Gottfried, brother of Brian Gottfried

It all started with Nick Bollettieri in Beaver Dam, Wisconsin. While he was exploring uncharted territory in tennis, Nick was also mentoring young people like myself who have gone into the tennis industry and were part of the tennis boom of the 1970s. In my estimation, Nick Bollettieri was one of the three or four people largely responsible for that tennis boom and consequently, for the wonderful industry that I, along with thousands of other people, now work within. I would love to see a "Nick Bollettieri Family Tennis Tree," as I am sure the branches would be plentiful and the number of Bollettieri-influenced men and women within the industry would reach four generations deep.

—Steve Contardi, USPTA Master Pro
The Club at Harper's Point, Cincinnati, Ohio

CHAPTER 5

Beaver Dam

I guess I was something of a hothead sometimes—it was "my way or the highway." But this was long before I started my Academy in Bradenton, Florida, and I couldn't call my own shots yet; more often than not, I had to take to the highway when there were disagreements with owners or management.

One time, for example, I had an argument with a woman at the Lake Bluff Racquet Club. She was rude and I responded in kind. She always complained that the courts were too dry and gave the maintenance crew a difficult time. I agreed that the courts were too dry, but it was because she and her friends continued to play on them long into the watering time. She ranted at me that it didn't matter how long they played, it was my job to keep the courts in tip-top condition. The next day, as she and her friends were playing at exactly the time that the courts should be watered, I turned on the sprinkler system and soaked the entire group. Dripping wet, she ran into my shop, yelling, "Do you know who I am?" My response was "Lady, I don't care who you are!" Well, it turned out that she was the wife of the president of the club. When I found out, I told her, "You don't like me and I don't like you. Either you stay out of my way, or tell your husband to buy out my contract." I finished the season and decided to move on.

At some point I recalled Vince Lombardi's advice that I belonged with children, and I called him in Green Bay to ask for his assistance in identifying another location for my summer programs. I was thinking about the Midwest. My wife's parents lived in Carlisle, Iowa; I had bought a house there and always enjoyed the time we spent there as a family. Vince Lombardi went out of his way to help, as did A.C. Nielsen, Jr. in Illinois, and the very next spring I found myself in a little community called Beaver Dam, Wisconsin, about 100 miles northwest of Milwaukee. The sign at the entrance to the town said that 14,000 busy beavers live there! I ran my summer programs at Wayland Academy, a private prep school that students from all over the United States attended, and Beaver Dam became the premier summer tennis camp in the world.

Beaver Dam Tennis Camp brochure featuring Jimmy Arias, Kathleen Horvath and me.

The headmaster of Wayland was Ray Patterson, Jr., a great sports fan with a phenomenal eye for talent. He later became the president of the Milwaukee Bucks and drafted a young basketball player from UCLA named Lew Alcindor, who soon after changed his name to Kareem Abdul-Jabbar. The following year, the Bucks became the fastest expansion team ever to win a championship title in any sport. Fifteen years later, Patterson did it again when he ran the Houston Rockets and selected Hakeem Olajuwon, who led the Rockets to back-to-back NBA championships in the 1990s!

Part of the deal that first year at Wayland was that I had to coach the boys' and girls' tennis teams in the spring. It meant I had to leave Dorado Beach in April, a few weeks early. In retrospect, it was worth the financial sacrifice. I had a room on the bottom floor of the girls' dormitory, so my family did not join me. Jeri and the kids stayed at our house in Carlisle, Iowa.

There were only four outdoor tennis courts. When I told Ray Patterson that they weren't enough for the summer program, he said, "So build some more." We did and, incredibly, managed to finish 11 additional outdoor courts just before camp opened in late June. As luck would have it, it poured down rain that whole first week. Fortunately, Wayland had a magnificent indoor dome with tartan turf, and we were able to share it with the basketball camp, which was run by Al McGuire, then coach at Marquette University. Nine years later, in his final season at Marquette, Al won the NCAA basketball championship. He later became a popular college basketball commentator for NBC Sports and CBS Sports.

We were always ready to improvise when necessary. One early summer, we oversold and didn't have enough courts for all the attendees. So we laid out four courts with two sticks for nets on a grassy field next to the tennis facilities and had kids serve and volley there so they didn't have to stand around while they waited for their turn on the regular courts.

I ran the Nick Bollettieri Tennis Camp in Beaver Dam from 1968 to 1983. We had kids come from all over the world. Many of the players who later made up the national tennis teams of Mexico and Israel got their start there. The mix of culture, ideas and talent gave me the idea of starting my own year-round program. It really was the genesis of the NBTA, and I developed some of the ideas there that I would later apply at the Academy—physical and mental training and discipline, plus complete immersion in the sport. The camp ran for eight weeks and my coaches and I put the students through the paces, conducting strenuous workouts. When they weren't hitting balls, I had them running in place. The approach included group lessons with teams of coaches and students, and individual sessions to assess a camper's game. If I felt people weren't giving it their all, I'd make everyone, staff and students alike, run laps on the nearby sports track, barking out orders like a drill sergeant.

Donald Dell, who was my agent at the time, had his two daughters come to Beaver Dam. His company, ProServ, also represented all the top professional American tennis players and members of the U.S. Davis Cup team. Through him, I got them all to make one- or two-day appearances (they were compensated for their visits). Over the course of the years, they included such greats as Marty Riessen, Dennis Ralston, Stan Smith, Bob Lutz, Charlie Pasarell and Arthur Ashe. That's where Arthur and I got to know each other better and discovered a mutual passion for teaching kids, which led to our important working relationship later on.

Stan Smith, who after his two-time Grand Slam singles titles partnered with Bob Lutz to become one of the most successful doubles teams of all time said, "Really impressed with the camp—the coaching is so thorough and enthusiastic." And Arthur, who could be sparing with praise, uttered just one word, "Unbelievable!"

I must say, I had a lot of fun at Beaver Dam. My family came along, although I had little time for them, coaching, running the show and dashing around in fancy sports cars, first in a red convertible Mercedes and later, a yellow Corvette. My love for fast cars was in high gear already! I even enjoyed the campers' annual show, in which they poked fun at me strutting around, yelling and sporting designer sunglasses.

Another important benefit of the camp was that it allowed me to recruit and try out coaches and staff, some of whom have been with me for 40 years!

Carolina Murphy and me in 2004.

One was Carolina Bolivar (now Murphy). I first met her at the Dorado Beach resort when her father, who was a local member of the club, brought her along when he played golf on Saturdays. She was 11 at the time and would hang out at my pro shop. She loved tennis from an early age, and I'd give her lessons. As she got older, she helped out at the shop and babysat Danielle and Angel when Jeri and I wanted some time off.

In 1972, when Carolina was 15, she attended Beaver Dam for three weeks and came back every summer after that. She taught tennis for a while as a junior counselor and went to the College of New Rochelle, graduating with a degree in psychology and elementary education. After that, she came to work for me when I started my tennis academy.

Another gem was Julio Moros. I had followed his career loosely from afar. I knew that he was born in Venezuela, played on the Davis Cup team there and was attending the University of Texas-Pan

American. One night in 1972, I called him up at two in the morning and offered him a summer job. He worked at Beaver Dam for two months from 6 a.m. till 9 p.m. without a day off before he asked me when and how much I was going to pay him. At the end of camp,

Julio Moros, 2005.

I somehow convinced him to join me at Dorado. He was head over heels in love at the time and wanted to get married. When he asked me for time off to do that, I told him that marriage was a bad idea—you might ask, who was I to give advice on marriage? After all, I was already on wife No. 3. But I gave him a weekend, telling him that if he wasn't back on Monday, he'd be fired. You can see the tyrannical kind of firebrand I was in those days.

Julio left Puerto Rico on a Friday, got married in Texas on Saturday and was back on the job in time. Good thing he didn't listen to my advice—he and his wife Irene are still happily married all these years later!

In retrospect, what mattered most about both Dorado and Beaver Dam were all the lifelong connections I forged with some of the high-profile guests. Many became incredibly important and my life and career would not have been the same without them.

Julio and I were always on the lookout for customers with children who loved tennis. Two such fathers came in and before we knew it, they bought nearly everything we had in the pro shop. Then they booked two of my assistant coaches and me to teach their kids all day long. We had our hands full with these kids. They were out of control, driving golf carts over the tennis courts, all over the golf course and finally getting stuck in the sand. One of the fathers, Dan Lufkin, could not have been more apologetic. The other dad, Louis Marx, just laughed and laughed. He tipped everyone with $100 bills and nobody complained.

Louis Marx was a wealthy man with a big heart and generous spirit. His father was the owner of the famous Marx toy company and once was on the cover of *Time* magazine. Mr. Marx—I always call him that—and Dan Lufkin were partners in the Pan Ocean Oil Corporation at the time, and he lived for tennis. He had a house outside of New York City, and when we were there he would invite us to

Mr. Marx, my wife Cindi and me at the 2006 U.S. Open.

come out on weekends. He was an excellent player himself, who had competed in the U.S. National Championships, and he wanted his sons to play college tennis. One of them, Louis Jr., became captain of the Princeton University tennis team.

Before long, I began talking to Mr. Marx about starting a bunch of camps, and we created a company called All-American Sports. We ran a series of tennis camps around the country; they were quite successful in terms of attendance, but didn't make very much money.

(By the way, Dan Lufkin was always kind enough to help out with any project of mine that Mr. Marx supported.)

One of the largest was in Amherst, headed by Harry Hopman and run by my staff and coaches. It was there, in 1974, that another of my loyal pros got his start. Chip Brooks came from east Tennessee as a summer instructor while in college. Upon graduation, he

Chip Brooks and Raúl Ordóñez, two outstanding coaches.

joined me at Dorado and has worked for me, on and off, until now. He liked to impress newcomers by taking a cherry stem, putting it in his mouth and tying it in a knot. He is a fine coach, and beneath his easygoing Southern charm lies a strong competitive streak. He is always willing to roll up his shirtsleeves when something needs to get done, and his ability to connect with others has made him invaluable in growing and running the adult tennis program at IMG. He now coaches the elite players there. He will always be one of my most trusted friends.

I got to know Jack Schneider, another close friend of Mr. Marx's, when he came to visit Dorado Beach with his children and his wife Josephine. As the managing director of Allen & Co. for more than 30 years, he later helped Andre Agassi with some of his investments. Jack has always been there to help me in whatever way he can and calls me every week to check up on me. He has taken me to every Super Bowl for the past 30 years!

Another important contact I met at Dorado was Harvey Mackay, now a famous businessman and columnist. At the time, he owned an envelope manufacturing company. Since then he has written five international bestsellers on business, including *Swim With the Sharks Without Being Eaten Alive* and *Use Your Head to Get Your Foot in the Door.* Harvey is an excellent tennis player and one of the most competitive guys I know, besides myself; and if you let him believe that he's a little better than you at whatever you're playing, things are fine. I can say this with impunity because he knows it's true and has a good sense of humor about himself.

Harvey introduced me to Dr. Glen Nelson and his wife Marilyn, who have become my dearest friends. I make an annual summer visit

Harvey and me at the Nelsons' in 2009 comparing rings
after I had been inducted into the Alabama Tennis
Foundation Hall of Fame: Which is bigger?

to their home in Minnesota, where they have built a tennis court into the side of a hill—the Nick Bollettieri Tennis Academy North. Their child Wendy is like a daughter to me; she and I have a very special relationship. I was best man at her wedding. Wendy first came to Beaver

77

Dam at age 12 when Harvey Mackay brought her and his daughter Jojo there, and I could tell right away that Wendy had talent. Later, she traveled to my academy in Florida often and spent vacation time there, too, competing and training. Jojo continued playing at a high level as well. To give you an idea of how important the Nelsons are to me: I always leave my job commentating at Wimbledon after the first week of the tournament, missing the finals, in order to visit them in the summer.

Raúl Ordóñez , Dr. Glen and Marilyn Nelson, me and Fritz Nau at the NBTA North in 1987.

Dr. Nelson is the former CEO of Medtronic, the first manufacturer of pacemakers. He and I enjoy watching action movies at night. Marilyn is a member of the Carlson family. Her father, Curtis Carlson, owns a number of TGI Fridays restaurants, Carlson Wagonlit Travel and Radisson Hotels. She has been chair of the board of the Mayo Clinic and gives motivational speeches at prestigious venues like the White House. She contributed generously to Camp Kaizen, a fitness and wellness camp for overweight young girls which my wife Cindi and I used to run. The Nelsons are very special people, and I can't say enough good things about their family.

Another important friend is Nate Landow, a real estate developer. He sent his two older children, Harolyn and David, to Beaver Dam, and they later ran it, collecting tuition, doing the scheduling and taking care of the pro shop. Harolyn is now Special Assistant to the General Manager, Major League Administration; David works in the family construction business. Nate and I are the same age, and we are like brothers. He's the one who gave me the red convertible Mercedes I tooled around in at Beaver Dam. (Nearly two decades later, I gave it to him for his 55th birthday. It had all of 21,000 miles on it and was in great shape.) Nate always starts his phone calls to me with "Hey, Guinea," (he writes it "Ginny") and I take it as a sign of affection. He tells me what he thinks without a filter, and no matter how much he knocks me down, I always say, "Thank you." He always makes time for me, and I love him for it. I have attended every Bar and Bat Mitzvah in his family.

I mustn't forget the Horowitz family: Monty, his wife Susan, and their three children Steven, Stephanie and Richard, who read *The New York Times* at age three! Richard, the older son, became a very good tennis player. Monty was a successful real estate developer in New York. He'd always tell everyone who worked at the camp that they would get a tip at the end of the summer, and they did. But we'd have to send someone, usually David Landow, to Monty's office on the East Coast to pick it up. David would return with a bag full of money—anywhere between $20,000 and $30,000—and I'd divide it up among the staff. Monty was an unbelievably generous man and never asked for anything in return. Later on, I was able to get him parking privileges at the U.S. Open, and he appreciated it.

On one of my flights home for the Christmas holiday, I met a young man named Tom Seavey. He seemed uncertain about his future and I suggested he join me at Dorado as a coach. I'm happy that he took me up on it because it changed the direction of his life. He stayed with me for a few years and when he left, I helped him get a position managing an indoor tennis club. Then he signed on for a long career in sales and marketing with Nike just as it was beginning to grow from a small company into a giant in the sport business. That led to a mutually beneficial association with Nike for me. Later, Tom went on to start his own businesses distributing athletic and outdoor brands, including Swiss Army knives, Deckers and Adidas. He has remained a good friend and supporter, and sometimes encourages my impulsive side: We own a ranch together in Arizona that I have never seen!

Angel, me and Danielle at Dorado.

Unfortunately, all good things must come to an end. In the case of Dorado Beach and me, it happened in 1976 when a *Sports Illustrated* management team took over the running of the resort. They planned to install Butch Buchholz, Jr., a well-known tennis player, as head of the tennis program. They were willing to keep me on if I was willing to work under him, but it would have been awkward with the many guests who knew me from before. Besides, it's nearly impossible for someone with my personality to play second fiddle. My dedicated assistant, Julio Moros, came with me. Butch later started the Sony Ericsson tennis tournament in Miami, and he and I have remained good friends over the years.

I did not have any definite plans, but wasn't worried. I figured I had plenty of irons in the fire. Little did I know that I was about to embark on the most significant step in my career.

The publisher of Tennis Magazine *called me and said that he knew I was going to interview Nick Bollettieri, and that I should definitely not put him on the payroll. A tennis writer for the* Chicago Tribune *simply said, "Don't hire him." Then I sat in my office with Nick for one and a half hours, knew he would be my perfect match, and hired him on the spot. I've never regretted it.*

—Dr. Murf Klauber

I first visited Nick's Academy in Bradenton, Florida in 1980 at age 13 because my dad felt I could not develop my tennis potential living in snowy Michigan. A few minutes after arriving, I was on the center court directly across the net from a semi-maniac who was shirtless, sunglasses on, well tanned, and firing tennis balls at me from the standard position near the net. He liked my forehand, which was really his coaching specialty.

—Aaron Krickstein

As a 14-year-old kid moving away from my home in a small town, I never thought that Nick would be the catalyst to open a closet full of dreams. I've known Nick for 37 years and as my life has evolved, so much of what I do and how I do things comes from key principals Nick has taught me over the years. Discipline, focus, desire and the ability to deal with adversity are keys to Nick's successes. He helped me learn as a player, how to dig in and get the most out of myself, day in and day out. As a coach, he helped me understand the psychology of dealing with individuals and educated me in the skills needed to be successful in helping others to maximize their potential.

—Paul Annacone

82

CHAPTER 6

The Birth of NBTA

Back in Miami, with no concrete plans for my future, I heard of a promising opportunity on the other side of the state. The Colony Beach and Tennis Resort, which was located on Longboat Key, one of the barrier islands on the Gulf Coast by Sarasota and Bradenton, was considering bringing on a new director for its tennis program. Longboat Key, Bradenton, Sarasota? I had barely heard of any of those places. What little I knew about that part of the world came from Mike DePalmer, Sr., a former basketball and football coach, who was then director of tennis at the Bradenton Country Club.

Mike and I had become friends when his two young children, Michelle and Mike Jr., both terrific players, came to Beaver Dam. They later became protour players. Michelle was in the top 100 before injuries halted her promising career. Mike Jr. also played on the

Skinny Nick and big Mike DePalmer— best friends forever.

professional circuit, worked as a teaching pro for me later on and coached Boris Becker for a while. His younger sons, David and Joe, worked for me as coaches, too. This was an athletically talented family and we have remained close ever since I first met them. At the time, Mike Sr. helped me get an appointment with the owner of The Colony, Dr. Murf Klauber.

Julio Moros and I hopped in my purple Cadillac—a lot of people made fun of me because of the color, but I didn't care—drove across Alligator Alley and then headed north on I-75. We arrived at the resort just in time for a beautiful sunset. Julio looked at me and said, "Let's settle down here."

The next morning, we met with "Doc" Klauber. He was originally from Buffalo, New York, where he'd been a successful orthodontist, and he was crazy like me—wild, passionate and nuts about tennis. At The Colony, he owned the recreation rights, the tennis courts, pro shop and the restaurants, but not the 232 villas and condos. That became a problem over the years when hotel management and the condo owners didn't see eye to eye, and today the entire resort is completely closed down, a sad ending to a fabulous facility.

At the time, though, The Colony was very much a happening place. Doc and I talked briefly about what he was looking for and the possibility of me starting a tennis academy while operating programs for guests. He was happy to support my plans so long as the needs of the guests and their families always came first. I assured him they would, he and

Me, "Doc" Klauber and his wife Susan.

I shook hands and I had the job. In all the time we worked together, we never had a single disagreement, and we have remained close friends over the years. The Colony experience turned out to be another life-changing opportunity for me, and I am forever grateful to Doc for giving it to me.

Mike DePalmer, Sr. knew just about everyone in the area, which helped us get a quick start. My pros and I gave lessons to the guests at the hotel during the day. Several nights a week, I also put on clinics at the Bradenton Country Club. Soon we added clinics for local junior players before and after The Colony guests used the courts. The guests loved seeing the kids play and many of the juniors hit with the adults.

We charged $35 a weekend for the junior sessions, and I gave all of it to my pros for putting in extra time. I didn't keep a penny of it. Both junior and adult lessons proved popular, and I am proud to say that The Colony became the No. 1 tennis resort in the world for the five years I stayed there.

Many of the people I met at Dorado Beach followed me to The Colony, visiting over Christmas and other holidays. Mr. Marx and his family were among them. A few years later, he bought a home on Casey Key, installed a private court and would fly down almost every weekend with the kids to play tennis with my staff and me. (Today Casey Key is home to well-to-do and famous people who value their privacy, like the author Stephen King and Rosie O'Donnell.)

Another was Charlie Reed, a close friend of Mr. Marx's, who ended up in real estate in Boston, Massachusetts. He attended camps at the same time as the Marx children and stayed in a house of his own close to mine on Longboat Key, and they all grew up together with me. His mother Annette is married to fashion designer Oscar de la Renta and is godmother to my daughter Nicole. They all have generously supported my family and my career.

One day a young girl and her father, Carling and John Bassett, showed up at the courts of The Colony. I had no idea who they were, but on John's request, I hit a few balls with her. Afterward he asked me what I thought and I told him that Carling had a lot of talent. He walked away, leaving her with me, and didn't come back for two weeks. Carling informed me that first afternoon that he wanted her to stay with me, and she became my first live-in student, staying at my home on Shinbone Alley on the north end of Longboat Key.

It turned out that Carling's mother's family had founded Carling Breweries in Canada (although they no longer owned it). John later became one of the Academy's great benefactors. He bought a bus for us when we wanted to take our players to state-wide tournaments, and he built a Har-Tru court for me at my house and included me in the development of a residential community next to the Academy. He loved sports and was instrumental in starting the World Football League (WFL). It was a shame that he died so young (he was in his early 50s). His widow, Susan, a wonderful woman, ended up marrying Murf Klauber.

Carling Bassett and me at The Colony.

Carling was always a fierce competitor. Her favorite saying was, "Watch out for me, I'm coming." She won a number of junior tournaments and reached the semifinals of the U.S. Open in 1984 as a 16-year-old. That was just a year after she had turned pro. She was fortunate to have a great agent, Sara Fornaciari, the first female sports attorney. Sara had gone to work for ProServ after she couldn't find work as a sportswriter—there were no female sportswriters then—

and pursued a legal career instead. Tracy Austin became her first client, and Sara eventually served on the WTA board and was executive director of the WTA Players Association. We became close friends when she began directing Carling's career. I appreciate her love of tennis and her pit bull qualities on behalf of her clients—she never raises the white flag! She is also a treasure trove of vital statistics and tennis trivia.

Carling achieved a ranking of No. 8 in the world by the time she was 17. At the same time, she pursued a career as a fashion model and dabbled in acting. In 1987, she married fellow tennis player Robert Seguso, and they have five beautiful children. In 2007 she was inducted into the Canadian Tennis Hall of Fame. We remain close to this day. Don't say anything negative about me in her presence. She'll punch you smack in the nose!

Another student who came to Florida to stay at my home was Kathleen Horvath. She was a talented youngster and my first protégé to be ranked among the top 10 female players in the world. One day I came upon her at my pool hanging upside down from a tree. When I asked her why, she said her father had told her that it would stretch her and make her taller. It's doubtful that that regimen had anything to do with her success. She won a number

Me and Kathleen Horvath at The Colony in 1979.

of junior championships, turned pro at 15 and two years later upset Martina Navratilova in the 1983 French Open—the only player to defeat Martina that year! But her career stalled and she left tennis behind in her early 20s and made her career with Merrill Lynch in New York.

Meanwhile, so many youngsters were visiting our Beaver Dam camp that in the summer of 1977, I told a number of the families at the camp that I was opening a boarding school for junior tennis players in Sarasota. I can still remember the surprise on Julio Moros' face when I told him that we'd have 15 to 20 kids arriving in September. He asked, "Where are we going to put them?" At that point we had no boarding facilities, so we ended up having the students live at my house and with the other pros.

One of our earliest boarders was Anne White, a delightful young woman from West Virginia, who ranked among the top 20 women players in the world before she turned 20. She stayed with Mike De-Palmer's family and later caused quite a stir at the 1985 Wimbledon tournament when she wore a full-length, formfitting, white Lycra bodysuit in her first round match.

As programs at The Colony expanded, I began large group instruction for the junior players. I had no choice because Julio and I were dealing with an increasing number of guests, and we had to find a way to teach all of our young players in the limited time and space available. So I put anywhere from 20 to 40 students on one court at a time. While one was hitting, everybody else was skipping rope, running in place and improving their conditioning. If someone missed a ball, it was push-up time. This was a revolutionary idea, and it worked quite well, although Kathleen Horvath didn't like it and insisted on getting personal attention. The successful experiment started the trend of mass teaching that is commonplace in tennis clubs and training facilities everywhere now.

When things finally got so busy at The Colony that the guests couldn't get court time, I bought a club in 1978 in West Bradenton that had 21 courts, (nine clay and 12 hard, 16 of them lighted). We called our junior academy the DePalmer Bollettieri Tennis Club and kept growing to the point that we needed our own student housing. We found a rundown, 20-room motel on Manatee Avenue in Bradenton that was for sale. I asked Louis Marx if he could help with payment, and he generously gave me the $50,000 needed.

By then Carolina Murphy had graduated from college and joined us, and one of her first assignments was to get the motel ready. Everybody pitched in, scrubbing floors, tubs and toilets, mopping and sweeping, so we'd have it ready for opening in September. When Carolina's mom heard about it during a phone call, she said, "That's what you're doing with a college education? Get out of there right now and come home." But Carolina didn't take that advice. She signed on for one year and has stayed with me for 40 more, holding a variety of different jobs. She is now the director of parent relations at International Media Group (IMG). Her son, John Ryan, attended the Academy's baseball program and is now on the roster of the New York Yankees.

The motel had small rooms designed for two people, but we arranged the bedding to accommodate four to six kids. Eric Korita, at 6' 6", was so tall that his feet would stick out over the end of his bunk bed. The rooms were so small that all the students' racquets, bags and personal items had to be stored by the shed in the pool area. The kitchen was set up for a family of moderate size and the pantry served as my secretary's office, so we turned two bedrooms into our academy commissary. We'd give our students breakfast and send them off in two rental vans, one to Bradenton Academy and the other to Saint Stephen's Episcopal School. Then we made sandwiches for lunch, which the students ate in the parking lot before their tennis lessons. A cook prepared dinner at the motel—spaghetti, Salisbury steak—easy stuff. Afterwards, it was time for cleanup, homework and room checks. There was no chef on Sundays, so we cooked bacon and scrambled eggs in a big frying pan for everyone. For dinner, we bought KFC or pizza—this was before I became more interested in nutrition and its effects on athletic performance.

Some of the players who ended up staying at the motel included Susan Smith, a nationally ranked junior and Frank Falkenburg, later an Ultimate Frisbee champion, who became an attorney and my personal manager for some time at the Academy. Paul Annacone also stayed there. Paul was an All-American at the University of Tennessee and spent a decade as a pro, winning a doubles championship at the Australian Open in 1985. Later on, he became a coach and took over as Pete Sampras' coach when Tim Gullikson got sick in 1994.

When Tim died two years later, it was a great loss for the tennis world. Paul also coached Tim Henman and Roger Federer for a time. His calm personality fit in well with these relatively laid-back players. He now coaches Sloane Stephens, who could become the heir apparent to Serena Williams in the next few years. I wonder how Paul will do coaching the ladies? I guarantee, it will be a different experience for him.

Paul Annacone at the Academy.

We were anything but laid-back at the new Academy. We went at breakneck pace and improvised whenever necessary. Picnic tables were set up in the driveway and the kids would eat in shifts. We didn't have a place for them to study, so we filled in the swimming pool and built a 1,200-square-foot structure above it to serve as a makeshift study hall. Chip Brooks personally laid some of the foundation blocks. Academy coaches served as cooks, bus drivers, maids and yes, tennis coaches. We worked 365 days a year with no time off, but I shared the profits we made with them (if we made any profit). I can't say enough about the dedication of my amazing staff from those early days, including Julio Moros, Chip Brooks, Ted Meekma, Greg Breunich, Steve Owens, Sammy Aviles and two other ball boys from Dorado Beach, Piri and Edwin Oyola. Many stayed with me for decades and worked tirelessly to help make my vision for a tennis academy become a reality. Some remain with me today!

I want to give special mention here to Steve Owens, a coach who worked with me through most of my career, from Dorado Beach to The Colony, at All-American Sports at Amherst, Beaver Dam and finally to the Nick Bollettieri Tennis Academy. Steve was a central figure in the lives of Mr. Marx's children, Geoffrey, Pearson, Lindsay and little Louis Jr.—he was like a second father to them. It was not

My staff at The Colony: from left, Steve Owens, Dee Mudd, David Brewer, Julio Moros, Ted Meekma, Laura Baxley and Mike Kruger.

unusual for Mr. Marx to keep Steve on the court 12 to 14 hours a day. Barbara Chin, Mr. Marx's able secretary, who was responsible for checking Steve's expense reports, one day noted that he was padding them.

Mr. Marx was well aware of it, and he didn't mind. He knew that only a few individuals could survive being with his kids day and night.

Did I mention that Steve is a force of nature? He could sell you your worn-out posessions and make you think they were brand-new. And he's a character. I never allowed my coaches to smoke. One day I was in front of The Colony Beach Hotel waiting for a ride to take me to my home on Longboat Key, seven miles away—I didn't drive my red Mercedes convertible to work because it would get all covered with sand from the beach. Steve was leaving the complex in his van, having no idea I was standing at the entrance. He passed me with a cigarette hanging from his mouth, and when he noticed me looking at him, he swallowed the cigarette! I thank Steve for all that he did for me and with me. He is a rare breed of human being and I will always call him my friend.

While my dedicated staff joined me willingly for the busy ride, my marriage did not survive the whirlwind of activity and my relentless drive to succeed. After more than a decade together, Jeri and I weren't getting along anymore, and she decided to file for divorce. She moved to Cincinnati where her sister Janet lived, taking the girls with her.

After a while Danielle decided to come back to Florida to stay with me. She didn't receive any privileges when at the house or on the courts. She became an excellent tennis player and won the state doubles championship with her partner, Mandy Stoll, who died in a tragic traffic accident a few years later. Danielle married Greg Breunich and they have given me two wonderful granddaughters, Willa Bay and Addie Sky, both excellent tennis players. Angel became a doctor of acupuncture. She was an outstanding equestrian who could have been a tournament rider. Angel now lives in Sarasota, and Danielle and her mother Jeri both live in Port St. Lucie.

During the two years after my divorce, I lived as a bachelor, spending time in hot spots on St. Armand's Circle, at the time the "in" place in Sarasota for tourists, resort guests and wealthy, famous people. Some nights we got pretty wild. My drink in those days was

Crown Royal whiskey, ginger ale and a wedge of lemon. One night, when I had had too much "ginger ale," I went to the bathroom and got into an argument with someone. It got so loud that some of my friends came rushing in to intercede. Turns out, it was me I was shouting at. I was cursing out my own reflection in the mirror.

But regardless of how late we stayed out and how much drinking we had done, we never let that interfere with the job. Six a.m. was reveille at The Colony, and everyone was there, ready to work, even if they hadn't been to bed. Tennis always came first, and my ambitions for an academy of my own kept me plenty busy.

Although we had the motel, some of the students still stayed with me in my home on Longboat Key. One of them was a young boy named Jimmy Arias. I first met him when he came to The Colony from

Jimmy Arias and me later on in my favorite training outfit—shirtless, working on my tan.

his home in Buffalo, New York. Although only 12, he was already the U.S. 14-and-under champion. He was 5' 2" on his toes at the time and had a slender frame, but he shocked us all by jumping off the ground, throwing his full body into his forehand and wrapping the racquet around his shoulder on his follow-through. Add to this his weird grip (strong semi-western) and you get a preview of today's game. He was smashing the ball around the court when others were just pushing it. His dad, an engineer who was also small, had taught it to him.

I called my staff over and said, "Here's the new Bollettieri forehand" and invited him to join me at the junior academy, offering him a scholarship. He first lived at Mike DePalmer's house and then moved in with me. I recommended switching him to a two-handed backhand, but his dad vetoed that and said if I insisted, just send Jimmy home. I still believe that he could have accomplished more, even though he rose to No. 4 in the world. Meanwhile, my other juniors started to imitate Jimmy's forehand, and it became the signature stroke of the Academy. I believe that it revolutionized tennis and that Jimmy Arias deserves credit for initiating the "power game."

During the late 70s, another revolution occurred when Prince brought out an oversized racquet. It had a larger striking surface than the traditional wood and steel racquets, which required precise hand-eye coordination. With the sweet spot increasing from two to about seven tennis balls, it made the game easier for everyone, eliminating the need for perfect technique.

Jack Murray, the president of Prince, and Howard Head, the inventor of the racquet, approached me and asked if I would use it in my programs. I said, "Are you kidding?" When they offered, "We will pay you for it," my ears perked up and I said, "Okay, I'll do it."

I became part of a Prince team, along with my friend Fritz Nau, to tour the country to introduce and promote the new racquet. Fritz had been with me for some time. He started out in tennis coaching a very talented young girl by the name of Susan Sloan, who was the No. 1 junior in the nation in the girls' 12-and-under division, and later went on to a world WTA ranking of No. 18.

We began the tour in California. Prince originally wanted to appeal to club players who hit off center more often than not, but I felt embarrassed traveling and playing with a "sissy racquet." It was an awkward-looking contraption, and a lot of people poked fun at us when we showed up with it. It helped, though, that I got paid $3,500 for my services. The racquet revolutionized tennis, ushering in the way the game is played today by elite players. I have been with Prince on and off for most of my career—the company now operates an innovation center at IMG Academy—and it has been a good relationship for all parties.

By 1979, my marriage life took another turn. Many evenings after work, my staff and I would start with drinks at The Colony's Lounge before heading out to St. Armand's Circle to party. On one particular night a waitress caught my eye. Her name was Diane. I asked her what time she got off and she said not until 10:30 p.m. I knew the maître d' at The Colony and asked him if Diane could leave early. He said, "Sure, Nick," so the entire group, including Diane, headed out. We went to the Patio, a local hot spot on the Circle and danced to "Saturday Night Fever" by Barry Gibb and the Bee Gees. Later on, I met Barry when his sons attended the IMG Academy. I was honored to be invited by him to Las Vegas to give a motivational "pep" talk to his team before one of the Bee Gees' last concerts.

A few weeks after that night at the Patio, Diane and I got married. She and her two beautiful children came to live in my house on Longboat Key, sharing it with Carling Bassett, Jimmy Arias, Pam Casale, Lori Kosten, Aaron Krickstein, Kathleen Horvath, the Marx children and a host of other kids. It was quite a circus—with Kathleen hanging from a tree outside, Dr. Krickstein calling me every night at 11 p.m., Jimmy Arias trying to explain to his dad on the phone why he lost one game in beating his opponent 6-0, 6-1, Louis Marx's secretary Barbara Chin calling 20 times a day checking on his kids to make sure they were on the court, not to mention having to feed this tribe of hungry kids. Add in the fact that I provided very little help around the house. So it was no surprise when I returned late one evening from a tournament with the players and found a note on the door: "Nick, I love you, but I have my two children. This is too much for me. Good luck to you!" The pressure I had put on Diane was just too much. And that was that.

The marriage lasted less than a year, but I didn't stay single for long. As if I weren't busy enough already, I decided to branch out and get into the restaurant business. I bought an Italian restaurant on St. Armand's. It was doing very well, but nobody knew that I was the owner. I'd go there in the evening and enjoy dinner without paying. Although the place was busy, we weren't making any money yet. The fact is, I've rarely made money on any venture I got involved in outside the sport of tennis.

But when opportunity knocks, I always open the door. One evening a beautiful young woman came over to deliver the check for my meal and Tomas, the maître d', intercepted her and told her that there was no check for me, because I was the owner. As I was leaving, I mentioned to him that I thought she was darned good-looking. He agreed and added that she was also doing a fabulous job for the restaurant. You guessed it; I started dating her and married her soon after in the backyard of her grandmother's house in Sarasota. Kellie and I lasted a lot longer than my previous marriage, and we had two beautiful daughters, Nicole and Alexandra.

Shortly after our dormitory motel opened for the new season, a television producer from ABC's "20/20" program was visiting The Colony with his daughter. They walked past me giving lessons to some youngsters, yelling at the top of my voice, as usual. Nonetheless, he asked if she could join the group, and I said, "Sure." Later he asked if I would like him to do a television piece on me and the tennis program. Of course, I would!

The "20/20" segment did a good job of presenting the program and my high demands, expectations of the students, and ability to motivate, although it wasn't entirely complimentary—it made no bones about my temper, ego and "my way or the highway" approach.

And it missed my fun side—me calling off practice anytime the waves were up, and leading the charge of a horde of kids to the beach to go bodysurfing. More often than not, we jumped into the waves still wearing our tennis clothes. The television program did not go over well with my mother. My dad later told me that she started to swear at the television screen in Italian when the program mentioned my not-so-wholesome qualities. Dad calmed her down, pointing out that *any* talk about me on national TV was a good thing; and, as usual, he was right. He said, "Let your son's results speak for themselves."

The "20/20" piece put us on the map and generated further interest in the tennis program. We had so many inquiries from parents and requests to take their children that we were working harder and longer than ever—if that was even possible.

We began to have so many kids in attendance at the motel that they had to eat in shifts under the direction of Bill Baxter, an ex-Marine drill sergeant I had hired to keep things organized. He was powerfully built and had the standard "butch" haircut. He treated the students as though they had enlisted in the Marine Corps. Beds had to be made with the blanket so tight you could bounce coins on it. Shoes and sneakers had to be neatly placed under the beds. During morning inspections, the students stood at attention. If they passed muster, they could then go to the outdoor mess hall and eat breakfast, one shift at a time. The boys and girls marched out to the busses taking them to school, and if they were going to the DePalmer Bollettieri Tennis Club a short distance away, they jogged there in double time. Bill Baxter's boot camp training methods may have seemed harsh, but without them we never would have succeeded. My coaches simply didn't have enough time to do everything. To this day I still wonder how we made it through the early days at all.

We were outgrowing our capacity and the time was ripe for my idea for the first live-in tennis academy in the world. Over Thanksgiving in 1980, when Mr. Marx visited The Colony—that was before he bought his house on Casey Key—I told him how well the junior program was doing. I talked about the expansion and needing a bigger, self-contained facility with courts, dormitories and food service to make our growth possible. He told me to work up a proposal.

I found 12 acres of land on 34th Street West. The area was sparsely populated with a housing complex nearby and a gas station at the intersection of 34th Street West and 53rd Avenue. This 12-acre parcel was clear but surrounded by hundreds of acres of tomato fields. We had to get zoning approval, which was not easy because the residents of the adjoining housing complex, mostly senior citizens, were fearful that we would have kids who were out of control and would disrupt their sedentary lifestyles.

Aerial shot of NBTA in 1981.

Luckily, I had a friend, Bob Farrance, who was a local attorney and knew the political ropes (he later became a judge); with a great deal of effort, Bob got a zoning variance for me. He explained that the development of this tennis academy would provide rapid growth to the Bradenton area. As it turned out, the original 12-acre facility, now known as IMG Academy, has expanded to more than 450 acres and offers elite academics and athletic training in eight sports.

When I showed the proposal to Mr. Marx, he didn't bat an eye. He not only wrote a check for $1.2 million, but also guaranteed the bank loan for the rest of the money to build the complex. All of his friends assured him that he would never see that money again, but he told me not to worry about it. If we didn't succeed, he would use it as a tax write-off. I was reassured but determined to prove his friends wrong.

We broke ground and laid out the courts for the Nick Bollettieri Tennis Academy (NBTA) early in 1981. Because the city of Bradenton didn't want to be stuck with dormitories if we failed, we built the initial housing for the students like condos with kitchen facilities. They would live in the bedrooms and could use the refrigerators, but were not allowed to cook there. The original buildings still stand on the grounds and are now used mostly for administrative offices.

That season was my last at The Colony, although from time to time, Dr. Klauber would call and ask me to conduct demonstrations for his guests. I would charge no fee and in turn, there would be free meals and accommodations when my friends visited.

The doors to NBTA, the first junior tennis academy in the world, opened in November of 1981, and we were on our way.

I first met Nick when I was at a national 12-and-under USTA tournament, where I was with Tracy Austin. I then became aware that he had just started the Nick Bollettieri Tennis Academy—a completely new concept in this country. Now, over 40 years later, everybody in the world is trying to copy him, but can't come close.

—Robert Lansdorp, tennis coach

The two back courts were like putting two tigers in there with a piece of raw meat to fight it out. Nick was not afraid to put the best into the playpen and see who came out alive.

—Jim Courier

The first time I ever saw a swing volley, because people were always critical of Nick that he didn't teach the volley, was with Carling, and she was at the Academy and was about 12 years old. She was skinny and scrawny, but she was fearless and ruthless and had great attitude. She would take the ball out of the air from a little bit behind the service box and just swing at it. She didn't have the height or even the technique, but she wanted the point. I am not crediting her with inventing the swing volley, but a bunch of kids at the Academy started doing it—taking the ball out of the air like that and using both hands.

—Mary Carillo

CHAPTER 7

NBTA Glory Days

The concept of a full-time, live-in training program for junior tennis players at the highest competitive level soon drew worldwide attention. *Sports Illustrated, USA Today* and *The New York Times* were just a few of the magazines and newspapers that conducted interviews or did feature stories on us. You can't imagine how proud we were to have such wide-ranging approval of our new facility.

Talented kids were flocking to NBTA from near and far, looking for a more competitive environment than their hometowns could provide. We already had Jimmy Arias, Aaron Krickstein, Kathleen Horvath and Carling Bassett, and with some of the new players arriving I began to imagine that we could beat national, even world-ranked players. But I soon realized that only one course of action would allow us to grow and continue to attract the most talented youngsters—beating the best players in Florida. Many parents struggled with the idea of giving up their children to a full-time training environment. Others had difficulty with the cost, which was close to $1,500 a month. So I decided to give the best talent full scholarships, which included having the Academy pay for the Bollettieri Traveling Team.

With the bus provided for us by John Bassett, Chip Brooks took our best players to tournaments all over the southeastern United States, including Flamingo Park (where my son Jimmy Boy is currently the tennis director), which hosted the most famous junior tournament in the world, the Orange Bowl.

We also attracted some unexpected attention. In 1982, the Academy became part of an international incident. I was visiting Washington, D.C., to meet with a potential donor for NBTA when I received an urgent call from my agent, Donald Dell. He had astonishing news. Hu Na, a 19-year-old tennis player from the People's Republic of China, had defected during the Federation Cup matches in Santa Clara, California. I was to fly to Los Angeles right away to pick her up and bring her to Florida, where she would train at the Academy while seeking political asylum in the United States.

I arrived in California close to midnight and checked into the Beverly Wilshire Hotel. At 1:30 a.m. the phone rang. It was someone from the U.S. State Department telling me they knew why I was there. I was getting just a little paranoid. In the morning, Frank Wu, the man who had orchestrated Hu Na's defection, came to the room. He was involved in tennis racquet manufacture, and I had met him once before at a junior tournament in Taiwan. He arranged for airline tickets to Sarasota, buying the one for Hu Na under an assumed name.

We met up later at the airport. It was like we were in a spy movie, with Frank Wu sitting in a telephone booth looking around to make sure he wasn't being tailed. When he thought the coast was clear, he brought out Hu Na and introduced us. She spoke no English and looked as nervous as I felt. Although we were supposed to take the red-eye in secret, I couldn't let such an opportunity slip by unnoticed and called a reporter at the *Sarasota Herald-Tribune* during our layover in Dallas. He met us when we arrived in Florida and interviewed me. His article initiated international press coverage.

A few days later, I got a call from the State Department warning me of rumors that the Chinese government was going to try to kidnap Hu Na. Soon, a federal SWAT team arrived with federal agents brandishing machine guns to protect us. I had visions of foreign agents attacking the Academy and killing everyone in sight. My ex-wife Jeri was going crazy because Hu Na was rooming with our daughter Danielle. She yelled at me, "Get her out of there!" So we got four identical SUVs and hid Julio Moros and Hu Na in back of one of them under some blankets. Then, we took off in different directions with the decoys and sneaked Hu Na to our motel until things blew over. And of course they did, because the rumors were false; we returned to our normal routine.

Three weeks later I received a call from the White House. It was President Reagan. He complimented me on being a very good tennis coach, but advised me to stay out of diplomatic affairs in the future. I all but saluted and said, "Yes, Mr. President." It was thrilling to get a personal call from him, and I told everyone about it. It wasn't until many years later that I found out it had been a prank call. One of my teaching pros had a brother-in-law who was a comedian and a very good impressionist, and put him up to it. But then, seeing how excited I was, he and his cohorts were too scared to tell me that it was all a hoax—a lot of people were afraid of me and my temper in those days.

From left: unknown, Lloyd Bourne, Chip Hooper, Greg Breunich, Hu Na, Tim Mayotte, Aaron Krickstein, me and Jean Claude Labout.

Hu Na was a lovely girl with a winning smile. She trained at the Academy for some time. Later, she played on the women's pro tour, but she never became a star. Her best showing in a Grand Slam tournament was a third-round finish at Wimbledon in 1985.

Meanwhile, Jimmy Arias kept developing like a shooting star. In 1982, two years after he'd turned pro, he ranked among the top 20 players. The following year, when he was 19, he won four singles titles, among them the U.S. Open Clay Courts Championships and the Italian Tennis Championship. At the 1983 U.S. Open, he reached the singles semifinals and finished the year ranked No. 5 in the world. He was still training at NBTA and his success was a big feather in our cap. Unfortunately, by 1984, shoulder problems and a bout with mononucleosis weakened his game, and while he returned to professional play, he never again matched his earlier, teenage triumphs.

Aaron Krickstein was coming into his own, however. In 1983, he turned pro and two weeks after his 16th birthday became the youngest player to win a singles title in Tel Aviv, Israel. The following year he broke into the top 10 and won the U.S. Pro Tennis Championships.

He had an extraordinary career despite being plagued by injuries, including stress fractures in both feet, problems with his knee and wrist, and the aftermath of a freak accident, when he was sideswiped in a New York taxi cab.

Aaron Krickstein

He reached the semifinals of the 1989 U.S. Open and the 1995 Australian Open. He got the nickname "Marathon Man" because of his tenacity in long matches. You wouldn't want to get into a five-setter with Aaron. His career record of 27-8 in that department was better than Boris Becker's. His forehand, which generated remarkable power and spin, was the precursor of all the great forehands in modern tennis—Federer, Nadal, Djokovic. Aaron has made a happy and successful life for himself after his professional career—he is now the director of tennis at St. Andrews Country Club in Boca Raton—and we have a great deal of affection for one another and continue to stay in touch to this day.

Carling Bassett was tearing up the courts as well. By 1985, she had reached the quarterfinals at the French Open and semifinals at the U.S. Open.

Holy mackerel, my crazy idea for the NBTA was working!

I kept going non-stop, pushing myself and everyone else—students and coaches at the Academy—as hard as ever. At the same time, I enjoyed many of the trappings of success that I could now afford. I bought a 38-foot Wellcraft yacht for $165,000 on the spur of the moment and hired an experienced captain to teach me how to operate it. I thought I was doing very well until the first time I tried to dock the boat. When I put one engine in reverse and the other in forward, the yacht started to spin and I clipped the dock with its bow, demolishing a good half of it. That was it for my naval exploits! I sold the yacht for $65,000.

Always on the lookout for fancy cars, I bought a black Ferrari in addition to my yellow Corvette. I also acquired a Clénet, a classy looking convertible roadster, for $83,000 and ended up selling it for $30,000. Sylvester Stallone also bought one and wrote an article for

Rolling Stone magazine, in which he said that only assholes would buy one of these cars. I wrote Sly a note, "From one asshole to another, I bought a Clénet too!" but I never heard back from him.

I nearly sold the Academy, too. One day, a neatly dressed man representing an Arab sheik showed up and told Julio Moros his client wanted to see the place. Apparently, he was crazy about tennis and wanted to buy a private facility where he and his friends could play. I said, "Sure, we'll show him around." Three months went by and nothing happened.

Then the man suddenly showed up again and told us, "The sheik's coming!" We weren't prepared, but I sent Julio to the airport to welcome him. The sheik arrived with his entourage—a small army of young Filipinos, his personal umpire and other retainers—in three of his private jets. He wanted to play tennis right away, so we teamed him up with Julio against Louis Marx and me. The Filipinos lined up around the court and acted as ball boys. Every time one of my or Mr. Marx's shots landed close to the line inside the court, the umpire would call, "Out!" Anything the sheik hit, even if it was out by a foot, was "In!"

For the next two weeks, the sheik stayed at the Hyatt Hotel in Sarasota; he then returned to the Academy a number of times over the following months. We had to set aside a room for him in one of the dormitories behind the clay courts, where he would perform his prayers in private. If Julio and I happened to be there at the time, we would have to get on our knees and pray with him. Although we gave the sheik racquets, balls and shoes, we never saw any money. At one point he brought four fancy watches for Julio and me and our wives. His representative told us they were each worth $10,000 and not to worry: The sheik would take care of us.

I did get nervous, though, and asked Mr. Marx to check him out. He did and said the sheik was the real thing, a full-fledged oil billionaire. But after three months passed and the sheik's account had risen to over $100,000 and we still hadn't seen a penny, I had Julio present him with a bill. The sheik acted shocked and said, "That is not mine. It is my understanding that I have been Mr. Bollettieri's honored guest all along. I never dreamed he would insult me this way." Then he got up in a huff, walked away and vanished along with his entourage. We never heard from him again. When we had one of the watches appraised, it turned out to be a knockoff worth all of $50. (He did pay his bill at the Hyatt.)

In the meantime, NBTA was attracting players from all over the world. Not surprisingly, some of them were from the country of my heritage, Italy. One of them was Raffaella Reggi. Her offensive weapons and physical stature may not have measured up to the best in the world, but she used all of her resources to win. She had an inner confidence that inspired the Italian players, both male and female. In 1985, she was the first Italian woman to win the Italian Open in more than 30 years. The

Raffaella Reggi and me.

following year she added a mixed doubles championship at the U.S. Open and later reached a career-high standing of No. 13 in the world.

Raffaella was a gritty competitor who possessed a never-say-die attitude that ranked among the best I've ever seen. I can still remember a match that took place on the red clay courts at the French Open in Paris. Annabel Croft, a highly ranked English player (now a top tennis commentator), seemed to have the match in hand because Rafaella was sick. She had been throwing up between games, and I wanted her to default the match; but she walked over to the fence where I was standing and said, "I'd rather die than give up." She went on to win the match.

Raffaella continues to be a role model for me to talk about to students, business associates, parents, etc. She always left everything on the court and will always be my "Italian Hero."

There were other talented Italian players in the early 1980s as well. Two of them, Giacomo Staiano and Umberto Rianna, came to me on the recommendation of an Italian touring umpire, Peppino DiStefano. Giacomo was an excellent player, but didn't have the killer instinct required to succeed as a pro, although he has become a very successful businessman on Capri. Umberto was also a very good player, and he is now the coach for the Italian Tennis Federation. The boys became very close to my family, and Giacomo's father got on a plane for the first time in his life to visit the Academy. Soon after, I made the first of my annual visits to their home on Capri.

Papa Staiano, me, Roberto, Mama and Giacomo Staiano.

The ancient and historic island is a vacation paradise, known for its famous Blue Grotto and the ruins of imperial Roman villas.

The town of Anacapri has a small, scenic harbor and a high panoramic promenade lined with villas. Limestone crags called sea stacks project above the sea. I either stay with the Staianos or at the Grand Hotel Quisisana, the most famous hotel on the island owned by Nicola Morgano and his family (his son was also a student at IMG Academy). There are tennis courts, of course, and I conduct teaching clinics while I'm there. Capri is one of the few places in the world where I can truly relax. If there were room for a golf course on the island, I'd move there permanently!

Giacomo Staiano and his family have essentially adopted me. I have brought some of my wives, my children, and my friends and colleagues along for some of the visits, and we are always welcome and treated as honored guests. Words can't fully express how my time with Giacomo and his family have impacted my life!

During the 1980s, NBTA had among its ranks just about every top junior in America. Among this group was a young man who had extremely effective, but ugly, strokes and knew how to put them to

A young Brad Gilbert.

use, constructing points to produce a winning result. The player I'm referring to is Brad Gilbert. Besides his unusual-looking game, he had the uncanny ability to get into the heads of his opponents, frustrating them to the point where their tennis suffered. He turned pro in 1982 and reached a ranking of No. 4 in the world. He won 20 tournaments during his career while earning well over $5 million in prize money.

Brad later became a sought-after tennis coach, working with top players like Andre Agassi and Mary Pierce. He is also one heck of a color commentator at Grand Slam tournaments. He comes up with witty names for the players and provides astute analysis of matches. Brad sent his son Zack and sister Dana to train at IMG Academy and at various times, comes to visit as a coach. Brad is a terrific friend and someone I will always respect.

In the 80s we were getting better known throughout the United States, and not just in tennis circles. Following Jimmy Arias' sensational showing at the 1983 U.S. Open, CBS' "60 Minutes" called wanting to do a segment on the NBTA. During the negotiations leading up to the taping of the show, I was worried that Mike Wallace would conduct the personal interview with me—I knew he was a tough customer and I was a little afraid of him. When I found out that it would be Morley Safer, I said, "Okay, we'll do it."

The program aired on January 1, 1984 under the title "Tennis Boot Camp," and became a huge boost for the Academy. Morley Safer didn't sugarcoat what we did and presented me as a demanding taskmaster, but it also made clear that the parents and their children came voluntarily, enjoyed the competition, and that the results spoke for themselves.

Soon after, I received a phone call from a man in Las Vegas who told me about his talented son Andre. Mike Agassi taught him tennis from an early age but felt he had reached the limit of what he could do for him. He wanted me to take over and make Andre a champion. Mike has gotten a bad rap for pushing Andre hard from an early age. He outfitted the backyard of his home in Las Vegas with all kinds of equipment and machines to develop his son's hand-eye coordination and tennis abilities. True, he was demanding and offered only "tough love," always criticizing, even when Andre started to win tournaments; but make no mistake, without him Andre would never have achieved greatness.

I agreed to help out and gave Andre a partial scholarship. Mike Agassi sent a check for $1,600 to cover the first two months at the Academy. When Andre first arrived, he played on the back courts against others his age, but I soon took notice. He was a relentless competitor and already had a powerful forehand. Two months into his stay, I gave back the check and put him on full scholarship.

A young Andre Agassi at NBTA.

Later that year, I also offered a scholarship to another talented youngster, Jim Courier. A Florida boy from Dade City about 100 miles north of Bradenton, Jim had a dogged determination to succeed. He and Andre were like oil and water. Although they roomed together for a short while, they soon became rivals on the courts. Jim was precise, serious and very organized. Although he didn't like drills and had to be pushed to practice, he had a tremendous work ethic and usually did what was asked of him. Andre was flippant, often confrontational and harder to manage. He had a love-hate relationship with tennis, with his overly demanding father and with me, but his talent and desire to succeed won out in the end (more on that later).

Another fine young player was David Wheaton. His caring, close-knit family relocated from Minneapolis to Florida to support him while he attended the Academy. His mother was very religious and sent him to Saint Stephen's while most of the other young players went to Bradenton Academy. She also became a major influence on Andre Agassi for a while, encouraging him to read the Bible and pursue Christianity. David was 6' 3" and had a powerful two-handed backhand. After a freak rollerblading accident at Stanford University in which he catapulted through a window and hurt his left hand, he developed a wicked slice backhand. He was a kind young man who would never hurt a soul. Perhaps that is why, despite his considerable talent, he never had the ferocious fire in the belly, the ruthless desire to win that characterized Agassi and Courier. Nevertheless, he had a good professional career, with a banner year in 1991 when he reached the semifinals at Wimbledon and the finals of the Grand Slam Cup in Munich, Germany, where he beat Brad Gilbert after getting into a huge argument with him and losing only to Jim Courier.

I also had a quartet of very talented young black players at the Academy: Rodney Harmon, Chip Hooper, Martin Blackman and MaliVai Washington, who all have made a career of tennis. Rodney Harmon reached the quarterfinals at his U.S. Open debut in 1982. He is currently the coach of the Georgia Tech women's tennis team. Chip Hooper has combined his expertise in martial arts and tennis, and is currently a private coach of elite players. Martin Blackman was a key component of the USTA's Player Development program and has his own tennis academy now in Boca Raton. MaliVai Washington reached the finals of Wimbledon in 1996 and achieved a career high No. 11 ranking in the world. I am proud of all of their achievements.

The year 1985 was perhaps when we had the most talented roster in the early days of the Academy. Jimmy Arias, now 21, was still training at NBTA. Aaron Krickstein and Carling Bassett, both teenagers, were doing well. Agassi and Courier were both 15; David Wheaton and Chris Garner were 16. My junior players were winning tournaments right and left.

I was in my mid-50s and saw nothing but a rosy future ahead.

The "Fab Four" and me at Mr. Marx's court—
Martin Blackman, Andre Agassi, Jim Courier and David Wheaton.

Nick has been extremely generous with me. He altered the path of my life by giving me a scholarship. I went from a boy to a man at the Academy. Fourteen to 17 is a pretty critical time in a boy's life, let alone in a tennis player's life. I went there as a diamond in the rough and left relatively polished.

—Jim Courier

CHAPTER 8

Jim Courier

One day I received a handwritten letter from Jim Courier's mother, Linda, explaining how pleased she was that Jim would be entering NBTA. Jim was just 14 years old when I offered him that full scholarship. He had started to play at a young age at his great-aunt's tennis club in Sanford, Florida. In fact, he played his very first

tournament at the DePalmer Bollettieri Tennis Club against Mike DePalmer, Jr. I had started to notice him when he competed against some of my players, and after he reached the finals at the 1984 Orange Bowl tournament—he was a high-ranked junior by then—I contacted him and offered him a place at NBTA. He later told me that it took him less than 10 minutes to make the decision to come, and it didn't take me much longer to realize this kid was a bull dog.

In her letter, Linda asked me to change his two-handed backhand. Jim loved baseball and was darn good; he was so good, in fact, that he could have been a professional baseball player. He actually struck his backhand the same way he hit a line drive with a baseball bat, using an unconventional grip—semi-western bottom hand and semi-western top hand. Before I decided what to do about Linda's request, I evaluated Jim's other strokes, his physical and mental attitude, and how competitive he was. My findings:

- Jim's forehand was lethal as he struck the ball with an extreme western grip.

- His powerful serve was sonic and he could change it to kick up so high, the receiver needed a stepladder to reach it.

- He was so competitive I almost nicknamed him "The Bull Dog."

- He was not a conventional volleyer, but he followed my instruction to just swing at his shoulder-high volleys.

My advice to him was, "Jim, my boy, forget about your backhands and hit all forehands." This is a very common practice today. Nowadays, you often see players like Federer and Nadal run around their backhands, but at the time, it was a new development in tennis.

I also told him to hit big serves, hit big returns and run for every ball. By the way, Jim's backhand, although unconventional, was pretty darn good, too.

In his first year at the Academy, Jim won the 16-and-unders at the Orange Bowl tournament when he was 15, and the 18-and-unders the following year. Only Björn Borg had achieved that back-to-back double before him.

Jim and my son Jimmy Boy became good friends—they both had an artistic streak; Jim was a drummer and my son, a photographer. At the time, there was a garage on our campus, where the Prince Innovation showroom is now, that was divided in half, with one side housing Jim's set of drums and the other serving as Jimmy Boy's photography lab. The two would do their thing well into the night as they both honed their skills with passion. Jim's drumming irritated a number of players who attended the Academy, including Andre. But Jimmy's interest was less intrusive, and he captured many of the players at the Academy both there and in tournaments in superb action photographs.

While Jim was always a stand-up guy, he wasn't a goody-two-shoes. When he wanted to visit his parents, he and Kenny Merritt would "borrow" a car from one of Jimmy Arias' friends and drive up north on the weekend. Kenny was from Florida, too. He came to NBTA in 1985 and did just about everything, from lawn maintenance to taking my daughters to school, to traveling with elite players to tournaments. He has always had a knack for sales and is now the head of promotion for Prince. In any case, he would drop Jim off in Dade City and continue on to visit his aunt and uncle. Then he'd return on Sunday, picking Jim up on the way, and they'd be back in time for curfew.

Jim Courier at a junior tournament.

Jim and Andre were my "special boys." They had a great rivalry going at the Academy. Jim resented that Andre got away with things that other students didn't, and that Andre didn't have to work as hard as others. He rightfully complained that he had to get up and start practice at 7 a.m., while Andre could show up at the courts at 11. I didn't realize at the time the depth of that resentment.

Throughout my career, I've always tried to treat my students equally and with compassion (the way I'd like people to treat my own children). But in 1989, around the time that Jim was leaving the Academy, I made a terrible mistake. We were at the French Open and Jim met Andre in the third round. I should have picked a neutral spot and cheered on both of my students, but I sat with Phillip Agassi, Andre's brother, and Bill Shelton, his manager. When Jim looked up and saw me, he was devastated. I could read in his eyes that he was wondering, "Why are you choosing Andre over me?" He later said, "I realized that Nick didn't want me to win and it kind of hurt me."

That didn't stand in the way of his performance, however. If anything, it got him mad and he played some of his most ferocious tennis, dispatching Andre (and me) in four sets.

To this day, I wonder why I chose to sit in Andre's seating area—when I loved both players with all my heart. How could I be so thoughtless as to not realize that it was an act of betrayal, a tacit admission of who I was pulling for? It was like a father overtly choosing one of his kids over the other.

As Jim grew into a man, he forgave me for my indiscretion and we became, and remain, the best of friends. He has always had a heart that is as big as all outdoors, and I am grateful to him for his unwavering support for what I do.

Jim stayed at the Academy for four years. His greatest triumphs, the four Grand Slam championships at the French and Australian Opens, as well as his No. 1 ranking in the world, came after he left and worked with other coaches. But he has always acknowledged the impact his time at the Academy had on both his game—laying the foundations for his success—and his personal development. Yet, he brought his unique personality to the game. Anyone who ever watched him compete could recognize his blood-and-guts, never-say-die style. He knew how to take what he had, make it better and reach for the stars.

Jim and me at the 2005 U.S. Open.

I met Nick at the 1985 Orange Bowl and he invited me, with a full scholarship, to train at his academy. Nick's academy was already world-famous, so I was excited for the opportunity. After I arrived I was doubly excited to be training alongside established pros like Jimmy Arias and Carling Bassett. In my former country, there were no indoor courts, so during the winter months I had to practice on a basketball court at crazy hours like 5 a.m. till 7 a.m. I know a few of his students complained about it being very military-like, but to me, I felt like a kid at Disney World.

Nick meant a lot to both my family and me. I know Nick and my dad didn't always see eye to eye, but they both wanted the best for me, and forever I will be thankful to both Nick and my dad for all they have done for me.

—Monica Seles

CHAPTER 9

Monica Seles

The first time I heard of Monica Seles was when one of my young female tennis prospects, Kim Kessaris, was trounced by her 6-1, 6-0 in the Sport Goofy tournament at Disney in Orlando. I just had to check out this 11-year-old phenom from Yugoslavia. The opportunity came two months later at the 1985 Orange Bowl. The tournament had several divisions, and only the older juniors played at Flamingo

Park. Monica was assigned to play at the Biltmore Hotel tennis facility.

By then, there already were rumors floating about that this young girl was darn good, but had a weird style of play. My staff and I were always on the lookout for new talent, so I was even more determined to see her for myself. The tournament director told me that Monica was playing on court four. I had to walk about 75 yards to get there. As I passed the clubhouse (the courts were hidden by shrubs), all I could hear was "heeee-heeee-heeee!" It sounded like a bird that had flown into a window fan.

When I finally came to the court and watched, I rubbed my eyes and cleaned my sunglasses in disbelief. Here was this tiny little girl who stood smack on the baseline—a toothpick on two spindly legs. You'd think a gust of wind would blow her over, but she was crushing the ball from both sides with a two-handed backhand and two-handed forehand. She had no need for the 21 feet behind the baseline. I thought that her motto must be to hit the ball hard, hit it early and never back up. Her determination and total focus on each strike of the ball was remarkable. She was pure, relentless, controlled aggression!

I offered her a full scholarship and invited her and her family to live in one of the apartments on the grounds of the Academy. She and her brother Zoltán, who was an excellent player in his own right and became a superb hitting partner for Monica, arrived  first. Two months later, her parents followed—Mama (Eszter) and Papa (Károly), a cartoonist by trade.

Early on, Monica practiced out in the open against some of my older female players and wore them all out. Keep in mind that she had one (and only one) style of play: Stand on the baseline and go for a winner each and every time. She did not believe in rallying or keeping the ball in play. She'd aim for the corners and blast winners. That's what made her such a formidable opponent, but an impossible practice partner. I had her hit against Agassi and Blackman, and she ran them ragged. I had her hit against three of my elite pros, Jose Lambert, Rene Gomez and Raúl Ordóñez, and she wore them out, too.

Monica quickly asserted herself. On one occasion, Jim Courier was practicing on court four of our indoor facility, while I was on court one working with Monica. I called him over to rally with her, and Jim obliged. He hit a ball to Monica and she blasted a winner. He hit another and she drilled that one, too. After she scorched the third winner, Jim yelled a few choice words and walked off the court, swearing he would never hit with her again. He didn't. They were both fiery characters.

When I mentioned this incident to Monica some years later, her recollection was kinder and slightly less graphic. She said, "Remember, at the time, Andre and Jim were not yet superstars. They were older and I was shy, so I never really interacted with either of them. I got to hit with Jim once, which didn't last long, as my tennis etiquette wasn't the best in those days. I would describe it more like I wanted to win every point and who cares about warm-ups, let's get down to playing points right away."

Another time I took her and Andre to Mr. Marx's winter home on Casey Key to play on his private tennis court. He and I sat on the small hill above and watched as the two began to warm up. I said, "You're looking at two kids who one day will be No. 1 in the world." He agreed with my assessment of Andre, but had his doubts about Monica, wondering out loud how "that skinny little girl" would ever succeed. After seeing her thrust her body at the tennis ball and squeak as she tore the wool off it, he began to understand—those two kids were destined for stardom.

Andre and Monica in 1986.

Unlike any player I have coached before or since, Monica worked tirelessly from dawn until long past dusk. Julio Moros, who arrived at the Academy at 6 a.m., would see her jogging, doing her morning run before she headed off to school. Our practice sessions were very intense. I changed her backswing because she was using too much wrist, which could have led to tendinitis. I changed the motion and toss of her serve. I spoke in detail about every physical and mental error. But

Monica never complained. She never put her head down and she never wanted to stop practice. Her focus, persistence and determination were amazing. Sometimes the sessions stretched until 8 or 9 p.m., and I often missed dinner and saying goodnight to my children.

I put in hundreds of hours with her, so much so that other parents began to get irritated. Dick Vitale, a former NBA coach of the Detroit Pistons and well-known ESPN broadcaster, was one of them. He and his lovely wife Lorraine moved to Bradenton so his two daughters could attend NBTA. Dick yelled at me once, "When are you going to pay some attention to Terri and Sherri? Why do you spend all your time with that little pipsqueak?" I told him, "Because she'll be No. 1 in the world one day." He looked at me and unleashed his famous expression, "Are you kidding me?" Dick was like every

Dick Vitale and me with his daughters Sherri and Terri, and Dick's grandchildren Sydney Sforzo, and Connor and Jake Krug.

typical parent. He wanted his daughters to become big-time pro players (they both received scholarships to Notre Dame and had fine college tennis careers). Dick now lives in nearby Lakewood Ranch and we have become great friends. As a former basketball coach, he understands my mentality from the inside out, and we have a lot of fun together. His five grandchildren are all young athletes with great potential and he's going bazooka, always asking me questions like "Should they go into this sport or that?" "Is this pro okay?" "Nick, what are we going to do?!"

Papa Károly was anxious, too, but in a different way—loving, over-protective and always concerned with security. After a while, we had to enclose Monica's back training court completely with canvas so that her sessions would be totally sealed from public view. No videos, no photos—Papa's rules! At first we kept the corners open to let the wind blow through, but at Papa's insistence, we closed those up, too. On three occasions, high winds blew the fence and canvas screening down.

At times, Monica's intensity and seriousness threatened to get the better of her, so I paired her up one year with Wendy Nelson as a doubles partner, and they toured the college circuit together. Whereas Monica was always serious and focused, Wendy was high-energy, joyful and sometimes too playful. They were complementary, emotionally, and became good friends and teammates. Wendy became an NCAA scholar athlete and captain of her tennis team at Northwestern, and then played on the pro circuit for a while after graduation.

When Monica was 14, she, Andre and John McEnroe were invited to play in a Nike shootout against Russia at its headquarters in Portland, Oregon. It was a serious competition, and both of my protégés easily beat their Russian adversaries. In fact, Monica smoked her opponent, Natasha Zvereva, who was a top 10 player at the time, 6-1, 6-2. It showed all of us that she was ready to compete at the professional level. When the matches were over, I instructed Monica to go to the far corner of the stadium and curtsy to a man sitting in a very special box seat. That man was Phil Knight, CEO and owner of Nike. She shortly thereafter signed a seven-figure contract with Nike (as did Andre).

Monica turned pro a year later, after her 15th birthday, and began her meteoric rise to the top. At Houston in only her second tournament, she ousted Chris Evert in the final, winning her first pro title. By the end of the year, she was No. 6 in the world!

When she didn't do well in the warm-up tournaments to the 1990 Lipton Championships in Key Biscayne, I suggested that we take a low-key approach. After all, she was only 16 then. I had Raúl Ordóñez working with her and Andre to get them both ready. The approach paid off because they both won. I was elated having two singles champions at the tournament. The following year, Monica became the No. 1 women's tennis player in the world, having won four Grand Slam titles already.

At some point, her father and I had financial disagreements and we went our separate ways. The Seles family moved out of the Academy and hired new coaches. In retrospect, it is unfortunate that we became estranged for a number of years, but I always kept a special place in my heart for Monica.

I was shocked and at a loss for words when she was assaulted and stabbed by a deranged spectator during her quarterfinal match in Hamburg, Germany in 1993. The attack halted her stellar career—she was No. 1 in the world at the time and had won seven of eight Grand Slams—and it took her some time to recover from the physical and mental trauma.

As she healed, she expressed some doubts about returning to competitive tennis. I know she reconnected with Wendy Nelson in Florida, who did her best to give her emotional support. I wrote Monica a long letter of encouragement, urging her to continue playing, and she answered it with a gracious letter of her own. It was the first contact between us for some time and initiated the mending of our relationship. We have become good friends since.

Monica made her comeback starting in the spring of 1995 with her usual determination and indomitable spirit, winning the Canadian Open and reaching the final of the U.S. Open, in which she lost to Steffi Graf in a thrilling three-set match. She ended up winning a number of tournaments, including two more Grand Slams, before she retired from the game for good.

I've worked with thousands of boys and girls. Some of them have become great players, but there are only a very few who can compare to Monica, not only because she became a tennis superstar, but because she is also a wonderful and kind person. Not many people in this world have the inner strength to forgive someone who has done them serious harm. Monica Seles is one of them. She has forgiven her attacker, understanding how disturbed a human being he was. We all wonder what she might have done had she not been stabbed at the height of her career. But she has never played the "what if" game. Instead, with a rare spirit she has accepted the ups and downs of her career and moved on with her life's journey. She has been rightfully honored by her peers and inducted into the International Tennis Hall of Fame.

People often ask me to describe Monica. My response is this: On court, Monica was a tiger, ready to do whatever necessary to win. But she always acted with respect and was true to herself, and she remains so to this day. Monica and I correspond regularly. She has always been kind to my children, and Cindi and my boys love her as well. She will always be very dear to me.

Me and Monica in 2004.

I will be forever thankful for Nick, who displayed not only a love of tennis, but also a love for Andre. He reminded me of my dad. Nick helped us navigate a world that was alien to us—agents, managers, media, practice schedules, tournaments and travel. As we moved on with our lives (notice I'm not saying that we "parted ways"), I've always known that Nick would be there if we ever called.

—Phillip Agassi, Andre's brother

I always felt that Nick was the perfect man to lead Andre through that time of his career. I sensed that he understood "the big time" of tennis and life. More, importantly, I sensed that Nick understood Andre… Nick understood that life on the "tennis road" is not easy, and he seemed to have an uncanny knack of knowing when to be serious and when to have a laugh. Sometimes, it's all about tennis and tactics and technique. Sometimes, it's about everything else. I enjoyed watching Nick demonstrate that wisdom. I have always respected his ability to teach and communicate.

—Gil Reyes, Andre's personal trainer

CHAPTER 10

Andre Agassi

Andre Agassi not only had a huge talent for tennis, he possessed the genius to change the game in ways that few have in its history. From his glowing, long, sometimes bleached hair, to his flashy clothes—image was everything. He was the first rock star of tennis, and he brought his brash, exuberant personality to a sport that was considered by many as somewhat lackluster and timid. If tennis was gentlemanly and pastel, Andre made it wild and electric. He catapulted it into public awareness in a new way and made it sexy like no one before him or since.

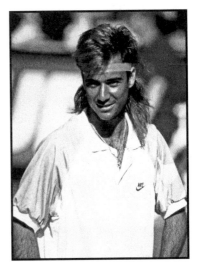
Andre in 1988.

At the age of 14, Andre was already a real character. It wasn't unusual to see him with red hair one day, blue the next, nails polished, sometimes even rouge. At the same time, he had a blistering forehand and the competitive ruthlessness of a champion. In his first year at the Academy, he won the National Indoor 16-and-under singles and doubles titles. In all, he won more than a handful!

Of course, that also made for difficult times for him and everybody else when he was acting out as a teenager. Add to that his love-hate relationship for the game, engendered by a trying relationship with his ambitious father, and it was a recipe for frustration all around. His testing of boundaries at the Academy caught everyone's attention. He defied curfews and once built a tower of empty whiskey bottles in his room (knowing that there were frequent staff inspections), although we never knew if it was just for show. Jim Courier and some of the others in my talented group of soon-to-be champions wondered why I hadn't thrown this brash rebellious kid out of the Academy. Some of my coaches thought he should go, too. At one staff meeting, they all voted to expel him, but I thought about it and vetoed the decision. I have the innate ability to look at a youngster's potential, and I saw something special in that little maverick. Call it gut instinct or a special gift from God—something inside me said, "Don't get rid of him."

I recently sent Andre a text message asking if he remembered exactly when he first came to the Academy. Within 15 minutes he responded. His reply was:

> *Ah, the challenges of detail. I came to the NBTA in March of 1984. I then got sentenced to my whole future by you finally seeing me play on the indoor Supreme Court, and we went to the phone together as I heard you tell my father, "I'm tearing up your check, you will not pay a penny now or in the future." That happened in late April. I lived in "Cell block C." All the buildings were named as cell blocks.*

My answer to him, as in the past, "But you had the key to all the locks!"

At one point when Andre was fed up with me and the Academy, he packed his bags and took to the road on foot. Julio Moros saw him leave and drove after him. Andre didn't know where he wanted to go, just "away," and it took Julio some time to persuade him to get in the car and come back.

That incident and others led to a memorable meeting between Andre and me. Fritz Nau, a longtime friend who was responsible for running the elite program at the Academy along with overseeing the adult program, advised Andre to let me talk without interruption until I had said everything I wanted to say. After that, and only after I was finished, should Andre begin airing his complaints. Andre did just so. When I was finished, Andre unburdened himself—listing all the things that upset him at the Academy. At the same time, he expressed himself with such maturity, clarity and poise, I knew that at the age of 15, he had finally reached a point where he was in charge of his own destiny, and our relationship changed from that moment on.

Fritz was a mentor, a confidante and an ally throughout Andre's career with me. When he and I talk about those times now, we often wonder how we managed to keep it all together! Another important member of the team was Andre's brother Phillip, who came to the Academy and dedicated his life to bringing a sense of normalcy and equilibrium to Andre's world. This was important because along with Andre's unique talent came a unique sensitivity and awareness. He never liked to be yelled at from the other side of the net. I could do it with Jimmy Arias, Carling Bassett and others, but not him!

One day while he was practicing on the old indoor courts, Phillip and I were standing behind him talking and laughing about a funny story. We were finishing up our training before heading to a tournament in Itaparica, Brazil. Andre turned to us and said, "Are you two laughing at me? Well, I'm not going!" And he walked away. We finally convinced him that we were laughing at something else and encouraged him to continue with his training. He won that tournament, knocking out the No. 13 and 15 ranked players in the world along the way.

Another time, we were at a tournament at the Longwood Cricket Club in Massachusetts. Phillip and I scouted Andre's first round opponent, a right-handed player, and were confident Andre would handle him with ease. What we didn't realize was that we had scouted the wrong guy—his real opponent was a lefty. Andre glared at us in disgust and immediately tanked the match, blaming his failure on our incompetence. He had a point, and I assured him that it would never happen again.

Andre's rise to stardom was a complex roller-coaster ride. Although our early relationship was often contentious, I committed myself to him wholeheartedly. I felt that Andre not only possessed a unique talent, but that the demons that haunted him were part of his genius; and I was willing to give him a great deal of leeway and support as he matured.

In a feature night match on the stadium court at the Sovran Bank Classic tournament in Washington, D.C. in July, 1987, Andre played against Patrik Kühnen. Andre was the talk of the tour—with his fancy clothes, wild hairstyles and big endorsement contracts. It irritated many of the established players and they wanted to teach this young, cocky kid a lesson. After the first set, Andre started to tighten up and doubt his ability to win and be a big-time player, and Patrik beat him handily 4-6, 6-4, 6-0. When the match was over and I left the coaches' box, Phillip and Andre's manager, Bill Shelton, told me that Andre was across the street in the wooded park area smashing his racquets. I walked up to him and asked in a soft voice what was wrong. He shouted, "I don't have it. I can't do it." I pointed to my left wrist and said, "Andre, am I wearing a watch? *Andre*, am I wearing a watch? There is no time clock on you. Your team believes in you, and we will stay with you every inch of the way." Andre looked at me with an expression of curiosity and doubt. I got a bit closer and in a near whisper said to him, "My boy, you will be a great tennis player."

The team packed up and we went to the next tournament, which was held at Stratton Mountain, Vermont. And wow, what a tournament Andre had! At that point, he was ranking 90 on the ATP tour, and he won four straight matches, including one against Pat Cash, the No. 7 player in the world. He lost in the semifinals to Ivan Lendl, the No. 1 player in the world! This was the beginning of his rise to international stardom.

As gifted and as talented as Andre was, he had self-doubts. This isn't uncommon when one is competing at the highest athletic level. It is vital for parents and coaches to understand that the wrong words can destroy a youngster. Finding the positive in their performance and encouraging them is critical. The power of self-confidence is terribly underestimated! One hundred percent confidence is an essential ingredient of becoming a champion.

Another important element is a great support team; I believe that can mean the difference between success and failure, and Andre was fortunate to have a good one. Besides his brother, Phil, it included Bill Shelton, the first black manager of a major tennis player, who passed away in 2011. He had a very good singing voice and did a great imitation of Nat King Cole. Andre loved to hear Bill sing.

Fritz Nau traveled to every one of Andre's major tournaments except the Australian Open, even though he hated to fly. He was a low-key, even-tempered presence, yet rock solid in his support for Andre and crucial in rebuilding his confidence after his first three Grand Slam finals, which he lost to Pete Sampras at the U.S. Open and to Andrés Gómez and Jim Courier at the French Open.

Another special person who hasn't gotten all the credit he deserves is Gil Reyes, his personal trainer, bodyguard and longtime friend. Gil did his best to manage Andre's fitness and diet, but Andre was a free spirit. I remember an occasion at the French Open when Andre sent

Andre beat Paul Annacone, another one of my students, on my 57th birthday. Paul told me afterward, "We kept it in the family for you."

Bill Shelton and me out to McDonald's. We came back with $200 worth of burgers, fries and sodas. Then Andre cranked the room temperature down to nearly 40 degrees and we all watched horror movies. As fitness and conditioning coach, Gil would cringe at this type of behavior, but it was the only way to keep Andre calm and relaxed.

We did other crazy things to keep us sane on the road. One year at the Italian Open, we all stayed in a hotel built on a hillside. We were on the fifth floor and bought balloons that we launched from windows and "gunned down" with rubber slingshots. People sitting outside on the lower balconies were startled, as were busses and cars whose roofs we pelted on the street below. At some point the police came, and we were lucky not to get arrested.

In his first Wimbledon tournament in 1987, Andre had to play his first round on No. 2 Court, which everyone referred to as the "death court." Top players hated it because so many upsets happened there. Andre's opponent was Henri Leconte, the No. 1 French player, and I had barely settled into my seat when the match was over. The score was 6-2, 6-1, 6-2. Andre said, "Let's get out of here," and decided like Ivan Lendl before him that "grass was for cows." He skipped the tournament for the next three years before returning. He may have been intimidated by the surface for a while, but that didn't stop him from getting that monkey off his back in typical Andre style.

A few days before the 1992 tournament, Andre called me at 3 a.m. at my home in Florida—12 midnight, Las Vegas time. He said, "Nick, what are we going to do for Wimbledon?" I said, "Andre, I've been waiting for you to let me know what you wanted to do." He suggested we go to Boca Raton to train for the next two days. Of course, I realized that was where his girlfriend, Wendi Stewart, was staying with Carling Bassett and her husband Robert Seguso, who together operated the tennis club in Boca.

So Fritz Nau, Raúl Ordóñez and I decided to pile into my Bronco and meet them over there; the three of us wanted to play some golf while we were there. On the day before leaving for Europe, Andre finally announced that he was ready to practice. Mind you, he hadn't hit a tennis ball since the French Open two months earlier! We found two green hard courts surrounded by lush green trees and pretended they were Wimbledon grass! After about 30 minutes of practice, Andre declared that he was ready, and I agreed, although I had my doubts. He had an amazing knack for picking up a racquet after not playing for weeks and hitting the ball as if he'd had no time off at all.

When we arrived in England, we conducted a clinic at a department store and a reporter asked him how his training was going.

Andre winked at me, smiled, and assured him that we had been training hard in Boca for the past two weeks and he was ready! I'll be honest: I didn't believe he had a snowball's chance.

He almost got bounced in the first round again playing Andrei Chesnokov, a dangerous Russian player. On the way to losing the first set, Andre made some off-color remarks—okay, he trash talked—and one of the linesmen complained to the head referee about it. Fortunately, the referee liked Andre and me so he ignored it—and Andre got away with a fine. The match was halted because of darkness, giving us time to regroup, and the next day, Andre won three straight sets and the match to make it into the next round.

After that, everything seemed to come together. En route to the finals, Andre defeated two former Wimbledon champions, Boris Becker and John McEnroe. The final was a nail-biter, a thrilling five-set battle that raged back and forth. Goran Ivanisevic had the biggest serve in tennis at the time and struck an incredible 37 aces. But Andre, the best returner in the game, didn't let it rattle him and answered him. When Goran volleyed Andre's final backhand into the net, Andre sank to his knees and raised his arms to the sky in celebration. He had claimed his Wimbledon title, the first of his eight career Grand Slams. Grass was no longer just for the cows. Andre owned it!

Andre and me at the Ball after his 1992 Wimbledon win.

For me, it was an indescribable feeling. It was my first Grand Slam victory, too, where I sat in the coaches' box rooting for my player. And at Wimbledon, no less—the biggest tennis tournament on the planet! For a tennis coach, there is nothing more thrilling than being the mentor of a Grand Slam champion! It was one of the greatest days of my life.

The following evening, dressed to the nines, we went to the Wimbledon Ball, which honored the champions. The women's singles had been won by Steffi Graf, who later would become Andre's wife when she retired after her stellar career. It was a fitting celebration of all Andre and I had worked to achieve.

But after he won Wimbledon, Andre had something of a letdown which lasted nearly a year. I sensed that things were beginning to change. Andre's childhood friend, Perry Rogers, replaced Bill Shelton as his business manager. Andre started to consult other coaches and I became increasingly uncomfortable, quietly wondering when I would be replaced. After much soul-searching, I reached the conclusion that after nearly a decade together, it was time to end our relationship and I wrote a letter telling Andre of my decision. That was one of the biggest mistakes I have made in my life. I should have flown to Las Vegas and told him in person. My second mistake was mentioning my decision to a reporter; Andre learned of our separation on the news before he got my letter. He was devastated—anyone would have been.

I have few regrets in my life; the way I handled that situation is one of them. Had I only jumped on a plane, sat down with Andre and told him why I wanted to leave the team, things might have been different. Sensitive issues deserve well-thought-out responses. And when dealing with friends and loved ones, the response should show the respect that the relationship merits. I know I was like a father to him, and I should have done better by him. Had I addressed the matter properly, maybe we would have remained a team, who knows?

At the time, we were both deeply hurt, and for some time we kept rubbing salt in the wounds, as I have discussed in greater detail in the book I wrote with Dick Schaap, *My Aces, My Faults*. Sometime after our professional relationship ended, Andre wrote his memoirs. I know that he was critical of me and called the Academy a prison. To be honest, I never read his book, not one word of it. But all of that is water under the bridge.

Me and Andre with my daughter Alex.

Over time, we gradually left the hurt behind. At the Canadian Open, we sat in the lunchroom and chatted for a while. We discussed my children Alex and Nicole, who always talked about how nice Andre had been to them. Andre was very good with children. Jack Schneider and Mr. Marx were both great friends of Andre's (Mr. Marx and Andre also did some business deals together) and I'm sure they told him that we had been too close to remain enemies. I certainly felt that way. I started to write notes to Andre. We began exchanging Christmas cards, updating one another on our families. And we talked whenever we saw each other at tournaments. Andre didn't attend the 30th anniversary celebration of NBTA, but he sent a video that was shown at the event, in which he said some beautiful things about me and our relationship. Today, he and I are the closest of friends. I know that if I needed anything, he would come to my aid, and vice versa!

I am proud of all we did for Andre at the Academy. I believe that, had it not been for his entire support team there, chances are he would not have achieved the level of success that he reached. The old adage that it takes a village to raise a child is especially true in Andre's case. That village was comprised of his dad Mike, his mom Betty, who was always laid-back and calm—the rock in an often stormy world—his brother Phillip and other family members, Fritz Nau, Gil Reyes, Bill Shelton and me. God sent me a message to keep Andre at the Academy and to appreciate his idiosyncratic behavior. Even though we had a seesaw relationship, I have no trouble admitting that our seven years together were among the most enjoyable times of my life.

Andre and me relaxing on the tour.

And let me also say, I'm not only proud of the tennis player that Andre became, but I am just as delighted by the man he has become! He has a fine family with his wife Steffi Graf and their two lovely children. He has opened a private charter school with an incredible graduation rate. He has raised millions of dollars for his and other schools in the Las Vegas area, and puts on exhibitions for inner-city children. He has grown into a thoughtful, generous man whose impact on the world goes far beyond his achievements as a tennis star.

Mark [McCormack] and Nick shared an abundance of genuine enthusiasm about people and their gifts. Then, they shared an amazing reservoir of energy and passion. They also shared great vision! I think Mark saw in Nick someone with more zest for life than anyone he had ever met. Mark couldn't wait to arrive at the Academy and find Nick and get the rundown on who was there and what Nick thought of them! I knew Mark had great respect for Nick's analysis and opinion of these young players. Mark had great respect for Nick's read on people period! Nick is so streetwise and Mark truly admired that.

—Betsy McCormack

All of us athletes should thank Mark McCormack for starting a business where athletes could monetize their image. He was a pioneer in the same way Nick was with the Academy. Also, the potential Mr. McCormack saw so early on at the Academy was very impressive. Betsy and I played tons of doubles matches and practices together. I learned from her how important fitness is to tennis. Plus, it was so great to have a friend to hang out with during tournaments. Together with Mark, we spent many fun dinners together that I will cherish for the rest of my life. My friendship with both Mark and Betsy was and is very special. I will never forget the love and guidance they gave me through the best times and worst times in my life.

—Monica Seles

CHAPTER 11

IMG

The concept and vision of NBTA—total immersion in a competitive environment, physical and mental fitness training, and the goal to turn young athletes into pros at an early age—were not only made a reality, but were producing outstanding results. We were getting kids from all over the world and turning out top-notch players. At the 1987 U.S. Open singles, we had more than three dozen of my players in the men's and women's singles draws.

We also attracted other elite players to the Academy. I always believed in an open door policy, even if it meant that players came with their own coaches to use our facilities. As a result, a very young Steffi Graf and her father paid us a visit. Pete Sampras and his coach Tim Gullikson trained at NBTA for some time. Over the last few years, other visitors who have come to use the facilities have included Andy Murray and Gaël Monfils and their coaches, and the Davis Cup teams from Colombia, Canada and other countries.

Pete Sampras training at the Academy.

At one point, Yannick Noah, the French tennis star, arrived to rehabilitate from a serious groin injury. He was a terrific competitor who won the 1983 French Open by sheer athleticism and determination.

I put him and his wife up at my condo on Longboat Key. His injury was so severe that he started his rehab hitting balls like a beginner and slowly worked his way up. Yannick had a wonderful, outgoing personality and even played soccer with the kids at the Academy. Later on, he organized a training session for coaches at the French Open where I spoke to a large audience. At some point, he stood up and said, "Only Nick Bollettieri could keep the attention of 1,000 tennis coaches!" I also attended the NCAA basketball final, when his son Joakim played for the Florida Gators (he is now with the Chicago Bulls) and won the first of their two national championships.

Yannick Noah

We seemed to be on top of the world at the Academy and there was no way for me to begin putting on the brakes. But dark clouds were gathering. On the court, we were producing world-class players, but off the court, we were losing money by the boatload. I don't regret my decision to give scholarships to many talented players—without that approach I never would have had the likes of Seles, Agassi, Courier and Krickstein at the Academy—but we were hemorrhaging. Too many scholarships to too many talented kids and a lack of financial oversight on my part led to the eventual downfall of the Academy.

It didn't help that I exhausted my savings buying homes, expensive cars and restaurants on impulse. I lost money on all of them. I just didn't have the knack for business. If I had only had the wisdom to consult a trustworthy financial advisor, someone who would have counseled me on each of these decisions, my life would likely be very different today. Sam Zussman, senior vice president of IMG, said that if I had him as a financial consultant then, I'd probably still own the Academy. He's probably right!

But I had nobody like that watching the books and it came to the point where I had no choice but to sell the Academy or declare bankruptcy. Fact is, had it not been for my closest friends, the moment of truth would have arrived much sooner. I'm sure they would have helped me out then, too, but I was too embarrassed to ask them.

My agent Donald Dell considered buying NBTA at the time but declined. He later said that it was the biggest mistake he ever made in his career. Instead, it was Mark McCormack, owner of IMG, who stepped in and bought us out for $7 million in 1987. He wanted to keep my name, which was becoming something of a brand, and we called it the Bollettieri Sports Academy.

At the time, Mark was, according to *Sports Illustrated*, "the most powerful man in sports." Tall, blond and Irish, he had been a promising college golfer at William and Mary, graduated from the Yale Law School, and practiced law in Cleveland. A man of unquenchable energy and entrepreneurial skills, he became the chief architect of the new sports marketing industry.

In 1960, he became the agent of a young American golfer named Arnold Palmer, striking the deal with a simple handshake. Soon after, he signed a talented South African newcomer, Gary Player, and another up-and-coming American professional, Jack Nicklaus. Either by chance or with incredible foresight, Mark had "bagged" the "Big Three," who would dominate golf for decades and promote the sport's global appeal. When he decided to branch out into tennis, he started with no less than Rod Laver. Mark was among the first to realize that athletes could earn extra money from endorsements and sponsorships. He negotiated a deal for Palmer to endorse Wilson sporting goods. Not long ago, IMG was responsible for the $100 million deal for Tiger Woods' endorsement of Nike.

Mark and his wife Betsy had bought a condo on the grounds of the Academy and always enjoyed their stays. Mark and I developed a relationship of affection and respect for one another. We also shared a good sense of humor. Mark loved to laugh and enjoyed it when people could poke fun at themselves. I could and often did, making him laugh on many dinner occasions.

Mark passed away in 2003, and one of the things I miss about him is his ability to give advice. He had the tremendous gift of knowing just what was best for those who asked him. If they needed career counseling, personal advice, or just some help achieving their goals, Mark took great pleasure in planning their next steps. He always carried a little notebook to put down reminders of the people he'd met, and no matter who they were, he'd always get back to them. I have tried to emulate him in that regard. I take great pleasure in assisting those who ask for advice, and I always try to make time and let them know not only that I care, but that I know what to say and how to help!

Mark McCormack and me.

Since then, Betsy and I have gotten to know each other quite well. With her now living at IMG Academy, I get to see her almost daily, and I am blessed to have her in my life as a friend, as we both were blessed to have Mark McCormack in our lives.

When Mark bought NBTA, I was at least able to send Mr. Marx a check for $2 million to repay him for his generous loans, and to take care of the bills that the Academy had amassed. I was left with $500,000, which soon went to settle my next divorce.

At the time, I was terrified what it would mean to have to take orders from a big, corporate outfit like IMG, but I needn't have worried. Mark and his right-hand man Bob Kain let me continue to be in charge of the Academy as before. They gave me complete freedom to run it as I saw fit, except in the financial area, of course. I could continue to do what I did best—turn out top-notch tennis players—and I will be forever grateful that they and IMG didn't try to change my style, but built on my natural abilities, just as I did with my athletes.

With the financial burden lifted from my shoulders, I actually had more time and freedom to focus on what I felt really mattered—my players. It was after the sale of NBTA that my great juniors, Courier, Agassi, Seles, all came into their own on their way to their greatest triumphs.

During this time there were other sad events in my life. Both of my parents passed away. They had moved close to the Academy for a while, but ended up in Deerfield Beach on the east coast of Florida, a three-and-a-half-hour drive away. For as long as he could, my dad would buy a new Cadillac Eldorado every year, usually yellow, and wash it every day. When my dad's heart finally gave out in 1989, he was in his mid-80s. I burst into tears when I got the news, just like with my younger brother. I thought the world of my father and I regret that we hadn't been closer at the end. Two years later, when I was named the U.S. Professional Tennis Association's Pro of the Year, I dedicated the award to him.

My mom soon followed him, also in her 80s. As I mentioned earlier, she willed everything to my sister, Rita, because she was worried that my wife—I was married to Kellie at the time—would end up getting it. Actually, the agreement was that Rita would leave half to me when she died. She was not in great health and didn't expect to outlive me. She spent her last days at the Windsor Rest Home, an assisted living facility near the Academy in Bradenton, and started to

Rita and me at the rest home.

suffer from dementia. When her time came, I found out that she left everything to her daughter, Mary Lou. Rather than make a big to-do, I decided to let it go.

As things turned out, my relationship with Kellie was not going well by then, in part because I spent so much time with my tennis players—I was on the road 36 weeks a year!—neglecting her and my daughters, Nicole and Alexandra. One night when I came home late again, we had it out. She gave me an ultimatum: "It's either going to be me and the children or that rascal!" The rascal she referred to was Andre Agassi. I didn't hesitate. I said, "I'm going with the rascal." I made my choice on the spot, threw my clothes in a plastic bag, got in my Corvette and left. I drove to Fritz Nau's house, which was right next to the tennis club in Bradenton I had bought a while back. He saw me getting out of the car with my belongings and knew immediately what had happened. Although he had been recently married, he was kind enough to offer me half his house until I could get a place of my own. Instead of going through a protracted legal battle, I gave Kellie the houses, boats, cars and other things, along with the money I had received from the sale of the Academy to IMG. She also received a handsome alimony for many years after the divorce, which was finalized in 1992.

Kellie went through some rough times later on, and I was unhappy to hear of it—I bore her no ill will. Nicole became something of a surrogate mom to her younger sister during that time, and both she and Alex have turned out to be wonderful young women.

In the meantime, the sale of NBTA allowed me some freedom to pursue other passions full throttle, especially my work with Arthur Ashe. There were also new talented young players entering the Academy, including Iva Majoli, Anna Kournikova and Tommy Haas.

Iva Majoli, an 11-year-old from Croatia, came to us accompanied by her father and brother, who was also a very good player and traveled with her to tournaments. Iva was not a standout right away and her physical stature was not overpowering, but she was a hard worker and had great determination. She turned professional three years later and

Iva and me in the early 90s at the Academy.

came into her own as a teenager, achieving a high ranking of No. 4 in the world. The following year, she upset Martina Hingis in the finals of the 1997 French Open with an aggressive baseline game, swinging forcefully from both sides with all her might and keeping Martina on the defensive throughout. It was the high point of her career. Since retiring, she has made her home in Bradenton, calls me often to see how I'm doing, and runs up to me like a young daughter to her father whenever she sees me. I will always love my Iva.

Late in the summer of 1992 I met a woman named Leah Rhodes at the Tampa airport as I was going to the U.S. Open. She had driven down from New York to help a girlfriend move and was flying back north. She was a flight attendant for American Airlines (and still is). We got to talking and when I found out that she was a big tennis fan, I promised to get her tick-ets to the tournament if she gave me her telephone num-ber. We went out to dinner while I was in New York, en-joyed a jazz club and ended up talking till late into the morning hours. We obvi-ously clicked. One thing led to another—and no, I didn't marry her. But we stayed to-gether for nearly a decade. She loved tennis and helped me in more ways than I can count. She traveled with me

Leah and me at the 2013 U.S. Open.

to some of the Grand Slams and other international tournaments and helped to keep things smooth and relaxed—a great gift in the intense, high-pressure cauldron of elite tennis.

Around that time, we moved into a large condo in Bradenton. It was originally five separate, attached units, but I had the walls torn down and made it into one large, no-partition villa, and Leah deco-rated it. At Christmas we had to turn one of the rooms into a staging area for gift wrapping because Leah sent out about 700 presents— she cared so much for my kids and the students at the Academy. We also had our own ice cream parlor and a fantastic game room with all sorts of video games. Leah was great with my children, and they all loved her.

Because Leah traveled to a lot of tournaments with me, she crossed paths with Venus and Serena Williams; they became close friends and, as far as I know, remain so to this day. Leah, who has a great eye for interior design, helped Serena with the decoration of her home. My friends often asked me why I didn't marry Leah. I would have, but she didn't want to marry me! We enjoyed each other's company, but I guess we both valued our freedom more. I still think of her as a good friend.

Meanwhile, I used the opportunity to focus on my elite youngsters, and after my split with Andre, I had the opportunity to coach other great athletes as well, notably Mary Pierce and Boris Becker. Both were on the comeback trail and had something to prove. Entering my sixth decade, I had something to prove as well. I wanted to show the world that I could do more than just develop talented juniors.

Nick puts his arms around you a lot more than he yells at you.

—Arthur Ashe

In a minute, people can step into each other's lives and together change the course of direction for others. You could say that is what happened when Nick Bollettieri and Arthur Ashe met and became friends. They shared a purposeful friendship and, while being two very different men, their purpose was fueled by a fierce passion to help empower youth, focusing on the inner city and the disadvantaged. Nick and Arthur believed in the power of tennis, teaching discipline and life skills through the sport to transform lives. They worked together with this common goal to improve the conditions and opportunities for kids in the inner cities.

—Jeanne Moutoussamy-Ashe

My most positive memory from the Academy was when Nick put together an event with Arthur Ashe. It was called World Hunger Day, and Nick brought in Arthur and some great basketball players and tennis players, and the whole sports world took notice. It was so cool to be a part of this special day.

—Kenny Merritt, longtime friend

CHAPTER 12

The ABC Tennis Program

When I first met Arthur in 1961 as a talented youngster play-ing in the Western Conference Championships in Springfield, Ohio, times weren't easy for black tennis players in America. There were many clubs that refused to admit them, and the fact that he and two other black players at the time, Bob Davis and Richard Russell from Jamaica, were "allowed" to play the Western, was a big deal. When he visited my Beaver Dam summer camp for one week, and also the Hopman/Bollettieri camp in Amherst, Massachusetts, he and I be-came fast friends. He enjoyed his visits and was very complimentary of my work with the kids. We soon realized that we had something other than our friendship in common; we both had the same agent, Donald Dell. He had arranged the camp visits for each of the players on the Davis Cup team, including Arthur.

Arthur was a humble young man who possessed a big serve and a cannon of a backhand, as well as a biting slice. His game continued to improve and he was selected to represent the United States on the 1963 Davis Cup team. He joined the ROTC while at UCLA and upon graduation was assigned to the U.S. Military Academy at West Point as a data processor. It was as a lieutenant in the Army that he won the first U.S. Open in 1968 and he was soon to become Wimbledon cham-pion. Although soft-spoken, he wore his social conscience on his sleeve and not surprisingly, became one of the finest ambassadors that tennis has ever known. I admired him for his insightful, generous character.

One day at the French Open, Arthur and I were sitting on a bench talking about the future of American tennis. He felt confident that the finest athletes in America resided in the inner cities, but without some intervention, would never strike a tennis ball. I assured Arthur that, together, we would create a solution. As we continued to talk, we both began to realize that inner-city youth needed much

Arthur Ashe and me at the 1987 French Open.

more than an education in forehands and backhands. They needed encouragement to stay in school, stay away from drugs and aspire to personal greatness. Before leaving Roland Garros we committed to each other that we would get together and devise a plan when we got home. We were both determined to create an impact on what Arthur felt was one of the great challenges facing America.

Back in the United States, we contacted Arthur's childhood friend, Bob Davis, who was managing his own tennis academy in upstate

New York and told him of our plan. Bob had run the largest private club in New York State and had the skills to manage the program we were envisioning. He bought into the concept immediately. We named the program the Ashe-Bollettieri "Cities" Tennis Program, ABC for short. We refined our mission statement believing that we could help reverse the current negative trends by introducing tennis, "the sport of a lifetime," into the schools and playgrounds of America's inner cities.

Bob, by the way, has dedicated his life to helping young children through his Panda Foundation. I have known him for more than 50 years and he is one stand-up guy.

Arthur was quite friendly with Sharpe James, the mayor of Newark, New Jersey, and we met with him to discuss his city becoming our first venue. He agreed and we launched the first ABC program there in August, 1988. Newark was the perfect model city to demonstrate the effectiveness of our program. At the time,

Bob Davis

it was the auto-theft capital of America. While the average high school dropout rate nationwide in 1991 was 8.6%, in Newark it was over 22%. Violent crime was rampant. On the very first day of the program, the mayor arranged for us to visit the program sites under police protection. The courts were littered with spent bullet casings—the first year we actually filled a gallon mayonnaise jar with them. Looking around, Arthur said to me, "Nick, is this a one-day event or will we stay here and make sure these kids are not just given false hopes?" I assured him that we were in this for the long haul. When we realized the scope of the challenge that we had taken on, Arthur asked again, "Nick, do we continue, or do we throw in the towel now?" I said, "We came to help, so let's forge ahead!"

Arthur was determined to include academic tutoring in our programming and believed that tennis could be a direct avenue to college. So we instituted after-school tutoring and shortly after the launch developed a relationship with the Children's Hospital of New Jersey. We called our health program "Urban Healthnet—A Partnership for Children." It provided information on the effect of drugs on the human body, stressed the value of proper nutrition, offered immunizations in the community and encouraged preventive health care. Each day, we refined the program to provide more valuable services to the children. We teamed with NBTA sponsor Adidas to create an academic awards program. Every student who received straight "As" would get a $100 gift certificate for Adidas products. Straight "Bs" would merit a $50 gift certificate and most improved would earn a certificate for $25. Arthur personally delivered the academic awards and shook the hand of each and every recipient. We realized that we were essentially paying—okay, bribing—the kids to achieve better grades, but decided that the education, self-respect and self-confidence they achieved were more important.

We reached an agreement with Rutgers University to provide administrative and financial aid to all of our kids wishing to attend college. More importantly, we wanted to show the children that getting a good education was not a "white thing," but something that led to college, careers and better-quality lives. And it worked! Not a single student in our program dropped out of high school. By the end of 1991, every one of our high school graduates went on to college. Arthur told me later that this program, of all the programs that he had ever been involved with, made him the most proud.

Newark was our prototype ABC program; we created operating manuals for every component and began considering other cities in which to establish ourselves. Make no mistake, when you do business with city government, the bureaucratic wheels turn slowly. The Newark program had an annual budget of about $350,000. We had an office and full-time staff, telephone bills, insurance, etc. While waiting for the city to pay the program invoices, there were times when we footed the bill, sometimes to the tune of $300,000. We always received payment, but I had huge lumps in my throat at times hoping that nothing would go wrong. I still get heartburn when I think of the risk that I was taking.

The program was so successful that other city governments and community leaders called us regularly to see if we could establish an ABC program in their cities. Using Newark as a template, we branched out to Albany, New York; Fort Lauderdale and Palmetto in Florida; both Kansas Cities, in Kansas and Missouri; Los Angeles, California; and Atlanta, Georgia.

Chanda Pinkney, one of the children in Newark's ABC program, was invited to speak to the U.S. Senate Committee on Labor and Human Resources. In her testimony she said, "Inner cities need more programs like ABC. To succeed I have had to overcome all the problems that teenagers must face—the many malignancies that are killing the people in my community and robbing them of their dreams—drugs, alcohol, teen pregnancies, school dropouts, unemployment and violence. It's hard to keep a positive attitude because we are surrounded by so much negativity. Most of the people in my neighborhood will eventually become a statistic. I myself could have done the easy thing and become a statistic. In-school kids, out-of-school kids, all kids—we are not bad people. We have had bad experiences. We can make something of ourselves and we want to. All we need is some support, some services and some sense of hope that our needs will be taken seriously."

Another component of our program was designed to help student athletes find fulfilling careers after college. We called it the Athlete Career Connection (ACC). Under the direction of Kevin Dowdell, a Princeton University and Wharton School of Business graduate and longtime friend of ours, ACC facilitated summer internships with a variety of companies. These internships kept the youngsters focused on their grades, provided experience in the business world and ultimately led to productive employment upon graduation. In just the first two years, participating ACC universities noted an increase of 205 more students using career placement services, a move toward more challenging coursework and a significant increase in efforts to secure summer employment.

Shortly before Arthur's death in 1993, we decided to rename ABC the Arthur Ashe Safe Passage Foundation Tennis Program. It had taken on a life of its own, and we agreed that this new organization would be totally independent. After Arthur's death, his wife, Jeanne Moutoussamy-Ashe, took over as the spiritual leader of the foundation. Jeanne shared Arthur's concern for the well-being of urban children and encouraged John McEnroe to become chairman of the board. We helped many children, but each program was extremely labor-intensive and expensive to run. As municipal budgets began to shrink, raising funds to support our programs became increasingly difficult. Over time we slowly closed each office until all were gone. The Safe Passage Foundation transitioned into a program offering financial support to deserving students under the auspices of the USTA.

Looking back at the life of the ABC program, it was a resounding success. We kept over 20,000 children off drugs and in school. When one considers the $30,000 per year that it costs to incarcerate a young man or woman, the ABC program would have been a bargain at 10 times the cost; and the value for the children who participated and benefitted was priceless.

I'm happy that Arthur and I established the ABC program and hope that someday, someone will decide that our answer to problems in America's urban centers is worth reviving. Sometimes offering someone a helping hand can work miracles. My dear friend Arthur Ashe spent his life offering helping hands. He was truly a "Citizen of the World."

Arthur and me in 1987 at NBTA
just before we launched the ABC program.

As I look back over my life, I now realize how much Nick really cared for me. He knew how to read my needs and how I would react to those people that came into contact with me. It's really difficult for the outside world to truly know Nick as more than just a coach. He is a character...who is vibrant, colorful and sensitive with a heart of gold. Put all of this together with his being an astute teacher who doesn't try to make all of his students play tennis the same way. He can give constructive criticism in a positive way. He acts like a kid—he has that gene and he works his ass off.

—Anna Kournikova

I think all the good players that came here to the Academy already had a good foundation. Nick was smart enough to take pieces from everybody and make them complete players.

—Tommy Haas

CHAPTER 13

Two Very Special People

I am on good terms with a lot of my current and former players, but there are two with whom I have a special ongoing relationship: Anna Kournikova and Tommy Haas. Both came to the Academy as youngsters and have remained close now that they are adults.

Tommy Haas, me and Anna Kournikova at the Academy.

Anna Kournikova came to the Academy in 1991. She had been playing a tournament in Italy when a sharp-eyed agent for IMG took notice of her. He suggested that she come with her mother Alla to IMG Academy to train. They accepted the invitation and arrived in February. I was skiing in Aspen at the time, but had heard about this young phenomenon. My plane arrived at midnight and the very next morning I went to court 40 to see her play. As I arrived, she bounced over to me with her blonde hair in a ponytail and said, "I'm Anna Kournikova and I'm ready for my lesson!" I knew right away that she was something special, but she was part of a package. Anna and her mom were inseparable. Alla was a former 440-meter running champion and she and I had many battles over Anna's training regimen, but they never derailed the overall plan we had mapped out for her development. Today, we laugh about the good old days.

At the time, we had about 300 tennis students at the Academy. Most of the apartments housed eight girls at a time, but we made special arrangements so that Anna and her mom shared an apartment with only two other girls. On the court, Anna also wanted my undivided attention and didn't like to have practices with others. When her game developed quickly, IMG signed her to a management contract when she was

Anna and me training hard.

only 10 years old. She was a hard worker, getting up early to practice at 6 a.m. for a couple of hours before heading out to the Bradenton Academy. After school, she would return for more training. Her mom thought it was too much, but Anna wanted to do it. Even at her young age, Anna was something of a con artist. She convinced her mom that it was me who insisted on her heavy training schedule. But I didn't mind being her scapegoat because her tennis was soaring.

I moved Anna into one of the units of my no-walls villa. There she became close to my two youngest daughters, Alex and Nicole, and to my son, Jimmy Boy. Leah was there, too, and Anna loved her.

I have always tried to treat my students the same, but with Anna this was difficult. She always wanted special attention and she was becoming part of my life. She often referred to me as her second father, because her dad, Sergei Kournikov, was in Russia earning a living.

Anna turned pro in 1995, but because of the age limit restriction, she was only permitted to play a certain number of tournaments. This restriction was troubling to her and she had a rocky  start. But she won the Orange Bowl at the end of the year, becoming the youngest champion in the 18-and-under division, and achieving a No. 1 junior ranking. That same year she reached her first WTA Tour doubles final at the Kremlin Cup. In 1996 she made her Grand Slam debut and reached the fourth round of the U.S. Open, losing to the world's No. 1, Steffi Graf. In 1997 she reached the semifinals at Wimbledon.

Her game relied on aggressive baseline play, great footspeed and agility at the net, which helped her become a superb doubles player. She had a never-miss backhand and a strong forehand, although it never quite reached the Bollettieri standard. She also could play devastating drop shots, which frustrated Pete Sampras when she played with him as a 10-year-old at the Academy.

Anna had her best singles season in 2000 when she rose to No. 8 in the world, but her greatest successes were in doubles. She and her partner, Martina Hingis, attained a No. 1 ranking and won the 1999 and 2002 Grand Slam women's doubles titles at the Australian Open. Unfortunately, serious back problems, including a herniated disk, ended Anna's professional career in 2003 when she was only 21, although she has played in exhibition matches for charitable causes since then.

She often drew bigger crowds when she was on a back court than many players on center stadium court, if it wasn't a feature match. It was the men, not the ladies, who would come to watch her. I wouldn't be surprised if it caused some friction between married couples. At one time, her website had more visits than any other website in the world.

But it isn't just her physical beauty that makes her so special. She cares deeply about others and has been involved in a number of causes focusing on children's health. Several years ago, I had a severe case of pneumonia. Anna called the hospital several times every day to keep track of my progress. She and Serena Williams sent me so many flowers, I could have opened up shop!

It is always fun to meet up with her. During the 2012 Sony Open in Miami, my son Jimmy Boy and I had dinner with Anna at the Ritz, and it sure was great talking about old times. It was during this meeting that we took our most recent nose-to-nose photo.

I often wonder how Anna's career might have been different had her mother dropped her off at the Academy the way Mike Agassi did Andre. Mike, the Couriers, the Kricksteins and Bassetts never got involved when their kids were on the court with me, so they didn't get mixed signals. Still, while Anna never won a major singles title, she was the first of a wave of players coming out of Russia who began to dominate world tennis. She took advantage of every opportunity that came her way and always gave it her all. In my book, she will always be my Grand Champion, and in my heart, "my little Anna."

Me and a young Tommy Haas.

I first met Tommy Haas when he was 11 years old. He arrived two weeks before the Orange Bowl, which took place in December just before Christmas. IMG put him in the dorms with seven other boys and he felt completely out of place because he spoke very little English. To make matters worse, his older sister, Sabine, who'd come with him from Germany, was away playing at the Orange Bowl. When Sabine returned to the Academy, she found that Tommy had packed his bags, saying he was headed home to Germany, never to return. But two years later, when it became clear that he had immense talent, his father decided to send him back to train with me. He returned in 1991 at age 13.

Tommy was always a strong-minded young man with many athletic gifts and a steely determination. His dad had been a professional martial artist in judo and had passed on his athletic DNA to his son. Just four years after he began training with me, Tommy achieved a junior ranking of No. 11 in the world. That same year, 1995, he reached the final of the Orange Bowl.

But make no mistake, his road to international stardom has been difficult, fraught with injuries that would have ended the careers of average players. In 1995 he broke his right ankle, in 1996, his left. That same year after he finished high school, he made his pro debut in Indianapolis as a wild card and reached the quarterfinals before losing to Pete Sampras. His injuries did not prevent him from becoming the youngest player to finish in the top 50 at the age of 19. In 2000 he suffered

Me and Tommy as a teenager.

from bulging discs in his back, yet he reached the finals of three tournaments. One can only imagine how much of an impact Tommy might have had on the sport of tennis had he not experienced so many debilitating injuries.

I decided early on that Tommy would play with a one-handed backhand. He periodically throws in some two-handed backhands, which, by the way, are excellent. One day I was with Tommy in Atlanta at an event featuring Ken Flach and Robert Seguso, the best doubles team in the world at the time. As they watched me training

Tommy, they both assured me that he would never make it with a one-handed backhand. I don't mind reminding them that today, Tommy's one-handed backhand ranks with the best the game has ever seen, right up there with Laver, Becker, Sampras and Federer.

On occasion I traveled with Tommy to tournaments, but I soon realized that he needed a full-time coach by his side. I selected David "Red" Ayme, who stood out in a crowd because of his fiery red hair. Tony Godsick, an agent from IMG, got the assignment to represent Tommy. Tony is married to Mary Joe Fernández, one of the best tennis commentators in the business. He now manages Roger Federer. Considering all the time I spent with Tommy and his support team, I wish I had videotaped some of the things that happened. They would have made for an Oscar-winning production!

I still laugh when I think of Tommy's antics at tournaments. His reputation as a young player was that anything could bother him during a match. Tommy had a litany of complaints: "It's too windy," "My shirt is too tight," "My racquet and strings ain't worth a SH*T!" He would look up at the coaches' box and yell at Red, "Why didn't you tell me that these courts were so fast, you are stupid and I ask myself why I'm paying you because you are a zero!" I often had to mediate and calm Tommy and Red down. Red would call three or four times a day when on the road. He would threaten to come home because of Tommy's disrespect, telling me, "He says I know zero about the game. How can I call myself a coach?"

Tommy's high-strung, volatile attitude would carry over into training sessions at IMG Academy. He was never disrespectful to me—not then and not now—but poor Red bore the brunt of his anger. Today, Tommy is quite open about how lucky he was to have someone who put up with all his crap and acknowledges that Red was an important part of his career.

Over time I became very attached to Tommy. When he was 18, I moved him into one of the units of my villa. By then, he had a car and went out a lot. To get to his unit, he had to walk through the others and he'd try to sneak past me when I slept on the couch. I'd stop him and we'd talk about where he'd been and what he was up to. I never stopped him from having fun. He became like another son to me and remains so to this very day.

Later Tommy signed on with other coaches, but he has always returned to the Academy to train in preparation for tournaments. He appreciates my eagle eye and the fact that I notice little things that help keep his game sharp. No matter where Tommy is playing, I send him text messages and tips about his game. When he recently hurt his shoulder at the Rogers Cup in Canada, I told him about the few things that he was doing to aggravate his injury, and he was amazed that I continue to be able to diagnose his strokes and identify the subtle causes behind some of his problems.

When we see each other now, we reminisce about our times together. I kid him about what a firebrand he was and he jokes that at least I never divorced my true first wife—tennis. He also likes to remind me of some of my less than stellar moments, such as the time I got a new car with a remote control button so I could start it before I got in. With my girlfriend Leah already in the passenger seat, I kept pushing it, but the car wouldn't start. Tommy tried to say something, but I shushed him while I wrestled with the problem at hand. I tried and tried and eventually gave up. When I finally let Tommy speak, he assured me that the car never would have started despite my persistence. Apparently, I had been pushing the button on the remote control for the TV!

I was delighted when Tommy became a United States citizen in 2010, and I was ecstatic when I heard that he and his wife, actress Sara Foster, had become parents of a beautiful daughter, Valentina. Sara came to train at the Academy when she was 12 years old; she was a talented young player. Her father, David Foster, the renowned music producer and performer—he has played with Diana Ross,

Celine Dion, Donna Summer, Kenny Loggins and Natalie Cole, to name a few—entertained us one evening during the Christmas holidays on my antique piano. Like many eager fathers, David hoped that Sara would become a big hit on the professional circuit, but I suggested that college was a more likely venue.

Sara has been a consistent source of encouragement through the many challenges of Tommy's career. She is his biggest cheerleader, and although some of the words that she uses to urge him on deserve an "R" rating, her support is undeniable. Tommy had hip surgery in 2010, yet two years later when he was 34, he became the oldest player in the top 50 and was named ATP comeback player of the year. He reached the quarterfinals of the 2013 French Open, losing to Novak Djokovic, and had a successful Wimbledon tournament as well.

Tommy has overcome more physical challenges than anyone I know, and his star continues to shine. His focus and rugged never-say-die attitude have served him well. It's a big deal for me that we have been a significant part of each other's lives for 22 years now. We have a special connection. It has been wonderful watching him grow into the man he has become. When he spends time with his daughter Valentina, the raging lion acts more like a puppy dog! I know that my family and I feel blessed for his presence in our lives. A small indication of how much he matters to us: My wife, Cindi, rarely watches tennis on television, but when Tommy plays, she follows his every move.

Nick always knew exactly what I needed to know or hear in just a few words and before my matches. I knew he was concerned for my well-being and me. He knew just how to work me hard, yet motivate and push me, and we always managed to talk on the phone if he wasn't at the tournament with me. Sometimes those talks lasted for just 30 seconds, but that's all he had to tell me for what I needed for that match. He was like a father to me. I know he cared, loved me and wanted the best for me!

My highest rankings were No. 3 in the world both in singles and doubles, and I consider him an important part of that accomplishment. I have a great deal of respect for Nick and for the tremendous contributions that he's made to the wonderful game of tennis. And by the way, I was always amazed that he didn't need much sleep to function daily.

—Mary Pierce

It is in the realm of interpersonal relations that his gifts have their most powerful impact. Combining his powers of observation with his emotional intelligence, Nick connects the dots to understand his players—as athletes, as emotional beings, as family members. In other words, he sees people "in context" and seems to instinctively know how to motivate and how to communicate. Combine this with eagle eyes that pick up on the tiniest physical clues, he seems to be able in a split second to review a freeze frame image and make a customized adjustment with amazing results.

—Marilyn Nelson, longtime friend

CHAPTER 14

Mary Pierce

When Mary Pierce first came to the Academy in 1988, she was 13 years old and already had a blistering forehand. Her father, Jim Pierce, a belligerent man obsessed with getting his daughter to succeed, felt that the competitive environment would help her improve more quickly. Although Mary lived in the dorms for some time, Jim continued as her coach.

Determined to maintain his control over Mary and her career, he soon pulled her out of the Academy. Mary turned pro two months after her 14th birthday and started to play on the women's tour. Meanwhile, her father was often abusive, unable to control his temper. He cursed at other players and their parents, and verbally terrorized Mary and her mother, Yannick. It got so bad that he was officially banned from tournaments. In the summer of 1993,  Mary finally succeeded in getting a restraining order against her father, but she and her mother traveled with bodyguards for a while.

I know those were traumatic times for Mary, although personally, I have never had difficulties with Jim Pierce. We have always been able to talk to each other, and I credit him with the work ethic he instilled in Mary and for helping her develop the smashing "Bollettieri forehand." I see him now occasionally, and he has become a gentler man, no longer afflicted by demons.

At the time, however, those demons plagued him and he often acted out in hurtful and damaging ways. With such a difficult background, it is no wonder that Mary was both a fierce competitor and a bundle of terrible insecurity about who she was and what she was capable of. During matches, when things didn't go well, she often looked to her coaches for help, even thought it was against the rules for them to signal advice to their players. She would also get down on herself, become irritated and tank matches when she ran into difficulties with her opponents.

I followed her career from a distance. By the time she was 17, Mary was ranked among the top 15 women players in the world, and I saw that she had great potential to do better. At some point when we ran into each other at a tournament, I mentioned to her that she was always welcome at the Academy to train and feel safe.

Soon after, I received a telephone call from her. She asked me to be her coach, and I agreed but I had conditions. I wrote her a note, "Mary, if I am to be your coach, there are two conditions that you must agree to: First, you are out of shape, in fact you are fat! You have to commit to a physical conditioning program that will get you into your top level of fitness. And second, I will stay with you until you not only believe in yourself, but also never need to look over to your support team, raising your hands in frustration and acting like a baby."

I was deliberately blunt to put her on notice that our work together would not be a walk in the park. After reading the note Mary came to me with tears in her eyes asking why I wrote such hurtful things about her. My answer was very simple, "It's the truth and it's my way or the highway." She agreed!

In 1994, our first full year together, Mary improved her ranking from No. 12 to No. 5 in the world. During the French Open, her road to the finals included beating defending champion Steffi Graf in two sets, 6-2, 6-2. Unfortunately, she ran out of steam against Arantxa Sánchez Vicario. That finish set the pattern for the rest of the year; she reached the finals of five tournaments, but won none.

I decided that we needed to step up Mary's training to get her to a new level. Toward the end of the year, I wrote her a long letter outlining both the physical and emotional aspects of her game that needed work, as well as what was expected of her off court. I do this with a lot of my elite athletes when I think their game needs a boost. Putting it in writing makes it real for them and allows us to go over things point by point, if necessary, so they clearly understand what the demands of their future success are.

Mary arrived in early December to get ready for the 1995 Australian Open—it would be my first time there, coaching her and Boris Becker. Mary and I went over the letter and although some of my comments rankled, she agreed with my assessment. For the next few weeks Mary trained as if she were preparing for a Navy Seal mission. In addition to her two on-court workouts each day, she also spent two hours in our weight room. Mary continued to work hard over the holidays with her full-time coach Sven Groeneveld and her conditioning coach, José Rincón. But after I returned from a week of skiing in Aspen and met her in Australia for the warm-up tournament, she still hadn't shed all of her extra body weight.

I confronted her about it and finally got through to her. That night, with a bit of help from Sven and José, Mary located all the junk food she had hidden in her apartment—her favorite indulgence was tiramisu—and threw it out. The next day she arrived for practice with a new attitude, all business and commitment.

Boris lost in the first round and generously told me to stay and take Mary to the championship. She breezed through the first three rounds in straight sets and dispatched Anke Huber, a German player who had given her problems in the past. In the quarterfinals, she faced Natasha Zvereva, a tough player from Belarus. I knew Mary could win, but I had a different problem. I had committed to hosting a Super Bowl tennis clinic in Florida and would miss the semis and finals.

Mary won against Zvereva as expected, and after the match I reminded her that I had to leave for the United States. I knew it would be difficult for both of us. I told her that she was ready—her game was technically close to perfect. The only thing she needed was confidence in herself to deal with adversity on the court, to look deep inside herself, not hope to find the answer in the coaches' box. She didn't need me or anyone else to win the tournament. We both had tears in our eyes as we hugged and parted.

Mary's opponent in the semifinals was the No. 3 player in the world, Conchita Martinez. I called Mary during my stopover in Hawaii and gave her the game plan Sven and I had worked out. I made it to Bradenton in time to watch the match on television. I was on pins and needles, but I needn't have been. Mary ruled the court, whipping Conchita 6-3, 6-1. After the final point, when she did look over to the coaches' box, her arms were raised in victory, and I knew the change had happened. At that moment, Mary came into her own; she finally accepted that she was a winner! I only wished I could have shared that moment with her by being there.

The finals were almost a foregone conclusion. She dominated Arantxa Sánchez Vicario 6-3, 6-2 to win the Australian Open. I was in heaven. When she called me, I was momentarily at a loss for words I was so happy. Then I congratulated her on her victory and told her, "Remember what I put in my note to you? I told you that I'd stay with you until you can stand on your own two feet. Today, you showed not only yourself, but the entire world that Mary Pierce is a winner. You were perfect and now you're ready to rely on your full-time coach, Sven Groeneveld." Then I added, "Go out, get the biggest tiramisu you can find and eat it all by yourself. You have earned it."

Since then, Mary's career has had its ups and downs. The year we separated she had some setbacks. But she also won the French Open singles and doubles titles in 2000 and the mixed doubles at Wimbledon in 2005, as well as a number of other pro tournaments. But whatever difficulties have come her way, she knew she could ultimately rely on herself to get things right. Our relationship is deeply affectionate at this point. I pray and hope that Mary continues to live her life with the same passion and warmth that she brought to tennis, and that she is able to convey those same traits to the children that she coaches and mentors.

Me and Mary at the Academy.

When I approached Nick to help me, I was lacking in motivation and inspiration. I had already achieved my goal of being No. 1 in the world, but I was bored. I needed someone who could motivate me to be the best again. When you are an accomplished player, you have your technique down pat and you're not going to change anything dramatically. But, in my case, something was lacking. The motivation and love for the game sometimes gets taken away. Nick still has a love for the sport and he has a way of talking and doing things that restores your confidence in yourself. Of course, Nick is a bit of a showman, but in this day and age that is good. He has this incredible exuberance—every day is a new day. It's contagious!

Every successful man requires a lot of dedication, discipline and hard work. You need to play to the very last ball and I think Nick and I both have those qualities.

—Boris Becker

CHAPTER 15

Boris Becker

I was very familiar with the name "Boom-Boom" Becker. After all, I'd watched him win Wimbledon as an unseeded player when he was only 17 years old. The following year I was there when he defended his title by beating Ivan Lendl, who was then ranked No. 1 in the world. Boris was an exciting player. I loved the way he dove for balls at the net to pull off incredible shots, pumped his fists, pranced around the court and served big aces, which gave him his nickname. When I traveled with Andre Agassi, I always said hello to him at tournaments, paying my respects.

By 1991, Boris had won five Grand Slam singles titles and was ranked No. 1 in the world for 12 weeks. The following year, he teamed up with fellow German player Michael Stich to win the gold medal in doubles at the Barcelona Olympics. He also won seven tour tournaments, including the year-end ATP World Tour Championships, defeating Jim Courier in three sets.

But in 1993, things turned sour. Boris went into a severe decline. His ranking fell to No. 17, the first time he was out of the top 10 in eight years, and he didn't make the year-end Grand Slam Cup Invitational. I was going through a rough patch myself, having parted with Andre Agassi in July. I was still coaching Mary Pierce, who reached the fourth round at the U.S. Open that year, but I missed being in the middle of all the action.

In late November, I received a phone call from Axel Meyer-Wölden, a famous attorney in Germany and Boris Becker's lawyer. He had visited IMG Academy that summer with his wife, Antonella, and their children Sandy and Agi (they later spent time with me as students for most of their teenage years). Now he was telling me that Boris was going to come for a visit. Upon arrival, Boris inspected every nook and cranny of the Academy—every court, every training facility. It was like he was checking me out. He hit a few balls with one of my pros, and he and I played a few rounds of golf. He seemed happy to be away from the army of paparazzi who followed him and his fiancée, Barbara Feltus, everywhere they went in Germany. As he left, I thanked him for coming, wished him good luck and thought no more of it.

A couple of weeks later, I went to Munich, Germany for the year-end Grand Slam Cup. This annual event was held indoors at the Olympiahalle from 1990 through 1999, and the best-performing men and women players were invited to compete. It was famous for paying out the highest prize money of any tournament in tennis, as much as $2 million during the first three years of the Cup's existence. Axel Meyer-Wölden and his business partner, Bill Dennis, ran the tournament, and I was there to help promote it.

At some point, I was invited to Boris' house for dinner. I had to make my way through a brigade of paparazzi because Barbara, now Boris' wife, was expecting their first child. During dinner, Axel and Boris sat on one side of the table and I sat on the other. Barbara, who was experiencing back pain, rolled around on one of those big plastic exercise balls (this was before they became popular in the United States). As we were finishing our meal, Axel pointed his finger at me and said, "We want you to be Boris' coach." Without hesitation, I asked Boris, "Do you really want to play tennis anymore?" and when he said, "Yes," I continued, "Why? What do you want to do at this point of your career?" He didn't hesitate and said, "I want to get back to the top again and will do whatever it takes." I reached my hand across the table and agreed to be his coach!

I was beyond thrilled—not in my wildest dreams did I imagine I would ever coach Boris Becker! At the same time, I knew I had my hands full. I had never coached a player of his stature—he was practically an icon in Germany. And he was very much out of shape. I decided to assign him David "Red" Ayme as his traveling coach. Red was from Louisiana where he had been a basketball, baseball and tennis player at Nicholls State. When he came to the Academy in 1987 just to work for the summer, he had made such a good impression—talented, hardworking and with a loud personality—I refused to let him go back to Louisiana, and he had been with me since then.

Boris and me during a training session.

We found a quiet court right outside of Munich to train. Did I mention that it was the Christmas holiday season in Germany? Boris wanted to train without my presence, so I went back to the States and didn't return to Germany until early February. I had been racking my brain how to approach Boris' training, though. I wasn't going to tell a three-time Wimbledon winner to change his game, tinker with his powerful serve, ground strokes, net game, or how he covered the court. So I decided to hang back, observe and wait for the right moment to put in my two cents' worth. When I got to Munich, it was cold enough to freeze your breath, but Boris was serious about this training. I was amazed and pleased about his work ethic. After the first week, Boris turned to me and said, "Mr. B., can you speak?" I said, "When I speak to you, I better know what I'm talking about." He stuck out his hand and said, "Mr. B., we will get along very well."

Boris, Axel Meyer-Wölden and me at the Grand Slam Cup.

Red accompanied Boris to play in a tournament in Marseille, France, where he lost early to Henri Leconte. They then traveled to Milan and Boris won the tournament. Had he lost there, his ranking would have dropped from 17 to 30 in the world. In Stuttgart, Germany, he beat his nemesis Michael Stich, who had replaced him as Germany's No. 1 player. (Although they had teamed up for the Olympics, there was no love lost between them.) When I attended his tournaments, Boris would turn to me shortly before each match and ask, "Mr. B., what's the plan for today?" and I would offer one tip concerning strategy.

We then played Palm Springs and began training for the Lipton Championships in Miami in March. The Lipton was the first tournament where Andre Agassi saw me working with Boris, and it made him angry. They faced each other in the third round, and Andre crushed Boris 6-2, 7-5. The match was more lopsided than the score suggests. At some point, unable to return Andre's serve, Boris gave his racquet to a ball girl suggesting that she might do better. Andre gently tapped a serve to her and she hit it back to the cheers of the crowd.

It was a surreal experience for me, sitting courtside representing Boris, while my friend Fritz Nau and former student Brad Gilbert, coaching Andre for the first time, were in Andre's corner. It was during the ensuing press conference that Andre famously said that I was insignificant to his career. The heart-wrenching hurt of our separation was still a raw wound, for both of us. When the press sought me out afterward and relayed the content of Andre's comments, I said, "He won Wimbledon, he's a Davis Cup hero, he's recognized as one of the best players on the tour and nearly every sponsor wants him to endorse their products. I wonder what would have happened if I were a significant factor in his career?" When reporters asked me to elaborate, I put them off by saying, "You can read about it in my book."

The quote appeared in *The New York Times* and the next day I received a call from Dick Schaap, a commentator for ESPN (and one of the very best in the business—like Charlie Rose, Dick was always well prepared and if he was critical at all, it was always in the spirit of helping you get better). Dick said, "Let's do a book." That's how my previous autobiography, *My Aces, My Faults*, got started. It allowed me to get out a good deal that was in my heart and also, I believe, begin the journey toward reconciliation with Andre.

Meanwhile, Boris and I didn't say too much about the loss to Andre, but he put his hand on my shoulder and reminded me that he would have another opportunity to play Andre and do better. That day came in a semifinal match at Wimbledon, 1995. Boris considered Wimbledon his second home and decided to stay there for two weeks. He treated all of us on his team royally. He provided a house for me in the Wimbledon village, close to the tournament site. My girlfriend Leah and I stayed there along with our hitting coach. Boris also rented a house for his physical trainer and his therapist. And of course, he, Barbara, their son Noah and the nanny had a house for themselves. The cost for all of it could have more than covered my tax bill, but Boris made sure that everything was first class. There was a private school a few miles away from the All England Lawn Tennis Club. Boris had two grass courts built at the school that were only for his and the school's use. We had a good week of training sessions.

Boris played well in the early stage and reached the semifinals, where the match he had been waiting for was about to happen. Becker vs. Agassi! After our daily training, Boris said, "Let's sit a bit and talk about tomorrow's match." This was the first time he wanted to go into greater detail than usual about a specific match. I was taken aback and asked if we could have the discussion in the morning. I realized that I had never considered the possibility of giving someone advice on how to beat Andre. But with a sad heart and a sense of duty to Boris, I offered this strategy:

- Andre will come out firing and beat the tar out of you for the first set.
- He'll probably take an early lead in the second set. (He did.)
- When you hit the big, booming serve for a winner, look directly at Andre and show him that Boris Becker will own this match!

I then followed Boris to the tournament site to prepare for the match. Most people don't realize that there are two locker rooms at Wimbledon. There is the main, big locker room where the majority of players shower and change, and another smaller locker room, guarded by soldiers, reserved for only the top players and their coaches. I sat in the corner waiting until Boris arrived wearing a beanie cap. He was carrying two bags, one over each shoulder. He walked slowly to his locker and gave a quick glance to all the others as if to say, "Why are you guys in my locker room?" I am absolutely certain that the other players felt his presence. He then went through his single-minded ritual, paying no attention to the steward who said, "Mr. Becker, five minutes until match time." If Boris heard him, he didn't respond—he was in a zone. "Mr. Becker, three minutes!" Boris started undressing, neatly folded his street clothes and put on his tennis clothes. Then he went to the restroom. "Mr. Becker, it's time!" Boris continued at his own pace to get ready. He was late, but nobody said a word to him. We left the locker room and I headed for the coaches' box.

The stands were packed like sardines, and so was our box. At Wimbledon the teams of both players share the same box. I had Boris' parents and Barbara Becker on my right, and Brooke Shields, Andre's wife at the time, on my left. Filling out the box was Nike personnel and Andre's manager. Leah sat nearby, although not in our box. The match was a gripping four-setter that unfolded exactly as I had predicted. Andre won the first set easily, but Boris fought back and took the next three, winning in a tiebreaker 2-6, 7-6, 6-4, 7-6. I was torn between exhilaration and dismay. Not too many coaches find themselves with a dilemma of having their two "sons" having to play against each other. That's how I felt. At the time, I wanted Boris to win, but it was a gut-wrenching experience for me. Richard Williams, the father of Venus and Serena Williams, has had the experience a number of times when his daughters have faced off, but few others have.

As we walked out of the stadium and to the black Mercedes that would take us back to our houses, Boris put his hand on my shoulder and said in a soft voice, "Mr. B., that match was for you!" Considering the physical and emotional wringer it was for him (and me), it was amazing that Boris won the first set in the final against Pete Sampras before bowing out 6-7, 6-2, 6-4, 6-2.

Shortly after that match, Boris traveled to Japan and had an awful loss to Robbie Weiss. He was upset because they put him on a side court instead of center court. He then traveled to Tokyo and reached the semifinals before losing to Michael Chang.

As the year went on, I started to feel a chill invading our relationship. I think there were some misunderstandings between us. I received a call from Michael Stich, Boris' archenemy, asking if I would coach him. I declined but when he asked if he could train at the Academy, I told him that he was welcome any time. When I happened to mention it to Axel Meyer-Wölden, he counseled me not to do it. But I stuck to my guns. I have always had an open door policy to any player and I wasn't about to compromise one of my fundamental values. Stich came for a week and soon after hired one of my coaches, Sven Groeneveld.

There were other disagreements between Boris and me, besides fraternizing with "the enemy"—I didn't realize how sensitive he was under his tough German exterior. In any case, the outcome was that by the U.S. Open, Boris had resolved to go his own way. He did not inform me directly of his decision, but had Alex Meyer-Wölden do it for him. When Axel told me while visiting the Academy that Boris did not want me at his side at Flushing Meadows, I was hurt and angry. I also realized for the first time how upset Andre Agassi must have felt when he found out in the news that I had let him go. Boris and I released a joint statement two days before the tournament that I was no longer going to be his day-to-day coach, but his tennis advisor instead, offering as an explanation that my busy schedule did not allow me to accommodate Boris' travel demands. It was utter nonsense, of course—I was always fully committed to him—designed to keep the media at bay and his head clear for the tournament. I went with Mary Pierce and left Flushing Meadows after she was eliminated in the third round.

I then flew to Minneapolis and visited the Nelsons; I noted with satisfaction that Andre beat Boris in the semis in four sets.

But I don't hold a grudge for long. And neither, to his credit, did Boris. At the 1996 Australian Open, he surprised everyone by winning his sixth Grand Slam. To my surprise, after he beat Michael Chang handily in the final, he told reporters, "Nick gets all the credit." It was a gracious acknowledgment that I had helped him get from No. 17 to No. 3 in the world, to the semifinals at Wimbledon and the U.S. Open, and to his final Grand Slam title. He later told *Sports Illustrated* that I was responsible for helping him find his game again.

Boris and I have a good, cordial relationship now. We greet each other warmly when we meet at tournaments and other events. I value his spirit, his great dedication to tennis and his deep understanding of the game at its highest level.

I remember calling Nick and telling him that I wanted to attend the 1991 Davis Cup match in Lyon, France. He told me not to worry and to make my flight arrangements. We were watching Andre Agassi play against Guy Forget, and Andre was being outplayed. Nick sent a note to Robert Seguso telling him that Andre was standing too far behind the baseline and he should step forward a few steps. As the note was delivered, Nick said, "Watch this!" Andre stepped in a few paces and handily won the match. Simply genius!

—Don Engel, longtime friend

Nick was always about being aggressive and being inside the baseline and taking the ball early and dictating the player. Those were his constant philosophies, but he was always evolving and trying to identify with how the sport was changing, whether it be with equipment or just the strength of the player and then trying to adapt and get players to adapt to those changes.

—Gavin Forbes, IMG agent

There are few coaches in sports who have accomplished what Nick has accomplished. Not only has he worked with the greatest tennis players in the world, his vision has changed the game. Academies around the world still try to emulate what Nick created more than 30 years ago. His charisma, endless energy, and love for the game of tennis are truly unique.

—Olivier van Lindonk, IMG agent

CHAPTER 16

The 1990s

The baby boomers like to say that "60 is the new 40." Well, I've never felt the need to keep score. I have been fit and full of energy throughout my life and haven't slowed down yet. In many ways, the 1990s were my busiest decade to date.

IMG Academy continued to grow in leaps and bounds. Using the model of total immersion, competition and elite instruction, it continued to add sports and acquired land in the surrounding area to build further facilities.

Meanwhile I had plenty to do, going to tournaments with my elite athletes and overseeing the development of new emerging players like the Williams sisters, Max Mirnyi and Maria Sharapova. Add to that numerous speaking engagements and tennis clinics in other parts of the country and the world, and I was more often on the road than at home.

One of the more interesting foreign engagements took me to Qatar, a small, but incredibly wealthy Arab nation on the Persian Gulf next to Saudi Arabia. The ruler of the country, Sheikh Hamad bin Khalifa Al Thani, was a tennis fan and invited me and my team to come and hold a clinic for him and his children on his private courts. He later championed the development of soccer in his country.

My daughter Danielle did research before our departure about the proper rules and protocol for us to follow. We weren't supposed to cross our legs in the direction of the sheik, and we couldn't touch him or look directly at him at certain times. And we weren't to pick our teeth in his presence. That warning was meant specifically for me. I was addicted to chewing on orange Stim-U-Dents (I now use

Soft Touch toothpicks). At the Academy my staff always knew how to find me by following the orange trail I left behind.

Greg Breunich, one of my coaches, and I arrived in Qatar late at night. We were picked up and driven into the desert in a caravan of jeeps. We were starting to worry about where we were being taken when all of a sudden we saw an oasis of bright lights ahead. As we got closer to the compound, we noticed a lot of young cows and a lot of security forces—guys with machine guns everywhere. We were shown to our quarters, small concrete block buildings. The air conditioning was freezing inside, so we stuffed towels into the vents to get some relief.

We conducted our clinic and one evening attended a feast with the sheik in a palatial tent. There were plates heaped with food, which turned out to be the calves we had seen when we arrived, and the meat stuck in my teeth. I wanted to use my Stim-U-Dents but I remembered that was a no-no. I didn't know what to do when all of a sudden the sheik pulled out a silver toothpick the size of a screwdriver. I looked at him and said, jokingly, "You're my man!" I told him what my daughter had said about not picking my teeth in front of him and proceeded to use my Stim-U-Dent. The sheik was amused and burst into laughter. International crisis averted!

Later the ruler sent one of his sons to the Academy while I was at Wimbledon. When I returned, I was supposed to check out some short-term students. There were five or six young players on the court and one of them was standing around, so I pointed at his feet and said, "You know those things down there?" He looked at me puzzled and said, "They're my feet." I said, "Yes, you're supposed to move them!" My coaches were freaking out, waving their arms, making faces and throat-cutting gestures from behind him. Finally, one of them pulled me aside and explained that I was yelling at the son of Sheikh Hamad bin Khalifa Al Thani and that I was in big trouble!

Nothing ever came of it then, but some years later when I was at the French Open, that same student, who now was an important minister in the Qatar government, met me there. He was visiting Paris for diplomatic reasons and wanted to say hello. I was a bit apprehensive at first, but he greeted me graciously. As we spoke, he recalled that incident and thanked me for talking to him that way. "No one else ever told me the truth to my face," he said, smiling. We parted as friends.

Another tennis workshop led to an unforgettable experience, a 43-year-old dream come true. In April of 1996, I was invited to conduct a tennis clinic in Pensacola, Florida for the Blue Angels in exchange for a ride in one of their planes. The Blue Angels are the U.S. Navy's flight demonstration squadron, which conducts exhibitions at air shows throughout the country. The pilots perform incredible feats of aerial acrobatics. They fly in such tight formations that they only have 18 inches from one plane's wing tip to the next—18 inches! Imagine the perfection required to pull that off. These pilots simply can't afford to have a bad day!

Angel, Danielle, Leah, Red Ayme and Ken Merritt all accompanied me to Pensacola where we spent the night. The next morning, we were to watch a demonstration of an air show, and I got to sit in on the pre-show briefing during which the pilots planned that day's formations. After the show, some of the pilots and maintenance team came out to the tennis clinic.

Then we all went out to lunch, but I didn't eat a thing since my ride was scheduled for that afternoon. Angel and Danielle were worried for me and tried to talk me out of going, but I wouldn't have missed it for the world. When we got back to the base, a man walked up to me clad in flight gear and introduced himself as Captain Scott "Yogi" Beare. He was going to be my pilot. They fitted me in a flight suit and we headed out to the runway.

The F/A-18 Hornet aircraft was an absolutely beautiful sight. It looked small from a distance, but once I got up close I realized how big it really is. At 56 feet, this magnificent machine was nearly as long as a tennis court and at top speed it traveled at more than one-and-a-half times the speed of sound (Mach 1.7). When they opened the canopy (which, by the way, was nearly 16 feet above the ground) and strapped me into my seat, I had no idea what I was in for. As they put restraints on my legs, chest and head, Yogi explained that they were there to prevent the G-force generated by the 90-degree turns from banging my head into the canopy. I listened as Yogi performed his pre-flight check and communicated with the tower. He went through emergency procedures with me, but I was so nervous that I'm not sure of anything he said.

Getting strapped in—too late to pull out now!

We taxied on the runway, and when we were next in line to take off, Yogi said, "Shortly after liftoff I'm going to say, 'Nick, hold on tight—three, two, one.' Do you understand?" I replied, "Yes, sir." We took off doing 100 miles per hour in a matter of seconds, then 150, and suddenly we were airborne. I heard Yogi say, "Nick, hold on— three, two, one!" He jerked the stick back, pointed the nose straight up and hit the afterburners. The thrust slammed me against my seat and left my stomach behind, I don't know where. I had never experienced anything like it in my life. All I could say (and I must have said it a dozen times) was, "Holy sh*t, Holy sh*t!" We finally leveled off and Yogi let me handle the throttle for a while, and I fulfilled my dream of piloting a fighter plane! Then he took over again and we did some maneuvers—rolling, hairpin turns, flying upside down. I had a plastic bag in my lap and wanted to throw up, but I couldn't. I was sweating like a bull dog.

We flew for about 45 minutes before coming in for a landing. When my feet touched the ground, I couldn't say a single word. I sat on the grass for what seemed like an hour—totally speechless. My daughter Danielle told me later that despite my deep brown tan, I looked pale as a ghost. I had waited for 43 years to live this dream and boy, I was not disappointed. I've had plenty of thrills in my life—watching my students win Grand Slams, skiing and parasailing—but nothing compared with the rush I experienced flying with the Blue Angels.

Not all of my activities involved teaching tennis directly. I continued to pursue my love of surfing, visiting Costa Rica seven times during the 1990s. On one of the trips, Giuliana Sotela, a student at the Academy, invited me to stay at her father Mario's large farm. It was a spacious place and had an artificial waterfall where we went swimming. Mario's mother owned most of the radio stations in Costa Rica—that's where he got his money. Mario and I hit it off immediately. He liked me because I was working with his daughter. At some point he said, "Let's start a zoo! Let's go in together 50/50." Like me, once he'd made up his mind, he went at it like gangbusters. He flew in giraffes, rhinos, and all kinds of other exotic animals, but it never came to anything. Somewhere in my files I still have the legal papers we drew up. Mario later became part owner of a soccer team, and Giuliana ended up marrying Marcelo Rios, a super talented player who also trained at IMG. I don't think the zoo is in existence any longer. I guess the animals roam the jungles of Costa Rica like the dinosaurs in Jurassic Park.

A different kind of development involved Wendy Nelson. After graduating from Northwestern, where she had been an NCAA athlete and captain of the tennis team, Wendy went to a ski racing camp in Wyoming and hurt her knee. She tore her ACL and meniscus and had to have two surgeries, plus weeks of keeping off the leg. She was getting so depressed that her parents called me, worried. I immediately said, "Get her down here." I knew that rehabbing among fellow athletes at the Academy would be good for her. I moved her into one of the units of my interconnected condo and put her to work in marketing.

Wendy Nelson and me.

I had had the idea of building a sports bar and restaurant for some time and decided to put it into practice. I figured with her parents being a big part of TGI Fridays, Wendy would be a natural for the project. When I told her that I wanted her to be in charge of building the Bollettieri Sports Grill, she looked at me like I was nuts and said, "You must be kidding." I replied, "No. Research it, get an architect, raise the money and build it." I reckoned that work would be the best therapy, and a challenge like that would take her mind off her physical situation. Plus, I was confident that Wendy had the smarts and determination to see it through. She didn't disappoint me. She took the time to learn how to start a new business, worked with the architect and builders, planned the menu with the chef, and oversaw hiring the staff. She did it all, and it turned out to be a beautiful place. Axel Meyer-Wölden, whose son played at the Academy, was one of the investors who helped with the down payment for the building funds.

My son Jimmy Boy created a large round bar with his sports photographs of me and athletes at the Academy under a polyurethane layer as the countertop. In the bathroom, there were piped-in sounds of tennis balls being batted back and forth—pow, pow, pow—along with crowd noises. Wendy brought in small bleachers, just like at a stadium, so fans could sit and have the full sports experience watching games on the TV monitors. I was so proud of Wendy and her achievement. She discovered a talent she didn't know she had, and soon after she enrolled in business school. When the place opened, it was an immediate success—the only venture outside of tennis in which I have made any money. I netted about $300,000 when I sold it. It is now the Anna Maria Oyster Bar Landside on the Tamiami Trail in Bradenton and continues to do very well.

I also continued to make friends with people who became important parts of my life and career. There was the Donato family, Lou and Liz and their sons Michael and Clay. All except Michael are tennis fanatics. Clay was a super athlete who came to the Academy full-time as a 13-year-old and later had a brilliant college career at Texas A & M and the University of North Carolina. Lou is a Canadian real estate developer who also has business interests in Sarasota, now mananged by Clay. We have a lot of fun together both here and during vacations on the isle of Capri. Spending time with Lou and his family feels a little like walking into one of the *Godfather* movies. He always tells me, "Nick, don't worry. I have your backside covered!" and I am grateful to him for it.

I had no idea when I was introduced to Mark Fisher that he would become such a huge part of my life. Both of his children,

Daniel and Jessica, have visited the Academy many times and have become very close to me. Mark is a smart guy who loves sports and betting—he puts small wagers on just about anything, but doesn't care so much about winning as making things happen. He "gets me" in ways most others I know never have. He is kind and generous to a fault, and what he has meant to me would fill a book and still not come close to explaining all he has done for me, my family and many projects. He has also supported numerous needy young players at IMG with scholarships, but would never want them to know it.

Me, Mark Fisher, Dick Vitale and John Calipari.

Don Engel has been a supporter of mine going all the way back to Dorado Beach. He was in the bond market where he worked for Michael Milken for a while, and is crazy about tennis and other sports. He sent his son, Chris, and daughter, Elisa, to my camp at Beaver Dam. Don is a character, and he has been more than generous with me and my family. In 1991, when my daughter Danielle got married and I was in financial straits once again, his wedding present was to pay for the entire wedding! The way it happened was that I called and told him all about it. As it turned out, the ceremony was slated to take place on the Saturday night of one of the Final Four NCAA basketball games. He said to me, "I'll pay for the wedding, as long as I can watch the game." So during the festivities, he was in the kitchen, glued to a telelvision set. Don has traveled to a number of tennis events with me and always looks forward to the U.S. Open in New York, where he makes the sky suite, owned by him and his partner Joel Pashcow, available to me for the duration of the tournament.

Don Engel and me at the U.S. Open stadium court.

Don's kindhearted hospitality has led to occasional snafus on my part because I tend to get lost there. One time, shortly after Cindi and I were married, I steered us mistakenly into the box of Donald Trump. He took one look at us and said, "You're not allowed, Nick, but your beautiful wife can stay!"

But of course, most of my life continued to revolve around tennis. After my breakup with Andre and two seasons with Boris Becker, I had the opportunity to coach a talented young player from Melbourne, Australia, Mark Philippoussis. I had first met him in 1989 when he came to the Academy for a two-week training session at age 13. I had followed his development as a junior from afar, and when I went to the Australian Open for the first time in 1995, I got together with Mark and his father, Nick, who had coached his son since he was six years old. My namesake was very much like me, a non-stop talker who didn't let others get a word in edgewise. He was considered an excitable, difficult and demanding parent, but we got along just fine. Mark claimed that I actually calmed him down!

At 6' 5", Mark was a giant compared to the rest of the elite men's singles players, who in those days included 5' 6"-tall Michael Chang. He was a forerunner of things to come—nowadays you don't stand much of a chance in elite tennis if you're under six feet. Mark had a good array of strokes and a phe-nomenal serve. It was once clocked at 142.3 miles per hour! He was also movie star handsome and as kind as he could be.

Over the next six months, we kept in touch. When Mark and his dad planned to attend the Lipton tournament in Florida, I invited them to spend the week prior at the Academy to use all of its facilities and prepare, and I sent one of my coaches to work with Mark at the tournament. By the time we hooked

Mark Philippoussis

up again at the U.S. Open, I was still coaching Mary Pierce, but Boris Becker and I were going our separate ways; Mr. Philippoussis invited me to spend time with him and his son. It was kind of a mutual evalua-tion or tryout time. Mark battled Pete Sampras for four sets before los-ing, earning everyone's respect. I was impressed and agreed to become part of the Philippoussis team. Not to direct it, mind you—Papa Nick took the backseat to no one.

I traveled with them to Japan, where Mark made it to the fi-nals of the Seiko tournament, losing to 19-year-old Marcelo Rios, the flamboyant Chilean who also trained at my Academy. In Tokyo, he beat Stefan Edberg handily in 47 minutes and lost once again in the finals, this time to Michael Chang. By the end of the year, he had moved from No. 307 to No. 32 in the world, and was the youngest player in the top 50. Nick Philippoussis was pleased with Mark's progress, and to my amazement he let me take over as coach—for a while. Mark continued to improve dramatically. At the 1996 Australian Open, he beat Pete Sampras in the third round in three sets before losing to fellow Australian Mark Woodford in the next round. But his father didn't step back for long. He disagreed with my analysis that Mark's forehand needed an adjustment, and we soon parted ways.

Mark's career has been a roller coaster since then. At one point he made it to No. 8 in the world and to the finals of both Wimbledon and the U.S. Open, but he never won a Grand Slam. I believe that part of what got in the way was his inability to fully focus on the game. He loved surfing and spent a lot of time doing that. With his rugged good looks, he was often distracted by other opportunities, including starring as the bachelor on a 2007 reality television dating show, "Age of Love." To my mind, he never reached his full potential as a player. But as a human being he was all aces—big-hearted, gentle and kind.

With his departure, I had more time to once again focus on the Academy. I had another crop of young, talented players to attend to, including Iva Majoli, Max Mirnyi, Marcelo Rios, Maria Sharapova, Jelena Jankovic and the Williams sisters, Venus and Serena—many of whom were on their way to becoming No. 1 in the world.

All these different cultures, all these different nationalities come here with the goal of becoming more disciplined, more determined, and end up kinder, more educated people, too. Those are all the qualities this place brings, and Nick is the head of all that, because on a regular basis he speaks to us. He gets to us whether it's on the outdoor bleachers or at the indoor center courts when it's raining. He teaches us life. He shares his life experience. He shares the life experiences of his friends. He's so determined that people come out of the Academy here with so much more than being tennis players.

—Max Mirnyi

CHAPTER 17

Max Mirnyi

Max Mirnyi's story is as much about his parents, who sacrificed their lives for their son's success, as about his own determination and desire. Max came to the United States from Belarus in 1991 as a 13-year-old when a management company signed Tatiana Ignatieva, a teenage tennis star, and brought her to America. Max came along as

her hitting partner. He spoke no English when he arrived, lived in an apartment in Brooklyn, played in junior tournaments, and earned extra money by stringing racquets. Eleven months later when his dad, Nikolai, arrived at JFK, Max handed him $300 he had made during the year at his side job. His mother Tatiana stayed in Belarus with his younger brother, who was only five at the time.

I can't remember how I heard about Max, but someone raved about this talented youngster and we raised the money to get him and his dad to the Academy for a tryout. I know they were nervous, and Nikolai had Max warm up for more than 40 minutes to get ready for what he expected to be a grueling evaluation session. The first thing I noticed when I was on my center stadium court was that the youngster was pacing up and down. It was as though he was on sentry duty, but I've seen that anxious pacing before. I called him over 15 minutes earlier than he expected and saw him gesturing toward his father with a "what do I do now?" expression.

Well, after three minutes of watching Max hit with my pros, I knew he was plenty talented and offered him a full scholarship. He already had a big serve, but he was still ordinary in size. I knew his mother, who had been a champion swimmer, was 5' 10" and his dad, who played competitive volleyball in the 1960s, was 6' 5", so I expected Max to keep growing. Nature finally caught up to him from age 18 to 22, and he just exploded, ending up as tall as his dad.

I also paid attention to his personal development. At some point early on, he took a test in his history class at school. When he tried to look up an answer in the textbook in his bag, the teacher caught him. Of course, it got back to me, and when Max came to the practice court later that day, I asked him about it. He was surprised because he figured he was at the Academy only to play tennis. Once I'd heard his side of the story, I said to him, "Don't you ever do it again," and suspended him from the tennis program for three days. During that time, I had him help a guy who washed and clearned my cars. Max later said, "From that point on, I learned two lessons: to never cheat in life and to always keep my cars clean." And he meant it!

Before going on with Max's career, I want to speak a bit about his father, Nikolai, a well educated man and geography teacher, who made the decision to give up his own career to give Max a chance at realizing his dreams. Nikolai worked as a dishwasher at a restaurant, drove a bus and became a clerk at a local department store to make a few extra dollars in order to get Max to tournaments and support his education. Just as inspiring is the fact that Max realized the commitment that his dad was making and worked his butt off to make the most of his opportunity. He also developed into a kind, generous and thoughtful man—very much like his father.

As Max continued to grow into his body, it became evident that not only did he have a big serve, he was also lethal at the net. After turning pro in 1998, he reached No. 18 in the world in singles, but his big serve, net game and aggressive play were perfectly suited to doubles, and he would go on to win world titles with a variety of partners, including Lleyton Hewitt, Jonas Björkman and Roger Federer. He ranked No. 1 in doubles in 2003 and holds 10 Grand Slam men's doubles and mixed doubles titles at Wimbledon, the French Open and the U.S. Open. In 2012 he carried the Belarus flag during the opening ceremonies at the London Summer Olympics and won the gold medal in mixed doubles with Victoria Azarenka.

Over a career that still continues as of this writing, Max has earned more than $10 million in prize money. But Max is more than his winnings. He is now 36 years old and works every day to maintain peak physical condition. As a result, he's still one of the best doubles players in the world. Max has been on full scholarship in all his years at the Academy, from the time he arrived until today, and he has given back more than we ever invested in him. Max is a role model and inspiration to so many youngsters. He and his family live within walking distance of the Academy and he can frequently be seen hitting with the juniors and offering words of support both on and off the court. He takes the time to listen to their questions and explains to them what the pro tour is all about. Let me assure you, this is not a typical practice among the best players in the world, but it is characteristic of Max's generous personality.

I am proud to have coached Max and grateful to continue to know him. He has been a blessing to his family—his lovely wife and three children—to the Academy, to my family and to the sport of tennis. My wife, Cindi, speaks about very few tennis players; he is one of them. In fact, Max is a gift to the world. He is an elite athlete who understands that being a champion on the court gratifies a player's self-image and ego, but being a champion off the court elevates humanity! Max is a man of integrity, for whom integrity is the first step towards true greatness.

It is challenging to communicate the anguish a parent goes through essentially handing off their child to someone else and entrusting them at such an important stage in their development. Nick, you know me well, there is nothing in this world I hold as dear to my heart as my son, Justin. Thus, I hope you can appreciate how much respect and trust I had in you when I dropped Justin off in your care. I stand today, 70 years of age, humbled, appreciative and forever grateful. My son never made it to No. 1 in the world or hoisted a Wimbledon trophy, but I consider him to be an amazing success as an athlete but more so as a person. His success is a direct tribute to you and your staff and the time he spent at your Academy. I'll always be grateful for what you did for Justin, and my family.

—Barry Gimelstob

CHAPTER 18

Marcelo Rios and Xavier Malisse

Not a day goes by that I am not asked the question, "Nick, who is the very best player that you ever coached?" There is no easy answer because I have coached many great players, and each one is unique and different in style, approach and temperament. Still, in my opinion the most talented player ever to train at IMG Academy was Marcelo Rios. Why? First, Marcelo was a lefty. He could make the ball dance and in a split second hit a forehand winner; or jumping, with both feet off the ground, he could hit a two-handed backhand from any position on the tennis court. I've never experienced gifts like Marcelo possessed. But he never came close to accomplishing all that his talent allowed.

Marcelo Rios

Talent is not and never will be the single determining factor that allows one to become the best in the world. Neither is beautiful or elegant form. There have been a number of players who were never beautiful to watch—Jimmy Connors and Brad Gilbert come to mind. Scrappy and indomitable, they won "ugly," often in thrilling matches, because they used whatever tactics they could, including mind games, to find a way to succeed. Brad trained at the Academy for a while and later became a successful coach with Andre Agassi and Mary Pierce, as well as a highly respected commentator at Grand Slam tournaments. He and I have had our differences in the past, but we are now the best of friends. He has become one of my biggest supporters and makes several visits to IMG each year to work with all of my students. And he always tells me that he should have sent his son Zach to me much earlier in his tennis career.

In any case, Marcelo had amazing gifts, and worked like an animal both on court and off. His physical regimen was second to none, and yet:

- He had no appreciation for the tradition of tennis and little respect for other players.

- He was rude to all spectators, especially children who waited for long periods of time to get his autograph.

- He did zero, zip, nada to promote the game in his homeland, Chile, to the tens of thousands of youngsters who looked up to him.

- He was so tight with his money that in the middle of the night he would leave his room to get free water that was set aside for the players.

I mention the last two points because I do believe that having a big heart is a requirement of a champion, and generosity goes along with that. Stinginess and miserly behavior are signs of something clenched inside, which often gets in the way and doesn't allow a player to soar. I'm not talking about personality—many champions are prickly, especially when under pressure—but how one conducts one's life at a fundamental level matters.

One of his coaches, Larry Stefanki, did one heck of a job and Marcelo achieved a world ranking of No. 1 in 1998. He held it for six weeks, even though he never won a Grand Slam title. I then began coaching him myself and at the end of that same year, he won the Grand Slam Cup in Munich, defeating Andre Agassi in the final 6-4, 2-6, 7-6 (1), 5-7, 6-3. His purse for winning that tournament was close to $2 million. Immediately after the tournament, I thanked all of the personnel, tipped the stringer who cared for Marcelo's racquets, along with our assigned driver and a few others. The total cost was a few hundred dollars. Marcelo went berserk on me. He also claimed that since the Grand Slam Cup was not a "regular tour event," I was not entitled to the bonus that was written into our contract. I won't spell out my response in these pages, but I did receive the money that I was due.

Today, Marcelo has mellowed considerably. He has a wonderful family and a daughter who is a very good player. We have a casual relationship but don't see each other very often.

Me and Xavier at the Academy.

Another player who never reached his full potential was Xavier Malisse. He came to the Academy from Belgium in 1997 on a full scholarship when he was 17 years old. He had talent beyond description—he was also a gifted junior soccer player—but his personality made it difficult for him to perform with any consistency. There was something of the young Andre Agassi about him. The Belgium Tennis Federation had thrown up the white flag and surrendered. When he first arrived at the Academy, I almost raised the white flag too, but something told me that this kid, or should I say, punk—he dyed his hair green for the first tournament he played with me—could be special. On the court, Xavier was in "Class E" (for explosive); off the court he was in "Class G" (for gentle). Our first challenge was to try to blend his talent and his mental qualities in such a way that they allowed him to win. He just wasn't motivated to use his gifts to the fullest.

Soon after his arrival at the Academy, he played the first round in the Eddie Herr International Junior Championships in such a lackadaisical style, I got upset. I called Fritz Nau and said, "I want you to go down to Xavier's court and tell him, 'Nick is watching you and if you lose, you will be one unhappy dude, and I mean that in every way!'" Fritz delivered the message and Xavier responded. He not only won the next match, but he won the entire tournament. He displayed such raw power and poise that he attracted worldwide attention, including that of Adidas, which signed him to an endorsement contract.

In 1998, Xavier turned pro, but his career has been like a seesaw. In his best performances he reached the semifinals at Wimbledon in 2002 and won the doubles at the French Open in 2004 with his fellow Belgian countryman, Olivier Rochus. By 2009, his world ranking had slipped to 205. At the end of 2012, he made it back to No. 47. There is no doubt in my mind, and many tennis experts share my opinion, that Xavier has fallen far short of reaching his potential. We all thought he had the talent to become a genuine top 10 player and was capable of winning major events. But talent without focus and unquenchable desire is not enough; it is one part of the equation for succeeding in tennis and in life.

Xavier retired from the professional game in October of 2013 after 25 years on the tour. He still lives at the Academy in the villa he owns and has become a coach, bringing his students there to train.

He is applying his talented hand to the game of golf—he has a very low handicap—and works as a full-time tennis coach. I miss him as a player. He has always been polite and caring toward my family and me, and I pray that he will find a way to enjoy the rest of his life.

Jelena has to be the most determined player I've ever coached. She may not have the strongest or biggest game, but she is so tenacious. She hates losing more than she enjoys winning. She never quits, never gives up. Playing her is like trying to put a cat in a bag. She fights you tooth and nail for every point, whether on the practice court or during a match.

—Chip Brooks, coach

CHAPTER 19

Jelena Jankovic

Jelena Jankovic came to the Academy from Serbia when she was barely in her teens. Training at the same time were two other talented young women, Tatiana Golovin and Maria Sharapova. They didn't

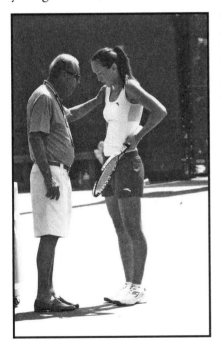

Me and Jelena. For once, Mom is nowhere to be seen.

socialize with one another. Each pursued her own fierce course dedicated to achieving greatness. It is a shame that Tatiana's career was cut short due to illness.

Jelena's parents were very much a part of her life. Her dad, Veselin, was a super basketball player, and there is no question that Jelena inherited much of his athletic abilities. Her mother, Snežana, an energetic ball of fire and likely the origin of Jelena's ferocious competitiveness, was not only a hovering mom, but also a bodyguard with the eyes of an eagle watching over her young. Mrs. Jankovic could always be found at Jelena's side, no matter what. She was there throughout nearly every match in Jelena's career. And when a call went against her daughter, Mom felt that Jelena was being picked on. At times, Jelena mirrored that behavior, looking to her parents and coaches when things weren't going her way on the court and getting down on herself too much. By the way, Jelena

209

divorced her coaches with about the same frequency that I parted with my wives:

- Can't get her serve in the box—get a new coach.
- His personality is negative—get a new coach.
- Coach and Mom disagreed—get a new coach.

Jelena trained at the Academy for all of her junior years and many of her professional years. She was, for a time, represented by IMG. Jelena has always been a super athlete with a tremendous work ethic. She has trained hard to develop her fitness and can do whatever needs to be done on the court—her technique, movement and ball-striking ability are outstanding. I share the view of key instructors at the Academy that she is one of the best athletes on the women's tour—you don't reach the No. 1 ranking in the world without being superior, both physically and mentally—though there are times when her mental focus drifts.

But Jelena has had a super career. As a junior she won the 2001 Australian Open and was ranked No. 1 in the world. She has reached the singles semifinals of the French and Australian Opens and the final of the U.S. Open. In 2007, she and Andy Murray teamed up to win the Wimbledon Mixed Doubles Championship. She is one of only a few players to have beaten both of the Williams sisters, Venus and Serena, in the same tournament, and she once again reached No. 1 in the world in 2008. After some setbacks and shaky years, she returned to fine form in 2012 and made her way back into the top 10.

I believe that in order to achieve the next level, Jelena needs to evaluate her own needs—not her mom's—and hire a top-notch coach who can satisfy those needs. That is the key to her becoming one of the best in the world once again. She also must look inwardly in difficult moments, not to her friends and relatives in the stands, and stop blaming others and circumstances for her difficulties.

That being said, Jelena and her mom have always been kind to me and shown concern for my wife and children. Never has Jelena been negative with me in any way and always credits me for helping her rise through the ranks of tennis. I will always be proud of being a part of her career and I will never forget her! She deserves every success that has ever come her way.

In addition to not aging—and I've known him for a number of years now—he's also consistent in terms of his principles, values and fundamentals. You know what you're going to get when you're dealing with Nick.

—Maria Sharapova

I started out as an intern at the Academy. Being around Nick for all these years has helped me become who I am today. He has taught me a lot about how to work with players and has given me the skill set needed to represent Maria Sharapova.

—Max Eisenbud

CHAPTER 20

Maria Sharapova

Maria Sharapova started playing tennis when she was four years old. At some point she attended a clinic in Moscow which was headed by Martina Navratilova. Although there were more than 100 girls there, Maria must have made an impression because afterwards, Martina went over to her dad, Yuri, who had been watching from the sidelines, and said "You know, your girl has talent and you should do something about it." Since it is hard to train in Russia, especially in the winter, he made the decision to take Maria to Florida. He had heard of my Academy but didn't know anything about it. Like Max Mirnyi's father, Yuri made enormous sacrifices to provide the opportunity for his daughter to succeed. He had to borrow money for the airfare to the United States. He and Maria arrived in Miami in 1994 with neither of

Maria Sharapova at IMG as a teenager.

them speaking any English. They got on a bus and headed west until they reached IMG Academy. Yuri took various menial jobs to support them until Maria was old enough to attend the program; at that point IMG signed her and put her on full scholarship. Her mother Elena joined them two years later.

When I met Maria she was eight years old and a skinny (and I do mean skinny) young girl. Yuri never left her side. At times, I thought their bodies were connected—that is, until her practice session began. At that point, Yuri would stand courtside with a pad and pen, taking notes on everything I said and everything she did. Sometimes I wondered if he was an undercover agent for the KGB.

Maria's practice sessions were always serious, highly focused events. If you've seen her play at a Grand Slam tournament, you know what I mean. She doesn't fool around, doesn't laugh; she hits ball after ball, concentrates on strokes and keeps her attention with laser-like focus on the mission: to win! The same was true of her practices. There were no smiles or cheerleading tactics. She berated herself for missing or mishitting. Everything was 100% business! A tornado could hit her and she wouldn't lose focus.

At times, Yuri and I, both Type A personalities, would clash over training strategies. For a while he'd take Maria to other coaches because he thought it would help if he could find different specialists for every aspect of the game—service, footwork, ground strokes—but he and Maria always returned to the Academy, and we always agreed on the overall plan of her training. When he was recently asked about his feelings toward me, Yuri said, "There are coaches here and there are coaches there. No one comes close to what Nick brings to the table. Not just in terms of coaching, but the entire environment in Bradenton. As for my conflicts with Nick, yes, there were times when we disagreed with each other. People have disagreements. What is important is that we agreed on the significant aspects of her training."

I never traveled with Maria and her team to tournaments. I realized that one of the best ways I could be helpful was to be there as support, guide and sounding board. At one point, when Maria was trying to decide whether to play with both hands on her forehand and backhand, I had her practice them with one of her hitting partners. After I observed her carefully, I told her, "I don't know what to tell you because you hit well with both, but you need to make a decision now. You can't keep going back and forth." She also tried playing left-handed for a while, but finally settled on a one-handed, right forehand. By the way, when she's on, it's lethal.

As a youngster Maria never practiced with her fellow students— never! In that regard, she was just like Monica Seles: She wouldn't associate with peers; she wouldn't even speak to them. She knew that one day, she would have to confront them on the court, and there was no benefit in developing friendships that might get in the way of the adversarial attitude she'd have to cultivate toward her opponents. When practice was over, Maria and her dad would pack up their bags and go back to their dwelling.

At age 13, Maria won the Eddie Herr International Junior Tennis Championships in the girls' 16 division. She made her professional debut the following spring on her 14th birthday on April 19. Because of age restrictions, she could only play a limited number of professional tournaments, so she entered several junior events and reached the finals both at the Australian Open and at Wimbledon in 2002. In 2004, she defeated Serena Williams in the final at Wimbledon for her first Grand Slam title.

I congratulate Yuri for recognizing when it was time to engage a full-time personal coach when she was 14 and about to turn pro. That was Robert Lansdorp, a top teaching pro from California and a good friend of mine. Maria got along well with him, and he provided valuable input during her climb to become No. 1 in the world. Working with him also led to Maria training on both coasts of the United States, depending on which tournaments she is preparing for. For a while, she also had a good run with a Swedish pro, Thomas Högstedt, who moved on to coach Caroline Wozniacki.

Maria has struggled on and off with a shoulder injury, but has rehabbed with her usual determination and work ethic. She has made a number of comebacks, winning the 2006 U.S. Open, the 2008 Australian Open, the 2012 French Open, a silver medal at the London Olympics and regaining her No. 1 ranking for a time. She now has a new coach, Sven Groeneveld, who was with me when he coached Mary Pierce, and he has the experience and temperament to match her personality.

I believe that I helped Maria on the court, and her IMG agent Max Eisenbud provided excellent guidance with her endorsements, scheduling and off-the-court activities. Throughout her career, whether she has been winning or going through a tough spell, I have always sent her notes and emails of praise, congratulations and encouragement. We are always glad to see each other at tournaments and at the Academy. I feel that Maria is a wonderful young woman and has been a super asset to tennis, IMG and her sponsors. On the court, she has the fierceness and determination of a lioness. Off the court, Maria has a gentle side. She might be seen hitting with one of the young juniors or signing autographs for a number of children gathered to watch her practice. She is polite and genuine, and I'm proud to have worked with her.

Nick is unquestionably one of the greatest motivators in sports history. His passion, energy and force of will are mesmerizing. When Nick turns on the juice, it penetrates to the very core of an athlete's psyche. A single dose of Nick can jolt players to new heights of self-belief, commitment and fighting spirit.

—Jim Loehr, Ed.D., Human Performance Institute

CHAPTER 21

Martina Hingis

My first look at Martina Hingis came at the French Open in 1995. She had just turned pro the previous October and made waves right away when she became the youngest player to win a match at

a Grand Slam tournament, reaching the second round at the Australian Open. My good friend, Mary Carillo, who is a sports commentator known for her insightful profiles of top athletes, came up to me while I was watching Martina play and asked what I thought of the talented 14-year-old. I told Mary that she would be a champion one day, maybe even the very best in the world. Mary wondered why I had such high regard for this girl. After all, I had seen hundreds, maybe thousands of talented kids who didn't

Martina Hingis

achieve world-class status. I said, "Martina has the nose of an elephant." I didn't mean her appearance, of course; Martina was an attractive girl already. I was referring to her ability to "smell" the ball, to know instinctively where it was coming to her and where to hit her response. Mary smiled and asked, "Are you sure?" I confirmed that I was. Martina possessed flawless technique—great anticipation coupled with great movement and balance. She was able to concentrate and never played out of her comfort zone. Like Chris Evert, she was not a power player, but a brilliant tactician, moving her opponents around the court at will. She did not have ballistic, killer strokes, but she never missed. She always looked like she was smiling, even when she was dead serious and going for the jugular.

Her mother, Melanie Molitor, who had once been ranked 10th in Czechoslovakian tennis, was determined that her daughter would be a champion from the get-go. She named her after Martina Navratilova and coached her from age two on. Both before their defection to Switzerland and after, she was always with Martina.

By the time Martina came to IMG Academy late in 2000, my prediction had come true in spades. Martina had burned up the court. For a while she was virtually unbeatable. She won five singles and eight women's doubles Grand Slam titles. She had been ranked No. 1 in both categories—only the third female player to do so. But something had changed that year. Although she had had considerable success, winning nine tournaments, she had not won a Grand Slam singles championship. In fact, she had made it only to the final of the Australian Open, where she lost to Lindsay Davenport.

Martina and her mother came to the Academy a week before the WTA Tour Championships. This was the final big tournament in 2000, the culminating event on the pro tour. It's considered the most prestigious competition after the four Grand Slams, and only the top 16 players in the world are invited. (This also happened to be the last time it was held at Madison Square Garden in New York City—what a shame!) I was thrilled to spend some time with Martina as a coach, especially after my prediction of her success had come true. The first thing I asked her mom was what she wanted me to do. In a quiet and somewhat frustrated voice, Mrs. Molitor told me that Martina had lost the zip, the hunger and the passion for playing the game, the fire in her belly to be the best in the world. Because of my reputation as a great motivator, I was her choice to rekindle it. I nodded in understanding, but inside I was jumping for joy! At the same time, I wondered how to handle this situation. Coaching an established world-class athlete, who is usually set in her ways, requires a great deal of sensitivity and intuition. So like a seasoned poker player, I presented a calm, composed exterior and agreed to take on the challenge.

I set up practices, including playing sets with strong hitting partners, and conditioning sessions. Martina's strokes, technique, foot and ball movement, and serve were as good as ever—among the best in the game. There was absolutely nothing for me to say. So I bided my time and waited for the right moment to have a sit-down, one-on-one talk. We went to South Philly, a family luncheon restaurant within walking distance of the Academy, and just talked. At some point I asked, "Martina, what's wrong? You just don't seem happy and full of excitement."

Her answer came with a sigh, and I had heard it before from other elite players whose parents are intimately involved in their lives as their coaches: "Nick, I'm tired of hearing my mother tell me to do this, do that and compete harder." Her tone of voice sounded as if she was feeling sorry for herself, but also begging for an answer. So I said, "Listen, young lady, if it were not for your mother giving up so much of her life, you would never be where you are. You are a star tennis player with a financial package that will allow you to live comfortably long after your career ends. Get out there and be the Martina that you used to be—because you can be that Martina again!" At the end of our week together, Martina and her mother thanked me for my time and flew to New York.

At the tournament, Martina breezed past the first round. On the Friday of the quarterfinals, I was on the golf course when a voice inside me said that I should fly to New York and watch her play. I hurried to the Sarasota-Bradenton Airport, booked a flight and arrived in time at the Garden to see Martina's match. Mrs. Molitor spotted me and asked me to sit in her box. Martina saw me there, and I believe she felt reassured by my presence. She was playing against Nathalie Touziat and took the first set 6-1, but tightened up and lost the second in a tie breaker 6-7. During the season, she had faltered in such situations, but now she shrugged off the setback, found her rhythm again and won the third set decisively, 6-2. Afterward she and I chatted for a while. I only offered a few comments, principally, that the quarterfinal match was over and in the history books. Now was the time to turn the page and concentrate on the semifinals. Martina did just that and took care of Anna Kournikova 7-6, 6-2. Once again I was in the unenviable position of having two of my players squaring off against each other. In the finals Martina beat Monica Seles in three sets, 6-7, 6-4, 6-4. To top it off, she also won the doubles championship (with Anna Kournikova)! Her faith in herself was restored.

In her awards speech, Martina said, "I want to thank the two people who helped me be the winner today: My mother—she has given me not only the foundation of my game, but love and support every single day—and Nick Bollettieri for his inspirational message to me and helping me to recognize who has always been at my side." By the way, Martina also gave me a check for $10,000.

Saying the right thing at the right time can be critical in an athlete's development and career. The game at the elite level is such a demanding roller coaster that it's easy to get off track, especially after an injury, with an emotional setback or from burnout. I credit Mrs. Molitor for recognizing that her daughter needed help to reenergize her, and I am glad I was able to do that. I applaud Martina for having the strength of character to reconnect with her inner core and draw on her champion desire to achieve success.

In her younger days, Martina was always pleasant and polite, but a little standoffish. Today, when she sees me at tournaments or exhibitions, she always gives me a big hug and a kiss. We reminisce and laugh, and she makes fun of me once comparing her to an elephant.

Nick has been a fabulous person throughout my life. Every time I see him, I think of some amazing moments in my career— whether it was him telling me to get it right on the court and what to do against opponents, or whether it was when we were all in Rome going out to dinner scared to death that something happened to Nick because no one could find him. He was found later lost walking in Rome at midnight still trying to find the restaurant. You see, that is Nick: He never stops.

My life would not be the same if I had never met Nick. I am happy to know him not as a coach but as my friend.

—Serena Williams

CHAPTER 22

The Williams Sisters

I met the Williams family when Venus and Serena Williams were nine and 10 years old. They were visiting the Academy with their dad, Richard Williams, after he had moved the family from Compton, California to West Palm Beach, Florida. He told me, "Nick, my two girls are going to be bigger stars than Michael Jordan." I didn't know what to make of him then. I soon came to learn that he knew exactly what he was doing. He had started training the girls at an early age and established one rule: When you left the tennis court, there would be no discussion concerning tennis. One day, Venus began a conversation about tennis while they were driving home. Richard stopped at a store and asked her to go inside to get something. As Venus returned, he told her she would have to walk home and drove off without her. When she made it back to their place and asked why he had done that, his response was, "The rule is that when we're not on the court, we don't talk about tennis. That's why you had to walk home." The rule may have been severely enforced, but it ensured that both Venus and Serena would develop interests away from the tennis court. As a result, when you meet them socially, they'll discuss a wide variety of topics, but never tennis!

My earliest impressions of Venus and Serena involved their incredible politeness. It was clear that Richard and their mother, Oracene, insisted on gentle civility, courtesy and good manners at all times, but tennis was another matter. On the court it was an entirely different story—100% focus on dominating and demolishing opponents with brutal power tennis and a ferocious will to win!

And that is still the case. Away from tennis, Serena is a sweet, soft-spoken young woman; but on the court, she is a lioness ready to devour her opponents (Venus is a tigress).

I often had to replace their hitting partners every 15 minutes because the girls tired them out, and I had two guys playing against each sister! I would stand behind the girls and watch in disbelief as they slammed each ball back into the court, even the out balls. They received so much attention around the Academy that my older male stars, Tommy Haas, Max Mirnyi and Xavier Malisse, started to grumble about the girls playing "queen of the court" and getting easy access to my primary teaching court. One time, when Tommy complained openly, the girls invited him and the others over to hit with them on center court. Venus and Serena showed no fear and held their own with the "big guys" very well.

It's really difficult to discuss the Williams sisters without understanding the family dynamic. Richard is a very confident and shrewd man who developed an early understanding of how best to use the system to benefit his daughters. Oracene has been the stabilizing force that kept the girls in balance as they dealt with the often unfriendly and alien tennis universe. I can still remember playing cards with Oracene and the girls. That's where I learned to appreciate the calm and the sense of normalcy that her presence created.

Richard's training was unconventional on the court; he believed that we all have two sets of eyes. When your eyes see the ball and the brain thinks about what to do, it's already too late. When your eyes see and the brain responds simultaneously, the impossible becomes possible. So another of his "crazy" rules was inculcated in the girls when they were six and seven years old. He had them chase down every ball and return it, even if the ball was out! That demand paid off and became a winning foundation for both Venus and Serena. They never wondered if they could reach a ball, any ball—they were convinced that they could! They simply reacted and their bodies responded. Their fast-twitch muscle fibers began to produce quick, powerful bursts of speed. That was the training regimen from early childhood and it served them well, as they became two of the quickest, most powerful women tennis players in the history of the sport.

Richard taught Venus and Serena to hit the tar out of the ball, no matter where it went. He taught them to warm up in a serious way before any match. When I say warm up, I mean the way a boxer warms up. By the time a boxer enters the ring his body is already wet with perspiration. And so it was with the girls from early on. Richard didn't allow the girls to play in junior tournaments until he was sure they were ready. The girls had received a great deal of publicity and sponsors, and USTA administrators were waiting for their debut matches. But Richard bided his time, sensing that he would know when the moment was right. As a result, he was roundly criticized for his parental leadership, and a number of people said that the Williams sisters were scared to come out and play the game.

Was he crazy? Perhaps. Crazy like me, I think.

Richard was also known for his tremendous sense of humor. When he brought his girls to the Academy for training, he told me the only reason he traveled the several hours from West Palm Beach to Bradenton was because he loved the free food he could get at the Academy dining room. Last year at Wimbledon when he saw me, he called out to me, "Nick, I have a very important question. My daughter Serena talks about you more than about me. I want to know who is her real father!" He cracked everybody up.

But make no mistake, his intense focus on the proper development of Venus and Serena's tennis game is always paramount. One time as the girls were training, I asked Richard what he wanted me to work on with them. His response was serious and direct. "Mr. Bollettieri," he said—he always called me Mr. Bollettieri—"if I thought I needed to tell you what to work on with my girls, I wouldn't be here! I trust you with my girls."

In retrospect, Richard and his family have created a new template for creating champions—he ignored conventional wisdom, broke with tradition and imagined a whole new way of training. Early on, many talking heads thought that the strategy used in the development of the Williams sisters was flawed and accused Richard of cynically pursuing a grand moneymaking scheme. Others called his approach the ranting of a wildly imaginative kook. I can relate to that, having been called crazy, egomaniacal, cavalier and arrogant myself for pursuing my vision of a tennis academy. I like to think of both of us as crazy idealists, crazy enough to believe in ourselves, crazy enough to follow our dreams.

In the case of the Williams sisters, the results have been nothing short of astonishing. Venus has won seven Grand Slam singles titles; Serena has won 17. They each have an Olympic gold medal in singles. Together, they have won 13 Grand Slam doubles and three Olympic golds. They each have two mixed doubles Grand Slams. They have been No. 1 in the world both individually and together as doubles players. Altogether, they have won more than 130 international tournaments.

Ever since Venus and Serena began to achieve their remarkable success, families across the world have tried to replicate Richard's strategy. But capturing lightning in a bottle is a rare feat, and he has accomplished it twice! I have been asked on many occasions what it was like being the coach of the Williams sisters. I am always very clear and remind people that I wasn't the coach—Richard was—but I was a proud member of the Williams team.

Venus is a remarkable human being and will be remembered not only for becoming one of the finest players ever to strike a tennis ball, but for her humility and compassion. At the Academy, Venus always gave 110% in practice and in matches, and never neglected to thank each of her practice partners. I could shout at Serena, but a quiet voice was the style that Venus responded to best. She and her sister always showed up 20 to 30 minutes early for their practice sessions.

Venus was the first African-American woman to win the U.S. Open and Wimbledon titles since Althea Gibson did it in 1958. When she reached No. 1 in the world for the first time in 2002—she did it two more times subsequently—she became the first black woman to do so in the Open Era (when amateurs and professionals compete together at Grand Slam tournaments). Her power and athleticism ushered in a new style of play in professional women's tennis.

A young Venus Williams.

Among active players, she is second only to her sister Serena in Grand Slam and total singles tournament wins. At the peak of her career, in elegant style reminiscent of Arthur Ashe and Billie Jean King, she became a trailblazer for human, civil and women's rights. It is rare for a top player to oppose the powers-that-be, especially when sponsorships are so lucrative and sponsors tend to be attuned to the sensibilities of the game's administrators. Yet, Venus decided to take on Wimbledon and the French Open and demand equal prize money for both men and women. At the time, the committees of both tournaments were completely opposed to changing the time-honored tradition of paying the men significantly more than the women. Venus met with officials from both tournaments, but her overtures were rejected.

The following year, shortly before the 2006 Wimbledon tournament, Venus published an op-ed piece in *The Times* accusing the tournament of treating women as second-class citizens. British Prime Minister Tony Blair and other members of Parliament publicly supported her arguments, but it took the joint effort of the Women's

Tennis Association (WTA) and UNESCO, with allies like tennis legend Billie Jean King and with Venus leading the campaign, to bring enough pressure to bear that Wimbledon agreed to award equal prize money in all rounds of the tournament starting with the 2007 competition. The French Open fell in line the following day. Credited with being the single most important factor in leading the turnaround, Venus said, "Somewhere in the world a little girl is dreaming of holding a giant trophy in her hands and being viewed as an equal to boys who have similar dreams."

Venus certainly has made her mark on the history books as one of the best female players in the game. Her outside interests have been wide and varied, including launching her own fashion line, acting as CEO of her interior design firm and, with her sister Serena, becoming part-owner of the Miami Dolphins football team. Like Arthur Ashe and Billie Jean King, she has changed the game of tennis in more ways than one. A hundred years from now, children may not know the name of Venus Williams; but women in tennis will continue to compete on an equal footing with the men. If anyone cares to look in the history books, they'll learn that they have Venus Williams to thank for the privilege. She and Billie Jean King have had an impact on sports that will affect young women for generations to come.

In recent years, Venus has had to deal with a series of medical challenges, most notably Sjögren's syndrome, an autoimmune disease which causes debilitating joint pain, swelling and numbness. At the onset, it caused her to pull out of the U.S. Open. But once diagnosed, she has done an excellent job of managing the disease through changes in her diet. And even at the height of her challenges, whenever her sister played, Venus could always be seen in the stands, rooting for her.

Serena was as hard a worker on the practice court as she was a ferocious competitor in tournaments. There were times at the beginning of her career when we were working for hours and hours until we got things right. But early on, Serena stood in her older sister's shadow and had a tendency to get down on herself.

2001 was a tremendous year for Serena, not because of the matches that she won, but rather for the losses that drove her to hate being in second place. She lost in the quarterfinals of the Australian Open, French Open and Wimbledon, and reached the finals of the U.S. Open, only to come in second to her sister Venus. One day, while training, Serena was seated under the canopy on my center practice court with her head in her hands. I walked over to her and asked, "Serena, what's wrong, dear?" Serena said, "Nick, I'm sick and tired of second place." Then she looked at me and added, "I'm going to start winning these tournaments." That singular decision started the ball rolling and Serena began her own march into the history books. The following year, she won the singles titles at the French Open, Wimbledon and

A young Serena Williams.

the U.S. Open, and a gold medal at the Olympic Games in Sydney, Australia on her way to a Golden Slam.

But it was not a straight upward trajectory, as she recently reminded me in an email. That fall, we were practicing and Serena was not having one of her better days. Being a perfectionist, she got so frustrated that she decided she was done, threw her racquet down and walked off the court. I went after her, grabbed her by the shoulders and said, "Serena, what the hell do you think you are doing? You get your ass right back on this court, and you don't leave until you get it right!" Apparently, no one had ever stood up to her and spoken to her in that way, not even her dad! She may have felt a bit embarrassed as other people looked on, but she got back on the court and did what I said. She did not quit and kept going. Shortly thereafter in 2003, she won the first of her five Australian Open championships, completing her first Golden Slam. Serena concluded her email, "More importantly, I never walked off a court again until I got it right. It was one of the most pivotal points in my career."

2001—Serena, what's on your mind?

Since then she has had her ups and downs. She went through a scary health experience—a blood clot in her lung, a pulmonary embolism after foot surgery that could have killed her. Another injury caused her to withdraw from the U.S. Open. She received 12 stitches in one foot and six in another when she was cut by glass at a restaurant in Munich, Germany. Each of these injuries had a profound and immediate impact on her ranking. But she hasn't walked away and has worked hard every time to regain her former dominant position.

Throughout her difficulties, Serena has been well guided by her longtime agent Jill Smoller, who is now senior vice president at William Morris Endeavor. Jill was a full-time student at IMG in the early

1980s. An excellent tennis player, she displayed great competitive spirit and played professionally after college, mostly in doubles. As one of the premier women's sports agents, she has worked with a number of high-profile athletes, including Florence Griffith Joyner, Pete Sampras and Kevin Garnett. She has always been a great supporter of the Academy and me, and I appreciate her dedication and commitment, especially to Serena's career.

Serena made an incredible comeback at the 2007 Australian Open as an unseeded player. No one gave her a chance, but she proved all the pundits wrong, beating Maria Sharapova in the final, 6-1, 6-2! Since then, she has completed another Golden Slam and, as of this writing, once again holds the No. 1 rank in the world. She was named the Associated Press 2013 Female Athlete of the Year. This is the third time she has been honored in this way, and she shows no signs of slowing down.

I am proud to have played a part in her accomplishments.

Serena and me in my
"Hall of Fame" room at IMG Academy.

I have the honor and privilege of knowing and working with Nick for many years. While Nick is best known as one of the most influential people in global tennis, this doesn't begin to describe this terrific man. Nick is renowned as a master motivator, a shrewd strategist and a gifted teacher. He possesses a unique wit and wisdom about tennis, business and life in general. He has spent the last six decades dedicating himself to working with children of all ages. Passionate about everything he does, Nick is charismatic, enthusiastic and has amazing spirit. In short, he is a "winner" we can all learn from.

—Mike Dolan
Chairman and Chief Executive Officer of IMG

I think Nick had passion to build tennis players and to make people do better and he has lived that. Nick has done well financially, but I don't think Nick measures wins and losses for himself financially; he measures wins and losses as his own personal state of mind and the happiness he derives from making other people better. In that category I would say he is extremely wealthy. To have the impact on people's lives that Nick has and to have the experience and success that Nick has had, I don't know what it is worth, but it is worth a lot.

—George Pyne, President, IMG Sports & Entertainment

Nick may not understand the business from a financial perspective or even from an operational perspective, but nobody understands better than him the dynamics, the culture, the kids, the development, the parents, the coaching and the staff; and how you put them all together. He is truly gifted in that.

—Sam Zussman, Senior Vice President, IMG

CHAPTER 23

Into the New Millennium

As we entered the new millennium and my seventh decade, I continued to be as busy as ever with tennis—no surprise there. I still traveled to tournaments, conducted clinics all over the world, and continued to do radio commentary for the BBC at Wimbledon and at the U.S. Open.

My broadcasting career started after some of my students, Maria Sharapova and the Williams sisters, won Wimbledon. Radio Wimbledon asked if I would join host Sue Barker on her early morning talk radio show for people on their way to work or heading over to the All England Lawn Tennis Club for the matches. The listeners enjoyed my sandpapery voice and my insightful and often accurate predictions. People even began betting on the winners I forecast.

Soon after, one of the U.S. Open's biggest sponsors, American Express, picked up on my show at Wimbledon and asked me to host a live, on-site radio show just before the last match each evening on either Ashe or Armstrong stadium court. I worked with two wonderful announcers, Tim Ryan and Al Trautwig. From time to time, the Jensen brothers and MaliVai Washington would also join the show. The success of the programs led to my appearances on Bloomberg News, Fox, CBS, the Charlie Rose show, The Tennis Authority podcast and the Ann Liguori show. Radio programs from across the world wanted to be part of the growing audience, including in New Zealand, Ireland, Germany and several South American countries, notably Brazil. It's always fun doing live commentary, but you have to be on your toes. There's no time for long-windedness—you have to know when to come in, have your say and get out!

At some point, the BBC approached me to start doing live radio commentating during the feature matches at Wimbledon. I was issued a press badge, which allowed me to attend all the players' interviews and sit in the press sections of every court, including center court. Then *The Independent* newspaper contacted me to do a daily column during the tournament. Before I knew it, it grew to two full pages a day and was a resounding success. I have since written for numerous worldwide sports magazines, including a regular Q & A for *Tennis Magazine* with feature writer Tom Perrotta.

Tennis legend Barry "The Bear" MacKay, loved by all, and me live at the U.S. Open.

The BBC was not finished with me. Apparently, the fans were intrigued by my voice, unusual wit, tidbits about the players and simple tips for recreational players; and so the station asked me to participate in some of its worldwide specials, including the Christmas show featuring Andy Murray. This turned out to be a popular program as well and led to assignments commentating for the BBC at the U.S. Open and the semis and finals of the Queen's Club and Sony tournaments. In addition, I now also do a night round-up with Peter Bodo at the U.S. Open.

It is always enjoyable to reconnect with other tennis broadcasters at tournaments. Many of them are former professional players (and in some cases, former students of mine) who are knowledgeable and passionate about the game, including Tracy Austin, Darren Cahill, Mary Carillo, Bud Collins, Dick Enberg, Brad Gilbert, Mary Joe Fernández, Cliff Drysdale, Martina Navratilova, Chris Evert Leif Shiras, Pam Shriver, and Patrick and John McEnroe. I think that perhaps John has gained respect for me and my tennis know-how by now. After all, he sent his son Sean to me for training at IMG. Mary Carillo is one of my biggest supporters and always entertained every-

Mary Carillo, Tim Ryan and me.

one with her imitation of my raspy voice, the result of years of yelling at students. Mary had originally trained with Harry Hopman at the Port Washington Tennis Academy. She played professionally for four years; her greatest success was winning the 1977 French Open championship in mixed doubles with her childhood friend John McEnroe. I first met her when she came to Florida and worked at a tennis club in Naples. She visited the Academy and I offered her a job, but things didn't work out. We didn't get to know each other really well until she started covering tennis as a broadcaster. Later on, her son Anthony came to IMG for two years in the basketball program.

Bud Collins visited the Academy and gave inspirational talks to the young players. He is, of course, most associated with Wimbledon, where he was much beloved as a television commentator and host of "Breakfast at Wimbledon" for more than 35 years, but he has also covered the U.S. Open. His signature bow tie and wild, colorful pants could scare a lion away. He is a walking tennis encyclopedia, a great promoter and historian of the game, and he was rightfully inducted into the Tennis Hall of Fame in 1994. He and his beautiful wife Anita are two very special people whom I will always cherish.

Mary Pierce and Bud Collins at IMG in the 90s.

Many years ago through my broadcasting and tennis career, I got to know Ken Solomon, who told me about a crazy idea he had—to bring tennis into every American home. Being partial to crazy ideas myself, we became the closest of friends; and as the founder and CEO of cable TV's Tennis Channel, Ted realized his dream. In November of 2013, I had the honor of introducing him at a special luncheon where he received an award from the New York Junior Tennis and Learning program for his contribution to inner-city tennis, an issue close to my heart. The event was attended by 400 officials from the USTA, the International Tennis Hall of Fame, the former mayor of New York City, David Dinkins, Jeanne Moutoussamy-Ashe and others.

Among them, I was pleased to meet up with Justin Gimelstob. I've known him for many years, first as a teenager when he spent time training at IMG Academy, and later as a college player at UCLA and then on the pro tour. When he retired from professional tennis in 2007, he stepped into a new career as a color commentator on the Tennis Channel. I took it upon myself to advise him about the dos and don'ts of broadcasting, and am delighted that his insight, wit and respect for his fellow players have elevated him to become one of the top announcers in the business.

Back when my broadcasting career hit its stride, my personal life once again had its ups and downs. In 2001, my girlfriend Leah and I parted amicably. For a while I was engaged to a young lady named Bobbie Lachiusa, who was a hostess at an Outback Steakhouse, but we broke up shortly before I met my sixth wife.

That event took place in Charleston, South Carolina when I was giving a tennis clinic for Fritz Nau, who owned a club there. One of the attendees was a very attractive young lady. I had Fritz check her out—she was the owner of an upscale antique shop in town—and he arranged a date for me. Her name was Elizabeth Flower and we had a good time together. After leaving Charleston I happened to bump into her in Boca Raton—I was at a tournament there, and I believe she was visiting her father—and I thought to myself, "Somehow, someway, I am going to end up with this girl." And of course, I did.

The evening before our wedding ceremony was to take place, I got a call from my close friend, Nate Landow. He said, "Guinea, you're making a big mistake. The lady you're about to marry has been married before. She didn't tell you that but if you go through with this, you'll be sorry." I said, "Nate, how can you call the night before my wedding with this kind of news? Besides, it's not like I haven't been married before!" and hung up on him. The next day, Elizabeth and I tied the knot in beautiful surroundings on the beach of The Colony. Judge Bob Farrance conducted the ceremony.

The marriage lasted about a year. I guess Nate was right. Elizabeth and I were from very different walks of life. She liked to mingle in artistic circles and took me to New York to museums, concerts and parties with her friends. While I enjoyed some of them, it was never my scene. I felt more at home on beaches and tennis courts with my shirt off, not at galas in tux and tie. It didn't help that Elizabeth and my kids never saw eye to eye. I was constantly caught in the middle of conflicts that developed between them. Elizabeth and I didn't part on the best of terms, but I've never made a habit of complaining about the women in my life, and I'm not about to start now. Let the record show that our combined marriages put us into double figures, and there was little chance that we would stay together.

After my divorce from Elizabeth, I dated another wonderful and beautiful lady named Kristy Allan Law. She was a waitress at Gio's restaurant in Bradenton. Notice all of the women in my life are beautiful! Like Leah, I didn't marry Kristy (although I proposed to her) and I sometimes wonder what life would have been like if I had married either of them. Kristy was a kind and generous soul, and we are still on the best of terms. I knew she was going to have a wonderful life, but it wasn't destined for her to have it with me.

At some point after my marriage to Elizabeth and my relationship with Kristy were over, I drove past Bobbie Lachiusa's house as she was tending to her garden. I stopped and we chatted for a while. She suggested that we give our relationship another try. Once again, one thing led to another, and we got married in Las Vegas soon after with one of my coaches, Greg Hill, in attendance. Bobbie was a beautiful woman, but it just wasn't meant to be, and our marriage lasted only a few months. We parted peacefully and my mind was at ease knowing she had the means to set up house for herself and her young son and was well taken care of financially.

In the course of 13 months, I had proposed to a girlfriend and been married twice. I think after Leah I was a bit at sea emotionally, looking for an anchor, and I didn't make very good choices. It worried two of my good friends, John Hendrickson and his wife

Marylou Whitney, who is better known as Miss Saratoga, the queen of horse racing. Her horse Birdstone won the 2004 Belmont Stakes, preventing Smarty Jones from winning the Triple Crown that year. John was one of my coaches in the adult program at IMG in the late 80s. I really got to know him and Marylou well when they had a winter home across from my house on Longboat Key. After my year of two unsuccessful relationships, they told me they were concerned I'd be loitering at the Outback Steakhouse looking for my next wife, so they made me sign a contract. It read, "I, Nicholas Bollettieri cannot marry anyone for one full year without express permission from John Hendrickson and Marylou Whitney," and we had it notarized.

In the meantime, they had bought a racehorse at auction and named it after me. Because he was too studdish, they had to remove his testicles, and many people suggested that they gelded the wrong "Nick Bollettieri!" Nick, the horse, won in his second start at Gulfstream Park and is now retired as a riding horse in Sarasota, Florida.

In January of 2004, a big change occurred at IMG when Mark McCormack's family sold the company—and with it, the Academy—to Ted Forstmann, the billionaire founder of a private equity firm, for $750 million. Forstmann, a wildly successful financier, had coined the famous term "barbarians at the gates" for the takeover of one company by another in the 1980s, when a lot of corporate buyouts were done with junk bonds, which he hated and called "wampum."

Ted was a great sports fan and a fierce competitor in golf and tennis. Winning was everything to him. He hosted the annual Huggy Bear pro-am tennis tournament that raised millions of dollars for charity. It took place on his private court in the Hamptons two days before the U.S. Open—no TV, reporters or sponsors present—and paired Wall Street bigwigs with elite professional players in doubles. There was gambling on the side with rumored six-figure wagers on a single point. Forstmann made sure to team with the best partners. The matches were intense, and any ball that landed close to the line was always in his favor.

I met IMG's new owner at the 2004 U.S. Open when Ted Forstmann invited me to join him for lunch. It was a bit daunting—he was all business and rarely smiled. But our common passion for tennis soon broke the ice. A few years later, he asked me to conduct a clinic at his Forstmann Little conference in Aspen, Colorado. Named after his private equity firm, it was an annual meeting of the minds with high-powered business, sports, media and political superstars exchanging ideas in a leisurely, beautiful setting. The mini-think tank took place over four days and was moderated by television host Charlie Rose, a good friend of Forstmann's. Monica Seles assisted me for the tennis clinic.

The night before I left, I met a good-looking gentleman with a beautiful woman on his arm. His name was Craig Kruse, and he recognized me because he loved tennis. He was a businessman from the Florida panhandle and planned to leave in the morning. When he heard I was going back, too, he invited me to join him on his private plane. During the flight home I told him about Camp Kaizen, a summer camp to help overweight girls shed extra pounds, and other projects of mine. When his pilot dropped me off at the Sarasota-Bradenton Airport, I thanked Craig for the ride and thought nothing more of it. Imagine my surprise when a substantial check from him arrived at my office at the Academy for Camp Kaizen. The next summer when he heard that we needed a bus, he provided the funds for it. He never asked for anything in return.

Sometime later, I received a call from Ted Forstmann. He was having difficulties with one of his teenage sons, Everest. He wouldn't listen to anything Ted was telling him. So he sent him to me for several months. Everest was a good athlete, but like Andre Agassi, he wasn't on time very often for practices. I worked with him for a week and gave him the "Nick treatment," listening to him, talking with him, encouraging him and offering occasional advice. After he returned home, I received a call from Ted. He said, "Nick, I owe you. You did for him what I couldn't do." I thanked him and said, "That's my job."

The IMG sale meant significant changes at the Academy. Over the ensuing years, Forstmann strategically brought in people from outside the tennis industry with related experience in other fields. In 2006, George Pyne was installed as president of IMG Sports & Entertainment, the division under which the Academy stood, following his 11-year tenure as NASCAR's chief operating officer, during which that organization experienced phenomenal growth. In 2009, Sam Zussman, vice president of business operations for the division, was appointed managing director of IMG.

For me it ultimately meant taking more of a backseat. I still remember the lunch meeting when George Pyne told me that he had a sensitive issue to discuss. He said, "Nick, everyone knows your name throughout the world. What we want to do is bring that same name recognition to IMG and no longer pursue individual brands. What would you think if we retained the Bollettieri name just at the program level?" It took me less than a second to say, "Do it."

I understood that it was strictly a business decision, and a good one. My name meant tennis, and IMG, which already had other sports programs at the Academy, wanted to expand and brand itself worldwide. I continued to build the tennis program with key IMG associates, including agents Gavin Forbes, Max Eisenbud, Olivier van Lindonk, Fernando Soler, Tony Godsick, Ben Crandell, Marijn Bal and Carlos Fleming, and worked with Athletics Director Greg Phillips, Director of Tennis Rohan Goetzke, and Vice President and Chief Financial Officer Chip McCarthy.

In the meantime, there were other developments—but not all of them were good news. It came as a shock to find out that Raúl Ordóñez, a longtime member of my staff, was diagnosed with amyotrophic lateral sclerosis (ALS), better known as Lou Gehrig's disease. I first met him while giving a clinic in the country of Colombia. Before we left, someone came to me and said that I had to see this kid, explaining that he would stay at the club from sunup to sundown hitting with anyone who needed a hitting partner. When I spoke to Raúl and looked into his dancing eyes, I could see the excitement as well as the warmth and compassion he possessed. After seeing him play against bigger, stronger opponents, I knew that I had to bring him back to America.

Over time, he became the regular hitting partner for my best players, including Andre Agassi, Monica Seles and Jim Courier. He was a brilliant player and an ideal practice partner because he was capable of beating any of them in practice matches.

During the summer months I used to visit the Carlson, Nelson and Gage families in Minnesota. Raúl and I would spend all day and night on Papa Carlson's hard court teaching their family members and friends. Raúl had a special quality. Throughout my marriages—and my girlfriends in between—all the ladies would say that if they had a daughter, they hoped they would find a "Raúl."

For an athlete who was so fit and active, ALS was devastating. As a neurodegenerative disease, it affects nerve cells in the brain. Before long, Raúl was paralyzed from the neck down and the degeneration continued until he could only move his eyes. Ken Merritt visited

Raúl while conducting a clinic in Cali, Colombia. Raúl's wife had just given birth to their daughter, and Ken was concerned that she would never have the opportunity to hear her father's voice. When Ken returned, he told me that Raúl needed money to purchase a machine that would help him speak. This remarkable invention is called an eyegaze device. As the user sits in front of a monitor, it tracks what he is looking at. If he wants to speak, he can look at the menu option for the alphabet and blink on individual letters to form words—the equivalent of clicking a computer mouse—and the machine converts them into "speech."

I contacted Andre Agassi and Jim Courier, and both immediately stepped forward and helped raise the $25,000 needed to buy the machine. After learning to use it, Raúl can now surf the Internet, control the air conditioner, turn on the television and change the channels. There is a video on YouTube showing him using it. Raúl was more than a coach. He had the rare gift of strength and tenderness in equal measure. He will always have a special place in my heart.

For me, the latter part of the decade brought several tributes that involved some of my former students. In 2008, I received an honorary doctorate from the New York College of Health Professionals. I am grateful to Lisa Pamintuan, one of my first students at The Colony, who became president of the college, for giving me that honor. It was fun to become "Professor Nick" in ceremonial cap and gown and "lecture" the assembled graduates on winning, character and following their dreams.

A year later I was inducted into the Alabama Tennis Foundation Hall of Fame. Once again, influential friends lobbied on my behalf, in this case the Falkenburgs, Frank Sr. and his wife Karle. Their son, Frank Jr., had attended NBTA in the early 80s. After college he became an attorney and was my manager for some time. The Falkenburgs have helped me and my family in many ways, including having my daughter Alex stay at their home when she attended the

University of Alabama to earn her master's degree. I can't thank them enough for their care and generosity.

In 2008, it was also time to celebrate the 30th anniversary of my original junior tennis academy. It was a memorable event at the Sarasota Ritz-Carlton. More than 360 people attended, many of them players, coaches and staff who had been with me in the early days. Most of the No. 1 players I had coached came, too. Andre Agassi and Jim Courier, who couldn't make it, sent video tributes, which touched my heart.

As a milestone, it was a good time to take stock. From 12 acres, a few tennis courts, dorms and administrative buildings, the Academy had grown into a comprehensive sports institution. It now covered 350 acres, offered five sports and housed 700 students, and it continued to invest in state-of-the-arts facilities and recruit world-class coaches. All academics were now provided on campus as well.

Today, IMG offers eight sports, including soccer, football, basketball, baseball, golf, lacrosse, track & field and cross country. It occupies 450 acres and features premier facilities like IMG Academy Stadium, a five-story residence hall, the Gatorade Sports Science Institute and the Prince Innovation Center. The campus hosts more than 100 events annually, including the Eddie Herr International Tennis Championships, which bring over 2,000 junior players from all over the world.

Tens of thousands of adult, professional and youth athletes have come through the doors of the Academy over the past few decades. While not everyone becomes a star athlete—in fact, only a few handfuls achieve that elite level—they all will tell you how their time at the Academy changed them and shaped their lives for the better.

While IMG's influence on athletics is worldwide, it also has had a huge impact on its immediate surroundings. In Bradenton, the Academy benefits the economy and social fabric substantially—from the 750 plus people it employs to the construction of housing for athletes and their families to the hotel rooms, restaurants and shopping venues frequented by visitors. IMG has put the city on the international map. I am pleased to have gotten the ball rolling, so to speak, and to continue to help it grow; and I was proud to be recognized by having the section of 43rd Street West that leads into the Academy named "Bollettieri Boulevard" in 2006, the only street in Manatee County named after a living person.

I recalled and forecast many of these developments when I spoke at the anniversary and listened to the kind words others said about me. They moved me deeply and reconfirmed in me a determination to go on with my work with the current crop of talented juniors—players like Sabine Lisicki, Heather Watson and Kei Nishikori.

County Commissioner Ron Getman, me
and Judge Bob Farrance at the
dedication of Bollettieri Boulevard.

Working with Nick is always different, but the one thing that makes him amazing is his energy. He always make me feel good walking off the practice court.

—Kei Nishikori

What makes Nick so special is that he sees the details that make a big difference. I'm getting closer to my goal. I lost in the final of Wimbledon this year, but next year, who knows?

—Sabine Lisicki

I love Nick! Everything that he tells me to do is right on. I can be hitting the ball okay and after two minutes with him, I'm hitting great! Equally as important, Nick has always been quite close to my family.

—Heather Watson

CHAPTER 24

Three to Watch: Nishikori, Lisicki, Watson

I have seen thousands of tennis players over the past 60 years and can identify only three who have had the gift of magic hands. I've already mentioned two—Xavier Malisse and Marcelo Rios. The third is Kei Nishikori.

*Dante Bottini, me, Kei and Olivier van Lindonk
at the indoor tennis center at IMG.*

I met and started to work with Kei because in the 1980s Arthur Ashe and I traveled to Japan to conduct a clinic for 500 youngsters. While there we toured many of the local tennis facilities. On the day of the clinic the skies opened with torrential rains, forcing us to move indoors. Arthur was panicked—how to deal with so many children at close quarters—but this wasn't a new challenge for me. We found a huge gymnasium and held two clinics, each for one hour with 250 participants. We had two lines running at the same time and each kid got to hit two balls. They all thanked us profusely.

I learned a few things that day about Japanese children. They were very polite, quiet and patient; but they watched our every movement and took in every word I spoke. They were so eager to learn, you could see their excitement as their eyes darted from me to Arthur to the interpreter and back again.

During our visit I was introduced to a kindly gentleman, Mr. Morita, whose family was the largest shareholder in the Sony Corporation. He loved tennis and wanted very much for Japan to develop a steady stream of world-class players. His passion for the sport and confidence in me led to a fruitful relationship that continues to this day. At the time, Japan's most successful male player, Shuzo Matsuoka, was in a class by himself. His highest ranking ever was No. 46 in the world, but both Mr. Morita and I believed that with focus, determination, and funding, more could be achieved.

So Mr. Morita dispatched Sato Nakajima to work at IMG Academy and act as a liaison for Japanese players. He also began to send youngsters there, all sponsored by Sony. One of those players was 14-year-old Kei Nishikori. Kei, who didn't speak one word of English at the time and had never eaten American food, housed in an apartment with seven other boys; not surprisingly, he was scared and took some time to feel comfortable. Not on the tennis court, though. It didn't take me very long to realize that he had talent. He was extremely quick and had those magic hands of a gifted shot maker. Like Agassi and Rios, he possessed innate skills that can't be taught, but need only to be channeled.

Mr. Morita continued to support him. Today, Kei is not only the highest ranked player from Japan on the ATP tour—he was No. 11

in the world in 2013—but one of the most celebrated sports stars in Japanese history.

His able team includes IMG agent Olivier van Lindonk, who sees to his schedule and business affairs, and his personal coach, Dante Bottini, who is quiet and unassuming but understands Kei. They relate well to each other. I continue to participate in the role of team advisor.

I was especially pleased to see Michael Chang coming to town to join Kei's coaching team. The last time Michael was at the Academy was in 1985 when he was 13 years old and training with his coach. Michael was a champion because of his movement, his recovery and his ability to avoid hitting defensive shots, not to mention an indomitable will. On the way to the 1989 French Open singles title, he had an epic match against Ivan Lendl, overcoming leg cramps, fatigue and dehydration in a remarkable five-set victory.

I watched Michael working with Kei and quickly identified what his plans were. He realized that magic hands were not enough but would make a big difference in combination with the right leg work. He showed Kei exactly how to load from the ground up which, in turn, got his racquet below the ball. This allowed Kei to apply more height, depth and spin, especially when he was out of position and behind the baseline. In the past, Kei's shots would land on the service line and get him in trouble. I applauded Kei's decision to add Michael Chang to his coaching team, alongside his regular coach.

Can Kei really compete with the best in the world? I know he can! But, he must learn to truly believe in himself—exactly what Michael Chang yelled to him in his first-round, five-set match at the 2014 Australian Open—and to know with every fiber of his being that he deserves to be on the court with the big boys. And he must deliver that as a potent message when he competes against top 10 players. I believe he will do it! Mr. Morita and I will continue to cheer for Kei.

Sabine Lisicki can best be described as a wild horse hoping to be tamed. This is a very delicate process because you don't want to hobble her tenacity, daring and her confidence in her shot making.

Sabine first visited the Academy from Germany when she was 10 years old. We had invited her dad, Dr. Richard Lisicki, who was getting his doctorate in sports science, to study our training methods. His thesis focused on power and precision in tennis, and he wanted his time spent at the Academy to lend credence to his doctoral presentation. Sabine stayed for a week trying to perfect the skills that her dad had taught her.

Dr. Richard Lisicki, Sabine and me at the indoor tennis center.

Four years later, Sabine moved into the Academy full time and signed a management contract with IMG. Tommy Haas and Mary Pierce, Sabine's idol, were training there then. One day Richard asked Mary's father, Jim, if she would be kind enough to hit with Sabine for a few minutes. He agreed and Sabine and Mary rallied for a while. Then Mary began to hit the ball harder and Sabine responded in kind. Before long, they were both smashing the ball back and forth in extended exchanges. They hit for more than half an hour. Mary was impressed with the power and control of this 14-year-old phenom. More importantly, Sabine got her first taste of being on the same court with a world-class player. She remembers the experience with pride and gratitude for Mary's largesse.

I worked with her dad to help Sabine achieve a better understanding of the game. Her dad did a fine job in her early development and continues to be a central character in her coaching. Chip Brooks, one of IMG's elite coaches, along with periodic tips from me, have been instrumental in Sabine's consistent improvement.

But there still is the issue of the team triangle—the player, parent and coach relationship. Throughout my career I know of only a few families who have managed to negotiate this triangle successfully: the Changs, the Everts, the Murrays and the Connors. I believe that Sabine and her dad need to identify a compatible personal coach to join the team. It will be difficult for her and her dad to accomplish reaching her full potential by themselves.

Since turning pro as a 17-year-old in 2006, Sabine has twice reached the finals at Wimbledon, once in doubles in 2011 and in singles in 2013, when she lost to Marion Bartoli. She has one of the most powerful serves on the tour and can dominate with her aggressive forehand. It will be interesting to follow Sabine's career in the coming years. She is now in superior physical condition, but still learning how to master the ups and downs that inevitably occur in tennis, both on and off the court. She has to accept that she cannot hit winners all the time and keep focusing on a winning strategy that involves her all-around game.

I met Heather Watson when she had just turned 11 and was already showing exceptional promise in dance, ballet, swimming and tennis. When her parents asked if she would like to focus on one of her skills, she chose tennis, and the search for the right training environment began. Heather and her family checked out tennis academies all over Europe, but her mom Michelle decided that their search would be incomplete without visiting the United States. During a family vacation in America, they looked at several academies, and IMG was their final stop. After a week, Heather excitedly decided that this was the place where she wanted to hone her skills. The very next year, Heather became a full-time student.

As a junior, Heather won the British under-14 championship in 2006. The following year she won the British under-16 championship and reached the semifinals of the British under-18 championship. In 2008 she won the singles gold medal at the 2008 Commonwealth Youth Games in India. That year, her mother left her job to travel full-time with Heather around the world.

Me and Heather Watson.

At the age of 15, Heather had the opportunity to practice against Sabine Lisicki, who had already begun her professional career. She beat Sabine during that practice session and has a 2-and-1 record against her since turning pro herself in 2010.

While the beginning of her professional career was quite impressive—she rose to a career-high No. 40 in the world and No. 2 in Britain, by January 2013 it became clear that something wasn't quite right. Heather was lethargic and constantly fatigued. It got to the point where she became depressed and wanted to quit playing. Her parents decided to have a doctor examine here, and two months later she was diagnosed with mononucleosis. Once the depression and fatigue had a name, her fighting spirit returned. Heather resumed training hard again and competing on the tour. Don't count her out. She is an immensely talented young woman with a kind and gentle spirit off the court. I'm proud to have been able to spend time with her.

Cindi and Giovanni behind Giacomo.

CHAPTER 25

Cindi
and the Boys

I used to give clinics (and still do) in Massachusetts at the Manchester Athletic Club (also known as MAC). One of the prominent members, Elizabeth Moore, was a tennis fanatic. She and her husband Stuart have five children, and some of my coaches and I would occasionally stay at their spacious, oceanfront guesthouse. Living there was Cindi Eaton, who worked as a nanny and house manager for the Moore family. Originally from the Northeast Kingdom of Vermont (the corner closest to New Hampshire and Canada), she had gotten her master's degree in social work from the University of Kentucky, and taken a six-month job with the Moores while getting her license to practice medical social work in Massachusetts. She ended up staying four and a half years. The family loved her and she loved them.

On one of my trips, I was with Scott Treibly, an IMG coach who is now a college advisor at IMG Academy. He and I spent a good bit of time talking to Cindi. She knew nothing about tennis, but she was fun, articulate and beautiful—and I was smitten. Before I returned to Florida, I asked for her phone number and she gave it to me. But when I called, over and over, I didn't get a response. Little did I know that she had left on a weekend skiing trip with a friend to Vermont where there was no cell phone service. I was discouraged, but persistent. I called Francisco Montoya, one of the coaches I had placed at MAC from IMG. I told him to contact Cindi, put in a good word for me and get her to answer or he'd be out of a job. When Cindi returned and we finally connected, we'd talk for four or five hours every evening. I invited her to visit with me in Florida for New Year's Eve, but she graciously declined. I finally convinced her to come by suggesting her childhood friend Caroline Lague accompany her. On the flight down, Caroline expressed some concern about our 33-year age difference. Cindi told her, "Just wait until you meet him."

When they arrived, I announced that I was having a quiet little barbeque with a few of my friends to welcome the two of them to Florida. In my world, "few" usually means a catered dinner for about 70 people, and this night was no exception. After everyone left, the three of us stayed up talking well into the night. I got up at my usual 4:20 a.m., went for a quick workout at the Academy gym and met my first student on court at 5. I worked all day at the Academy and came home to get ready for the big New Year's Eve dinner and party that evening. Once again, we all stayed up into the wee hours and

Cindi and me. That's one lucky guy!

then I left to go to work early the next morning. After three days of the same schedule, Cindi and Caroline went home to New England exhausted. On the flight back, Caroline said, "You've got to find someone older than Nick because you'll never be able to keep up with him."

If Cindi wasn't quite sure yet about me, I certainly had made up my mind. I knew what I wanted and asked her to marry me—five times. On each occasion I gave her a necklace or bracelet. By the time she had turned me down four times, I was beginning to think that she just wanted to grow her jewelry collection, but I somehow had a hunch that it was really about children. Cindi was 39, great with kids, and had always wanted a family of her own. Over dinner one night—we did get together from time to time in person between our marathon phone conversations—I told her I would love to be a dad again and to have more children, and that broke the ice.

There was another hurdle, though. She told me that she was an old-fashioned girl, and I'd have to talk to her parents, Peter and Nancy, before we could make any decisions about marriage. I agreed, but I was scared sh*tless. I had never asked for permission in any of my previous seven marriages (maybe I should have). I knew that Cindi's dad was a retired captain for the U.S. Border Patrol and it didn't escape me that he was likely to be armed and dangerous (when he wanted to be). But I took a plane to Boston, rented a car and drove to an restaurant in New Hampshire (a halfway point for the big "meeting"). In the parking lot as I got out of my car, I saw a tall, distinguished-looking man who resembled Andy Griffith and was seven years my junior, walking in my direction pointing at me. He was still quite a distance away and I could only hope that he was pointing a finger and not a gun. He came up to me and said, "Are you the old man that's trying to steal my daughter away?" I said, "No, sir, I don't want to steal her, I just want to borrow her!" He asked, "Are you going to take good care of her?" I said, "Yes, sir, I will." My future father-in-law gave me one of his famous bear hugs and said, "Welcome to the family!" And that was that. I was accepted as a member of a large, loving family from Vermont!

Cindi and her folks put our wedding together in a mere three weeks. Because her favorite number is 2 and mine is 4, we decided to get married on 4-22-2004 (Earth Day) at 4:22 in the afternoon.

The ceremony was conducted by Rev. John Hughes at the First Parish Church in the beautiful village of Manchester-by-the-Sea, Massachusetts with 35 family members and some of our dearest friends in attendance, including Lou and Liz Donato, Chris and Bonnie Covington, and Tom Seavey. The Moores hosted a wonderful reception for us at the very same guesthouse where I had met Cindi four years earlier.

Like the Donatos, the Covingtons entrusted one of their sons to work with me at the Academy. I speak with Chris regularly and value his and Bonnie's friendship and opinion greatly. I knew the Covingtons would "approve" of Cindi, and I was right. However, there was another couple who were not so thrilled at the prospect of my marriage.

Remember my promise of no marriage for one full year without express permission from John Hendrickson and Marylou Whitney? I had to call them in Saratoga, NY and say, "Johnny, I've got to break the contract." They weren't happy and didn't really want to meet Cindi at first, unsure of how long this marriage would last, but they finally agreed, and we went out to dinner in Florida. I could tell as the evening progressed that Cindi had won them both over just by being herself. At some point, when I asked Johnny what he thought of her, he said, "She is a lot different than your other wives." I shouldn't have asked how, because of course, Johnny never holds back with me. He replied, smiling mischievously, "The others just wanted a great lifestyle now. Cindi is smarter. She wants to make sure she has money to fund her lifestyle when you're dead." He didn't think Cindi heard him, but she did and kicked him under the table hard enough that he yelped. They have loved her ever since.

I must say that Cindi has been a tremendous stabilizing force in my life—overseeing every aspect of our personal and my professional life, including my globetrotting schedule. This was no easy task—the fabric of my life is complicated to say the least (remember, seven ex-wives and five adult children!). She also had to learn the ins and outs of the Academy and the world of tennis. I will never forget the time Cindi said, "I saw on your schedule that you have a really important client coming to town who has booked you exclusively for private lessons for two consecutive weeks! Who is this Roland Garros?" I almost burst out laughing, but I composed myself and explained that Roland Garros was the official name of the French Open.

But make no mistake, Cindi is one of the wisest people I've ever met. Before I had her, I was like a roller coaster without any brakes—it was always a thrilling ride, but a lot of people, including myself, got hurt along the way. In the early years of our marriage, she compared herself to the chief of a fire brigade, made up of my coaches and staff, who were doing their best to put out fires I had started while I was off tossing newly lit matches. She is organized where I am not, calm when I am explosive, sensible when I am idealistic, realistic when I am a dreamer. We not only love each other, but we make a great team.

Cindi was instrumental in making my passion to fight childhood obesity a reality. Fitness has always been an important part of my life. During my entire career I have been surrounded by young people who are motivated, athletic and in optimum physical shape. Whenever I travel in the United States, I am always saddened by how many chubby kids I see at the airports and restaurants. I often feel I am on a different planet than the one I live on at the Academy. After hearing me gripe about the problem for the umpteenth time, my good friend and golfing buddy, Richie Harding, told me if I didn't like what I saw, I should do something about it…so I did and started a summer camp for overweight young girls.

As with most of my projects, I dreamed it up and then handed it over to someone else—in this case, Cindi. We liked the name "Kaizen" because it means "continuous improvement" in Japanese. That's pretty much been my life mantra, and hers as well. With the dedication and hard work of many, including Christine Wolfert, Allen Young and Cindi's sister Tami, and financial support from us and good friends like Jonnie and Celeste Williams, Mark and Jennifer Styslinger, Mark Fisher, Craig Kruse, as well as the Carlson Foundation, to name just a few, Camp Kaizen opened its doors in 2005. As with the Academy, the idea was to totally immerse the campers in a new environment and introduce them to a new lifestyle. For five weeks each summer, overweight young girls from all over the U.S. and beyond came to the Burke Mountain Academy campus in northern Vermont. Many had never experienced rural living before. There was lots of fresh air and time spent outdoors with no access to electronics. Instead, they learned to dance, sing and play games, and took nutrition, exercise and cooking classes. They also learned proper table manners and how to meet and greet people with confidence. Several times a week, we'd bus them to Breezy Hill Farm, our home in Craftsbury, where they could swim, bike, hike and learn about organic gardening, archery and arts and crafts.

By the end of camp, the girls had not only shed considerable weight, they had gained a whole new perspective on life. They arrived with a lack of hope and left with excitement for what they could accomplish in life. When the parents arrived to pick them up at the end of the five weeks, they were often moved to tears when they met their beautiful, confident, and genuinely happy daughters. I was as proud of each of those young ladies and their tremendous efforts as I was of any of my champion players.

The pond at Breezy Hill Farm, where we set up the tents for the campers.

And the positive changes stayed with them. Many of the campers went on to join academic and athletic teams, drama clubs, band and chorus, and volunteer organizations—activities they never had the confidence to try before. They continue to keep in touch with each other, their counselors and our staff. I give all the credit for the camp's success to Cindi and her team.

Unfortunately, running a camp where most participants received full scholarships (much as at the Academy when I ran it) is extremely expensive. As the largest financial donors, Cindi and I considered it a privilege and responsibility to live modestly in order to provide financial aid, and we kept Camp Kaizen running as long as we could. But even with the generous help of friends, the time came when, with heavy hearts, we had to close the doors in 2012. We continue to stay in touch with campers and love to hear all of their amazing success stories.

Even with all the mad number of activities going on in our world, Cindi and I never lost our desire to have a family together, and after five failed IVF procedures, two surgeries, and two heartbreaking miscarriages, we decided to pursue adoption. One night at dinner, we each took a piece of paper and secretly wrote down the name of the continent from which we wanted to adopt a child. When we exchanged the papers and read them, we found that we had both written "Africa."

Because of 9-11, adopting internationally has become an incredibly complex, time-consuming process. I could write another book just on what we went through. Again, had it not been for Cindi's persistence, hard work, and ability to organize the right support team, it never would have happened. The first stumbling block came when we went to have our fingerprints taken. After decades of holding a tennis racquet, I had worn away my fingerprints. I'm not kidding. Neither the normal inking procedure in Bradenton, nor the two times with special laser equipment in Tampa raised the slightest imprint. We were told we had to find a judge willing to testify that I was an upstanding citizen. Our good friend, Judge Bob Farrance, did the honors.

Then we needed to obtain the official divorce decree for every one of my prior seven marriages. Remember when Nancy, my second wife, went to Mexico by herself when we split up? I had no document verifying the divorce. It took Cindi and her squadron of sleuths several months to track down Nancy and find out where and when she had gone south of the border. It turned out it was in the city of Juarez, just across the border from El Paso, Texas. Juarez was now one of the most dangerous places in the world—there were international news accounts of daily killings, beheadings of judges and gang wars.

Who could we send? Who would go? Fortunately, I knew an attorney in Mexico City whose children had attended the Academy and he promised to take care of it. When his people finally located the document in a file at the Juarez courthouse, it turned out to be a wrinkled old piece of paper that had never been signed. All my marriages and children since Nancy were illegitimate! Fortunately, the local judge, after hearing the story, decided to put his signature on it right then and there. Phew, another hurdle cleared!

Cindi and I chose Wide Horizons for Children in Waltham, Massachusetts as our adoption agency, which was affiliated with Ethiopia. The process took almost two years from start to finish. When we finally got the long-awaited phone call that we had received our referral, Cindi was in Vermont at Camp Kaizen and I was at the Academy in Florida. We each sat by the computer, she surrounded by family, friends and staff, I by coaches, students and staff. Slowly, the face of a beautiful four-year-old boy appeared— our son, Giovanni—and there were tears of joy, loud cheers, hugs and offers of congratulations all around. But we still had to wait several months for an appointment with the U.S. Embassy in Ethiopia.

In the meantime, Cindi put together a book of photos of us and our world, which we sent to the orphanage so our son could get to know us ahead of time. In mid-November 2009 we received a call giving us all of eight days' notice before we had to be in Ethiopia to pick him up.

After an exhausting 26-hour flight with a layover in Dubai, we finally reached Addis Ababa, the capital of Ethiopia. The man from the agency who met us at the airport asked if we wanted to go to the hotel first to freshen up or head directly to the orphanage. What a question! Of course, we wanted to see our son right away. But when we arrived at the orphanage, it was nap time. As each child woke up her or she would come out into the concrete courtyard to play. Finally, Giovanni emerged, rubbing his eyes from sleep. He looked up, saw Cindi, shouted, "Mommy," ran to her and threw his little arms around her. He kept kissing her face and repeating the word "Mommy" over and over like he couldn't believe she was real. Then he looked at me—said, "Daddy"—and gave me a big hug. We bonded instantly and I was a dad once again!

Like most of the orphans there, Giovanni knew only three words of English. Within four months in the States, he was completely fluent. As soon as he could say his nightly prayers in English, he started praying for a little brother. We started the whole process again.

With Giacomo, who is three years younger than his brother, the process was equally cumbersome. The authorities once again wanted my fingerprints (I guess they thought they had magically "grown back"). By then, the adoption laws in Ethiopia had changed, so this time we were required to fly there twice, once to "pass court" in front of an Ethiopian judge (a meeting that lasted less than five minutes), and then two months later for our U.S. Embassy visit. At that point we could then bring Giacomo home. Again we were given just a few days'

notice of when we had to be there! But we overcame every bump in the road and almost two years to the day of when we picked up Giovanni, we brought home my third son and seventh child—little Giacomo!

Both of our boys are smart (like Cindi), athletic (like me) and bring a whole lot of fun to our family. If mothering were a professional sport, Cindi would be a world champion. She is truly a wonderful mom who makes parenting look easy (a sign of a true expert). I give her all the credit for creating a home where our boys

Giovanni and Giacomo

are loved beyond measure and a strong foundation that will serve them well their entire lives.

When it came time to choose godparents for the boys, Cindi asked her sister Tami to be their godmother. Tami had trekked with us to Africa both times to pick up the boys. Together with her husband she has raised seven great kids, and I know she would love our boys as much as we do and would give her life for them. Cindi told me I needed to pick the person I wanted to be their godfather.

I thought it would be an easy task, but there are so many great people I know who would love these boys as their own. I have been incredibly blessed with having so many wonderful people in my life. I could have chosen an army of godfathers for the boys if only Cindi had let me. When I finally narrowed my list down, I gave Cindi six names. She asked, "Are these your finalists?" and I said, "Nope, I want them all."

All of the six godfathers—John Hendrickson, Steve Shulla, Giacomo Staiano, Richie Harding, Mark Fisher and yes, I included Wendy Nelson—share similar qualities. They are great athletes and all are hardworking, kind, loving, philanthropic and blind to differences like race, wealth, gender orientation or religion—traits I would wish both Giovanni and Giacomo to possess.

When we decided to adopt and I told John Hendrickson, he asked, "Why?" and pointed out in his inimitable style that as soon as the kids would be coming out of diapers, I would be going into them. He now takes his godfather responsibility very seriously. This past Christmas, he sent the boys a full drum set, an electric guitar with amplifier, a keyboard and a Karaoke machine. I'm still waiting for the earplugs he promised to send. The boys call him Uncle John Jib Jab because he is always creating and emailing them funny cartoons that usually have me wearing some type of tutu or tiara.

I have already mentioned Giacomo Staiano, Mark Fisher and Wendy Nelson and their marvelous qualities.

I met Steve Shulla at The Colony when he was a Florida junior tennis champion, and he has been a huge part of my life for close to 40 years. I have never met a man with more integrity and honor. Steve is the one I call in the middle of the night to run something, anything, by. He stays calm when I go ballistic and is one of the few people, other than Cindi, brave enough to deliver unwanted news to me. Steve knows my life and the world of the Academy better than anyone else, including me. Yes, tennis drew us together at first, but Steve, his wife Becky and their three children have become family!

Richie Harding is a hardworking, self-made man with a heart of gold. I got to know him and his lovely wife Cindy when they sent their daughter Allie to the Academy as a teenager during her school vacations and summer breaks. I helped her get into Villanova and her entire tennis team would visit and train at IMG. The Hardings support just about every project I have been involved in. Richie would give anyone the shirt off his back (in fact, I have a whole closet of beautiful Robert Graham shirts from him, some of them literally off his back). I love hanging out with Richie and his family, and in many ways, he fills the void in my heart created when my little brother died.

Actually, I enjoy spending a lot of time with all of the godfathers and completely trust them with my own well-being and that of my family. I hope I'm around a long time to see Giovanni and Giacomo grow up into the great men I know they will become. But, if for some reason I am not, I feel reassured knowing there are so many people who will be there in my place to care for them.

I couldn't discuss my boys without mentioning my dear friend, Hassan Chaouqi, one of three brothers from Morocco (the other two are Kareem and Mohammed). They have been on court with me for almost 20 years and an important part of the Academy. I have the utmost respect for their loyalty, work ethic and devotion. Hassan has been my right-hand man for so long, he could write his own book on my life. He loves our boys and is almost a daily presence in their lives. He is incredibly patient and able to teach them all the things that I can't—like the secret to working remotes and tire pumps, putting up and taking down Christmas trees, fixing and moving furniture, swimming like fish, and dancing like a true northern African. If my boys have half the honorable character and kind spirit that Hassan has, I will consider myself a very lucky father.

Cindi and me vacationing on Capri.

Another great blessing in my life because of my relationship with Cindi is our farm in Vermont. Besides the isle of Capri, Breezy Hill Farm is the only other place in the world where I feel at home away from the tennis court. My friends thought I had "lost it," unable to believe that I could leave my action-filled life even for a week and survive in a place that doesn't get cell phone reception. True, it takes me a day or two of going through withdrawal not being able to text and get instantly in touch with others throughout the world. But then I slow down a little and start to relax. I find myself outside a lot picking blueberries, riding our ATV Mule, harvesting corn (one time a whole month before it was ready!), stacking freshly cut logs in our woodshed and kayaking with Cindi and the boys on Little Hosmer Pond, where we are often all alone, except for a loon or two. In the winter I shovel snow, ski in nearby Stowe and keep the huge stone fireplace going pretty much around the clock.

The sign was given to us by Wendy Nelson.

The farm also gives me a chance to spend time with my Vermont family: Poppa Pete, Nana Nancy, Cindi's brother Tim, her sister Tami, their spouses Penny and Allen, and all of my nieces and nephews. I enjoy sitting at the little kitchen table chatting it up with Clair and Sandy, our two neighbors who stop in every day to check on us. We just added three cows to the property, so it feels like a real working farm now. I have come to love Breezy Hill Farm and really look forward to our visits.

When I see Giacomo and Giovanni out playing at the farm, I think back on my own own childhood and remember the pleasure Grandpa DeFillipo had with his garden in the back of the house in Pelham. He grew fruit, vegetables and flowers and even kept chickens. Sometimes, I wish he could be part of my farm. I also regret that my grandparents and parents could not meet the Eatons. I believe they would be happy that their "Sonny"—me—has finally found a large family where there is great love and readiness to help in whatever we may need, just like I had growing up.

Giacomo, Giovanni, Cindi and me in Vermont.

Alex, Nicole, Jimmy Boy, me, Angel and Danielle
at Jimmy Boy's 50th birthday party.

CHAPTER 26

My Children

Throughout my life I have become so close to some of my students that I sometimes say they are like a son or a daughter to me. Yet, I'm not sure I was always the best father to my own children. Although I have always tried to assist them whenever there was a need, there have been some very difficult times that have caused tears, anger, sorrow and distrust. In the early days when I was developing NBTA, I would be on the road 36 weeks every year. That didn't leave much time to devote to my children. I can only imagine how difficult it must have been for them to deal with separations, new women in my life and my many marriages.

There is no question that I didn't give my children a full father relationship; I chose my career over them and acting in the traditional male way, I let their mothers take care of them. But if I hadn't done that, I wouldn't have been able to do and give them some of the things and opportunities they have had.

Do I feel guilty? No. Do I feel lucky that they all turned out the way they did? Yes! I am proud of each and every one of them.

In recent years, I have made a deliberate effort to mend bridges and have a good relationship with all of them. I think I have succeeded in part because as they have gotten older, they have forgiven me and we can appreciate each other better.

So I asked my five biological children and my two adopted boys to write about me and their relationships with me—no holds barred —while I wrote about them before I read their responses. Here, in abbreviated form, is what we came up with:

Jimmy Boy, my oldest son, probably should have been a priest. There is no evil in him. His mission in life is to help others and to be a good person. He went through all of my marriages and all of my life experiences with me. Not many people could relate to the many different personalities he's had to deal with, but he has been a kind soul to all of my wives and other children, every one of them! And he has always taken care of his mother Phyllis.

He worked for me at the Academy as the director of all recreational activities. Early on, we had no television in the rooms, and he

organized all the entertainment for the young players—dances, skits, movie nights. He taught photography to the kids and acted like a big brother to them, and they all came to him for advice. For a while, he also was a traveling coach for my elite players, including Jim Courier, David Wheaton, Mark Blackmore and Chris Garner.

He is now the director of Flamingo Park and North Shore Park on the east coast of Florida, which

Jimmy Boy in the early 1980s.

allows him to focus on his two loves: tennis and surfing. I'll always remember him as a boy running up to me: "Hey, Daddy, the waves are up!" And we'd drop everything we were doing to go surfing.

Jimmy Boy on Nick:

My dad is afraid of areas that may hurt him, so smoking is taboo, drinking not so much. He doesn't like being idle. He likes action. My dad was a phone freak long before cell phones and iPhones. His use of the phone has always been the same. He calls you and thinks you know what is going on; he thinks you are there with him.

He is full of zest at all times. That is a unique quality that most people do not have.

To be associated with my dad you have to be in some kind of sport. You could go to dinner with him or go and watch a good war movie, but it doesn't go much further than that. He has a lot of respect for athletes. If you don't stay on those grounds you are going to lose him.

He doesn't degrade anybody in any way. He has made mistakes along the line, but you will never see him put anybody down. He always tries to bring you up. He leaves the welcome mat out even to people who have wronged him or who have been disloyal. He's willing to take them back in.

From early on, **Danielle**, my oldest daughter, has been like my personal bodyguard. I think she believed that everyone was out to get me, so it was up to her to watch my back. It was a difficult decision for her to stay with me when Jeri and I split up while her younger sister Angel went with her mom; but I guess she felt strongly that I needed someone to take care of me.

Danielle was a good tennis player and traveled with me to many of the camps I conducted. I admired her for never complaining when she

Danielle, Willa Bay, husband Greg Breunich and Addie Sky.

had to share living quarters with eight or 10 others and got no special treatment as my daughter.

My strongest memory of her dates back to the time when Hu Na defected from the People's Republic of China and came to NBTA. Danielle shared a room with her in the dorms, and when we got word that Chinese terrorists would attack the Academy, the place went bonkers. Danielle never lost her cool. She never said, "Daddy, take me out of here."

That sense of calm and courage continues to this day. She is married to Greg Breunich, one of my former coaches, and they have two wonderful daughters, Willa Bay and Addie Sky, who both have severe peanut allergies. I admire how Danielle has dedicated her life to safeguard them from harm at all times.

Danielle on Nick:

Through all of the chaos and constant dysfunction on the homefront over the years, it is safe to say that I am still Daddy's girl. I can't say that his lifestyle didn't take its toll on me—the drama because of all of his wives, the players, the parents of the players and everyone else in between that consumed the majority of his time…all of his time. It took me a long time to realize that he tried and as a father, did what he was capable of doing and gave it his all when it came to raising and providing for me.

I did get to travel with him and experience the world in a way that few people could ever imagine. The times I most fondly remember are my dad shirtless, basking in the sun; constantly washing and Blue Coral waxing his cars; having the music blasting—the Bee Gees, Barry White, Marvin Gaye, George Benson. Then, a two-hour break at the beach, bodysurfing; the phone ringing; people all around, sizzlers on the grill. My God, it was never ending!

Even when we were in the public eye, his behavior could surprise you. Who else would shoot spitballs on people in the unlikeliest places, or burp so loudly that everyone would stare in disbelief? He has never cared what people say about him, and I have always liked that about him.

Angel was the horse girl—a super athlete who had all the abilities of an Olympic equestrian and the mental toughness of a winner. I remember at one big horse show, her mount crowded the sideboards and she got a gash in her leg with blood gushing. But Angel did not let it deter her and rode on to victory!

When Jeri and I split, Angel decided to go with her to Cincinnati. I think it was tough for her to accept my new families and all the wives that followed. But she returned to Florida at some point and is now an acupuncturist in Sarasota and doing very well. I have always been amazed about her ability to talk to animals—and how they listen and talk back to

Presley, Angel and me.

her. When we were at Dorado Beach, the lizards would come out to wherever she walked. She has about 20 cats living with her now.

What I appreciate most about her is that she pulls no punches with me. She always tells it like it is!

Angel on Nick:

My dad is a great motivator—he has the special ability to make you want to do your best. Even when his voice bellows from several courts away, his energy travels. He hates confrontation. He is selfish, yet has a huge heart; narcissistic, yet humble in his own way; obviously confident, yet secretly insecure (not so secret to those who really know him). He thrives on being in the limelight and seems oddly uncomfortable when the subject matter is not him. He loves to put smiles on others' faces. He has a boyish silliness about him. He always made our family trips fun—spitball fights in airplanes, races down the ski slopes, riding the waves...

He has not made the best choices with most of the women that he brought into his life which, sadly, has led to deterioration and strain in his relationship with his children for many, many years. We don't get to choose our parents but we do get to choose how they affect our lives. Life is about accepting people for who they are and what they are capable of. It's just a little more challenging when it's a parent. If you expect more, it is a lifetime of disappointment.

I have always had a love/hate relationship with my father, with the root being sadness, but I love him deeply and only wish him happiness.

Hudson, Nicole, Jameson and Brad Kronig.

After my divorce from Kellie, **Nicole** was like a second mother to her younger sister Alex. I know, because both of them lived with me for some time at my condo. She also lived at IMG when she was in high school and we got to spend good times together, which I still cherish.

My best memory goes back to when I was in the hospital room when her son Hudson was born. She couldn't believe I was there because I'm afraid of hospitals. I had to look away, but I'm glad I was there. (Nicole's husband, Brad Kronig is a leading model for international fashion designers. That's how Karl Lagerfeld became the godfather of both boys.)

Nicole is very focused on details, which can drive me crazy. What I appreciate most about her is what an unbelievably good mother she is to both of her children, Hudson and Jamison.

Nicole on Nick:

I loved to play baseball. My dad would often come to the games and always was a huge supporter from the stands. I loved seeing him cheering me on and loved knowing he was there.

When I was young, I used to get so sad when he would travel. I used to help him pack and then we would walk him out to the driveway and watch him drive away. He would always fax us to tell us how his trip was going and that he missed us. Every time he went overseas he would bring me back a piece of Swarovski crystal. I always looked forward to each special piece.

When I was leaving for college my freshman year, I remember going to the Academy to say goodbye to him. After giving him a hug, I looked at his eyes through his glasses and saw tears. It was a moment I will never forget. He had never really showed emotion to me like that before.

I think my dad and I have a good relationship. We are able to talk through issues that arise and have a good understanding of one another. I try not to hold on to any hurt feelings that have come from the past because it only harbors negative energy and I don't want to live like that. "Life is 10% what happens to you and 90% how you react to it." It's funny because I learned that from my dad. He has always been able to pick himself up from any situation and move forward. I respect that quality in him. I may not always agree with all of his decisions, but that's life. I love him very much and am pretty darn lucky to be his daughter.

My youngest daughter, **Alex**, can be very dramatic. She looks more at the negative side of things, while I try to always see the positive. But I have come to appreciate that her complaining is strategic. When she wants something, it's her way of getting it, and she usually succeeds. I believe my divorce from her mother was very hard for her. But she moved on and developed her creative side by attending the Fashion Institute of Technology in New York with the help of Oscar de la Renta.

My best memory is being at graduation when she got her master's degree in management from the University of Alabama. I was so proud of her. She is now the manager of a department store and I know she can go a long way if and when she is ready to stand on her own two feet.

Alex and me.

Alex on Nick:

Growing up in south Florida, Daddy and I would cruise to the beach to go bodysurfing. We'd have the windows down in his car, groovin' to "Breezin" by George Benson. He is the only man I will give my hand to for a dance. I know I'm biased, but he is the best dance partner ever! We always have an absolute ball! His laugh when he finds something hysterical is priceless!

Favorite times—summer vacations in Capri, ski trips to Aspen. The best part is being on the chairlift up to the mountain with him. You never know what he's going to share with you about life. And of course, Grand Slam tennis tournaments: I always felt most connected to my dad on those trips because I could sit back, just listen to him, see him in action interacting with others. I am so incredibly proud of my father and take much pride in being his daughter. Listen to one of his speeches and I promise you, you will feel something deep inside you—your heart, head and soul.

Giovanni—Gio—is a kind soul, very much like Jimmy Boy. He's very bright, thoughtful, even-tempered, calm in difficult situations and a good athlete. He's also responsible, a little gentleman. If anything drops on the floor, he is the first to pick it up. He wants to be a "real" rescue hero when he grows up, preferably a fire chief.

My youngest son, **Giacomo**, is the opposite. I think he comes closest to resembling me as a kid. He loves to have a good time, lives to make everyone laugh, can't sit still to save his life, loves sports of any kind, and is impulsive with a flair for the dramatic. He will either end up a charismatic minister, a professional athlete, or a stunt man.

Both boys are very attached to their mother, who spends lots of time with them, and I like that. Keeping up with them is a challenge; they keep me young. I can't imagine my life without them. They teach me something about myself every day and constantly challenge me to be a better person.

Giacomo, me and Giovanni.

Giovanni on Nick:
My dad is loud except when on the phone. And he loves to exercise.

Giacomo on Nick:
He is happy with us and with his wife. My dad is nice.

Even knowing about his passion for the game and what he accomplished, I was blown away to see the Academy that came from his "crazy dream." The IMG Academy, top in its class, would not be here if it wasn't for his passion.

—Rohan Goetzke,
  Director, IMG Academy Bollettieri Tennis Program

We came from Serbia to your Academy in 2001 when I was seven and my sister Sara was eight, and we spent 11 years there. Sara now goes to Florida State University, and I am at the University of Connecticut on a full athletic scholarship. We always thought of you as more than just a coach. You were a huge figure in our lives who taught us a lot more than the game of tennis. Without your dedication, warmth and kindness, we would not have developed into the young ladies that we are today.

—Sarna Stosljevic, former student

My full scholarship to the Nick Bollettieri Tennis Academy provided by Nick is the single biggest moment in my life that shaped me for who I am today. Without Nick and his incredible team in those days, particularly Julio Moros and Carolina Bolivar Murphy, my life would never have gone in the positive direction that it has. Nick taught me that winning matters and taking risks with a work ethic that does not stop is where the fruit is in life…. I love you, Nick, and I know I will help young people like me for the rest of my life just as you helped me.

—Bobby Blair, former student

CHAPTER 27

Summing Up

I celebrated my 80th birthday like George Herbert Walker Bush, by jumping out of an airplane. I figured if our 41st president, who was not nearly in the shape I was, could do it, so could I. I went to West Point, where Colonel Steve Fleming was my jumpmaster. It had been nearly 60 years since I had skydived as a paratrooper in Kentucky, North Carolina and Japan. As someone who had coached others for years, I appreciated someone who would coach me through the experience, and Colonel Fleming was superb. I felt comfortable and in good hands as he secured my jumpsuit and the tandem harness, although they were strapped so tight I felt like we were Siamese twins.

After we ascended to 10,750 feet, there was that moment of excitement and terror when the door to the airplane opened and the cold air rushing past invaded the cabin, and then we were off. It was everything I wanted it to be—a thrilling experience, the wind rushing loudly past my face during freefall, and the amazing silence that follows when the parachute opens. It was a clear day and we could see across the Hudson River into the Cascade Mountains. It was beautiful but I couldn't wait to touch down and have my feet back on solid ground.

I didn't have time to do any celebrating, since I had to fly immediately after to Ethiopia for the adoption of my second son, Giacomo. But when I got back, a big surprise awaited me. IMG had dedicated a room in the tennis administration building as my personal "Hall of Fame." The walls were covered with photos and framed articles about my achievements, documenting various milestones in my career. Also on display were mementos like Bing Crosby's golf putter, which Barry Gibb of the Bee Gees had given me as a present. I was deeply moved by the expression of affection on the part of IMG and all the staff members who contributed to give me this remarkable gift.

It also gave me pause and started me thinking about my life up to now and my legacy. I know I made some big blunders in my career, some of them causing hurt to others. I count among them sitting with Andre Agassi's entourage the first time he played Jim Courier, and later on, breaking up with Andre by sending him a letter rather than going to see him in person. I've made big mistakes not paying attention to finances, spending money as quickly as I earned it, although I don't regret a single scholarship I gave to anyone in my camps and at the Academy.

Notice I've never said that my prior seven marriages were mistakes. I call them unbelievably costly experiences! But they have all enriched my life in important ways, and I have no regrets about any of them.

I am proud of my five children, two adopted boys and four grandchildren. They and their families provide more than I could ever have hoped for as a family.

Overall, I think I have done more right than wrong.

I am an innovator and have always been willing to explore different roads to success. To that end I started the first live-in academy in the world. It changed the way tennis is taught at the junior level.

When we got started, there were no free-standing tennis academies that housed and trained students year-round. Now they exist in every part of the world—Japan, Croatia, Spain, you name it—and other sports have modeled their training after it. More importantly, the impact on individual students has been immeasurable.

Some of my teachings have had a lasting impact on the game, including:

- I was a leader in developing the killer forehand.

- The Bollettieri Traveling Team in the 1980s was the talk of the junior circuit.

- The swing volley. They said I didn't know how to teach the volley, so I said to my students, "Swing at it!" And I had Andre Agassi, Jim Courier and Monica Seles do it, as well as Brian Gottfried and Serena Williams, two of the best swing volleyers in the game!

Some people have criticized me for being too demanding on players and causing hurt by harsh critiques of sensitive, impressionable youngsters. Others have argued that I spent too much time with my elite prospects—many of them on scholarship—to the detriment of less talented players who were paying full bill. While there is some truth to these comments, I have always found time to see every single student—whether full- or part-time—and I continue to do so today at IMG Academy. And the results speak for themselves. At last count, more than 150 Grand Slam tournament winners have done substantial training at NBTA and later on at IMG Academy.

One way or another, I have been coaching not only tennis, but almost everyone I have ever met.

Here is what I think good coaching is all about: It requires the ability to read others in order to bring out everything they have and motivate them to reach their full potential. That also means finding a way to blend all of their various talents and abilities into a winning package. Timing is important, especially while communicating what you know and have others accept it so they use it to reach their maximum performance.

Beyond that, I believe it is also important to demand of athletes an awareness of sportsmanship, respect and dedication. Above all, no matter what it takes, they must learn to always guard and nurture what's deep inside them. That is their character and the source from which their achievements come. I always say, "Your character is not for sale. Never!"

Something happened recently that put everything in perspective for me.

It was August 9, 2013, and I was in my office under the indoor tennis dome at IMG when who do you think stopped by with his physical trainer to say hello? It was Tommy Haas! He said, "Nicky, how in the world do you stay in this hot box, you should have IMG put in air conditioning!" Only a few people call me "Nicky," actually just my first wife Phyllis, Fritz Nau and Tommy. We sat down and chatted for a while about this and that. At some point I asked him how he felt about spending 21 of his 35 years with me. Tommy said that I was like his second father, someone he confided in and relied upon—in much the same way as with his biological father. It was at that point that I had an epiphany. I thought about all the kids who I mentored, cared for, advised, housed and yes, fathered during the early years of my academy. Agassi, Courier, Wheaton, Arias, Kournikova and others all lived with my family and me during the early years. Not only did their parents trust me with them—a great honor—but many, including Tommy's father, also permitted me to be a surrogate and mentor to their young children.

About six years ago Mark Styslinger and his lovely wife Jennifer brought their son Mac to me. Mark had been a student at NBTA in the 1980s. He was a fine tennis player (later a two-time all-American at Southern Methodist University) and has become a staunch supporter of many of my projects, including Camp Kaizen. I watched Mac hit a few balls. He was a shy boy, but I could see the positive qualities in his game. When I asked the Styslingers to leave him with me, it brought tears to Jennifer's eyes; but they said yes. Mac trained at IMG for the next four years and also became one of my private students—I hired David DePalmer as his coach to develop his game. Mac grew and matured and became one of the top juniors in the United States. I encouraged him to go to the University of Virginia. In 2013, his freshman year, he and his doubles partner Jarmere Jenkins won the NCAA Championship. I'm sure Mac will join the pro tour at some point and do well.

As I pondered my relationships with all of the youngsters I have mentored, I began to think about the ones that I sponsored, supported or encouraged who would never have recognizable names; kids who would grow up to have productive lives, pay their taxes and become good citizens of the world. I wondered about the children from the Boys & Girls Clubs of Sarasota, Florida who had received more than $2.5 million in scholarships to IMG Academy via my good friend Dick Vitale and me. I wondered about the kids who were inspired to become doctors, accountants and lawyers. I wondered about the 20,000 inner-city youth that Arthur Ashe and I trained in the ABC tennis program in nearly a dozen cities across America.

At a recent U.S. Open, my daughter Alex and I were invited to sit in the President's Box. A gentleman came up to us, introduced himself and reminded me of how I had saved a young man's life when he had called me years ago on behalf of his mother. Allister Martin, a young man of Haitian descent, had dropped out of high school even though he was an excellent tennis player and outstanding student. He described himself as a "directionless punk." His mom was advised by local police to relocate him into another area lest he come under further attack from gang members who had recently beaten him up so badly that she didn't recognize him. We arranged to bring him to IMG on an affordable package, where Allister spent six months training with me. He graduated high school, received a scholarship to Rutgers University, where he played Division 1 tennis, was voted the team's most improved player and made the Big East Conference Academic All-Star team. He graduated from Rutgers with a 3.85 GPA and went on to Harvard Medical School. His mom felt that IMG's assistance and I had refocused his attention on his goal to become a doctor and, in effect, saved him. Allister is an example of how, sometimes, a helping hand is all it takes to change a life.

I recently received an email from another former student, Bobby Blair. I first met him in 1980 when his mom, who sadly was ill and dying, dropped him off at the motel that served as housing for my

Bobby Blair, me and Aaron Krickstein in the early 1980s.

Academy before NBTA opened. He had two tennis racquets, two pairs of Kmart tennis shoes and $10. I accepted him with a full scholarship and he went on to become one of the top junior players in the United States. Bobby played professionally and became a well respected tennis coach. Today he owns a newspaper and magazine. At the end of August in 2013, Bobby released his book, *Hiding Inside the Baseline*, and came out of the closet about having been a gay athlete, coach and entrepreneur. I was honored to speak at that event, and I can't say enough of how proud I am of Bobby for all he has accomplished and continues to do to bring equality and understanding to the world.

There are other, equally important examples coming from my partnership with Arthur Ashe as we provided tennis, health education, immunizations and other services to thousands of children in inner cities across the country. Whenever I go to a tournament or event, people come up to me thanking me for what I did for them, or their children and families. I realize that my staff and I have made an impact on thousands and thousands of people—young and old—who in turn will make an impact on their children and generations to come.

As I sat talking with Tommy Haas, I wondered if my most important contributions to this world might very well be my service to others. Yes, I'm known for training 10 No. 1 ranked tennis players, but maybe when the final accounting is taken, what will matter most is what I have done for others and the positive impact I have had on the lives of God's children who did not come from a world of success and privilege and needed a helping hand along the way.

Bobby Blair and me in the fall of 2009.

From December 13-20, 2009 I hosted our third USO Christmas tour to visit our troops in Afghanistan and Iraq… At 78 years of age, Nick had moved just beyond middle-age and I was concerned with how he would relate to our young men and women whose average age was about 20.

Man, was I wrong to be concerned… He was magnificent. He let these young men and women know how important they were, how important their mission was, and how much the American people appreciated and supported them. He was an incredible inspiration for us all. I could not have been prouder of Nick and what he did to bring a little bit of our great country to so many superb young representatives of America so far from home. It was a signature USO performance that had Bob Hope smiling from above.

—Admiral Mike Mullen, retired
Former Chairman of the Joint Chiefs of Staff

If you have never heard Nick speak from the stage, you have missed an unusual opportunity. He is up there with the greats— Lou Holtz, Billy Graham, Tommy Lasorda… From Harvard to Oxford to Barclays Bank, he has spread his message near and far. And I'm not talking about just tennis. I mean life lessons, business and success.

—Harvey Mackay

When Nick sold to IMG, we formed a partnership so he could continue who he is…he acts as an ambassador ready to do whatever is needed to be done, whatever is called upon.

—Chris Ciaccio, Vice President of Marketing & Sales,
IMG Performance

CHAPTER 28

Tennis Ambassador

During my travels, I have always promoted tennis. But in recent years my role at IMG Academy has changed. In addition to being on the tennis court, I have become even more of an ambassador for the sport, advocating on its behalf worldwide through writing, commentating at major events, holding clinics and speaking to a variety of groups.

I believe that tennis is a training ground for character and life's challenges. The determination and commitment to excellence required at a high competitive level translates very well into other endeavors, be they in the business world, in the military or in people's personal lives.

Not all of my "diplomatic missions" involve speaking to groups. Sometimes, because of my many years of experience in tennis, I'm called on to consult and offer advice. In 2012, Stacey Allaster, the head of the WTA, asked me come to the headquarters in St. Petersburg, Florida, about 45 minutes north of IMG, and share my thoughts in a discussion concerning a matter that has been highly controversial for years—the pervasive grunting and screaming during matches.

My answer was simple and based on what I thought was best for the sport. I never taught it to my female (or male) players, but I defended it because a number of my champions, notably Monica Seles, Maria Sharapova and Serena Williams, have made it part of their arsenals of weapons on the court. It can disturb, distract and intimidate opponents. In addition, it is now so much a part of their game, that to demand they stop would severely damage their ability to compete.

If we wanted to get rid of the screaming, my suggestion was to phase it out gradually by starting with 10 to 12 year olds. Have the umpires announce before matches that they will issue first a warning and then start to deduct points. Do it consistently, across the board, and the "problem" will soon go away. It's not clear to me, however, that the will is there on the part of the governing tennis organizations to make that happen.

While I am always willing to offer advice, I have been especially honored to share my ideas with individuals and large groups of people under extraordinary circumstances. A few years ago Chad Bohling,

Me addressing students at the Academy.

who worked on IMG's mental conditioning team, asked to speak to me. The program was originally founded by Dr. Jim Loehr in the early 80s to develop the mental aspects of the game—toughness, confidence, handling pressure. He'd also help them break the habit of "chucking" their racquets into the fence when they got frustrated. A pioneer in the field of athletic performance, Dr. Loehr is now perhaps the foremost sports psychologist in the world. He has written numerous books on and has worked with elite athletes in a number of different sports to help them raise their game and improve their performance.

Chad was doing a good job running the department. A good-looking, personable athlete, he was not usually emotional, but that day, as we sat outside at the bleachers by the tennis courts, he teared up. He had received an offer to head up a similar program for the New York Yankees and didn't want me to feel that he was leaving because he was unhappy about working for the Academy and me. I assured him that IMG would be pleased to see him move on in his career because we're in the business of developing people, and that I was genuinely happy for him.

Chad and I kept in touch over the years, and in the spring of 2013 I received a letter from him informing me that I had been selected to give a motivational speech to the Yankees at their spring training facilities in Tampa, Florida. Only two speakers are chosen each year and the event is attended by the major league players, team managers and the farm teams. What an honor! My mind flashed back to my childhood days growing up just north of New York City. Whenever my father drove into Manhattan—and once in a while I'd go along for the ride—he had to go by Yankee Stadium in the Bronx. In those days there were three teams: The Yankees, the Brooklyn Dodgers and the New York Giants—I was actually a Giants fan. But with 18 division titles, 40 American League pennants and 27 World Series championships—all Major League Baseball records—the Yankees are the most successful franchise in baseball and all of professional sports. Forty-four of their players and 11 managers have been inducted into the Baseball Hall of Fame.

I was beside myself with excitement and called several of my friends to give them the good news. Then I thought about what I could say. I often made impromptu remarks when I spoke to my assembled staff and players at the Academy or other small speaking venues. But this was too important an occasion and I couldn't just wing it. So my manager Tim Westervelt and I spent considerable time writing my speech.

We drove to Steinbrenner Field in Tampa and met Chad, who took us through a warren of corridors which were filled with posters of past Yankee champions. He introduced me to Coach Joe Girardi, who welcomed me warmly and said that, regretfully, his wife couldn't be in attendance. She loved to play tennis and had very much looked forward to meeting me. I arranged for Prince to send her new racquets and a racquet bag when I got back to IMG.

Then Joe and Chad took me to the locker room. Joe invited me in and introduced me. There were players everywhere, some wrapped in towels, others getting into uniform. I was shaking from head to toe, but I took a deep breath and decided to rip up my prepared speech; I wanted to speak from the heart. I started to tell the assembled players that I had seen quotes from Babe Ruth, Joe DiMaggio, Lou Gehrig and others in the corridors and understood that when they walked onto the field, the fans and the opposing team knew that they had come to win! Yes, they were paid for their services, but Yankee pride was what drove them to excellence. Babe Ruth signed a contract that would pay him $100,000 in 1919, a laughable sum by today's standards, but he was proud to be in pinstripes. And like him and those other greats, the men before me were driven by the same pride. I said, "This team was drawn together by a simple, yet powerful phrase: "We Are Winners."

Then I told them that at night before I go to bed, I ask myself four questions:

1. Did I do all that I could do today?
2. Did I do my best?
3. Would others say that I did my best, too?
4. Did I tell the truth to myself?

When I finished, one of the questions asked was, "Nick, why are you working 14 to 16 hours per day at this stage of your life?" I answered, "If you had to pay alimony to seven ex-wives, you would be hitting homeruns to get a bigger bonus yourself." It got a good round of laughter before I assured them that my eighth wife was a keeper. Andy Pettitte winked at me and said he'd send me an autographed picture for my hall of fame room!

Later that day, as I was standing behind the batter's box with Derek Jeter, he said to his teammate during batting practice, "Remember what

Mr. Bollettieri said and tell yourself the truth: You can't hit a lick!"

It was a wonderful experience to spend time with these remarkable athletes, many future Hall of Famers, whose pride inspired them in their daily efforts to achieve greatness.

I've had other fun moments in my speaking engagements. At the 2013 ITF Worldwide Coaches Conference in Cancun, I was asked to speak along with Patrick McEnroe, Dr. Jim Loehr and Judy Murray, the mother of Andy Murray who earlier that year had won Wimbledon. (Andy visited IMG Academy with his coach for a week as a younger player. When I saw him practice, I knew he was a heck of an athlete. His ability to move and his effort to run down every ball impressed me.)

I got to know Judy as the coach of British players for the Federation Cup, the premier international tennis competition for women, when one of my students, Heather Watson, played on the British team. Judy also sent other players, including Laura Robson, to practice at the Academy in anticipation of cup competitions. I developed immense respect for Judy and her efforts on behalf of tennis and also for the stable, balanced family environment she has created for her sons competing at an elite level.

A young Andy Murray at IMG.

(Jamie Murray, Andy's older brother, is a top tennis player as well. He and Jelena Jankovic won the 2007 Wimbledon mixed doubles.)

Judy and I have a good relationship and when I spoke at the ITF conference right after her, I joked that I was so impressed by her, I wouldn't be surprised if she just might become my ninth wife.

Well, someone put the comment on Facebook and one of our friends who saw it mentioned it to Cindi. Fortunately, she has a good sense of humor. Her comment: "There goes Nick again!"

Judy Murray and me.

Another memorable speaking engagement came about as a result of me being part of an American Express show at the U.S. Open that included Tim Ryan and Al Trautwig. Members of the West Point men's and women's tennis teams were in attendance and after the show, I walked over to them and answered their questions. The next summer, many of the cadets worked as tennis counselors at the IMG Academy's Bollettieri tennis program. Soon after, I was invited to West Point not only to speak to the tennis teams, but also to address the entire corps of cadets. When I close my eyes I can still see that ocean of young adult military men and women sitting in front of me wondering what I could say to them that would have an impact. It helped that I was introduced as a former officer in the U.S. Airborne.

The thrust of my speech was about what it took to become a winner. I held their attention by telling them stories about Agassi, Courier, Becker and the Williams sisters. At the end of the speech I received a round of applause that rocked the building and was presented with a West Point saber that I proudly display in my trophy room at IMG today. The commanding general called me into his office and said, "Lieutenant, you spoke our military language today and conveyed what we always demand from our troops. It's all about winning! Playing the best you can is impressive and makes you a valued member of our team. Your athletes play for trophies, scholarships and for money. But, our soldiers play to stay alive and that means that they must win!" I was deeply touched by his compliment.

But perhaps my most powerful experience came in December of 2009 when retired Brig. General John Pray, the head of the USO, asked me to participate in a tour. The USO is the entertainment arm of the military that produced the famous Bob Hope Christmas show. Bob Hope brought joy and excitement to tens of thousands of our troops overseas, often performing inside active war zones. General Pray selected comedian David Attell, singer Billy Ray Cyrus, tennis sensation Anna Kournikova and me to join the tour.

We didn't really know many details of the trip—how we would travel, the exact times of our departure, or where we would perform. We were simply told to report to a certain location, follow orders and maintain complete secrecy. When we got to the appointed location, we were driven to an airport and given a complete body search. Then we were spirited off to an airplane for departure. Did I say airplane? It was Air Force Two! We had a complete suite with every accommodation we could imagine. The icing on the cake was the arrival of Admiral Mike Mullen, Chairman of the Joint Chiefs of Staff, and his wife Debra. They greeted us and advised us of our destinations: Iraq and Afghanistan!

Altogether, we made 10 stops. I spoke in hangars, in fields and in the desert to as many as 2,000 soldiers at a time. It was an indescribable experience and a special honor to address the troops fighting to keep America safe.

A few months after the trip, IMG hosted four "wounded warriors" and their families for a week. Everyone participated in sports activities, their wives and children, too. I hit tennis balls with some of the veterans. It was only a small token of appreciation for what they had done, but it turned out to be a wonderful experience for everyone involved, and I can't thank General Pray enough for making it all possible.

Despite his amazing record of accomplishment, or perhaps because of it, Nick has never changed. He's always upbeat, friendly, shrewd and purposefully a little crazy. His devotion to tennis, his players and his Academy is unquestioned. If Nick lives to be 100, on his birthday I would expect him to be on the court, shirtless, sunglasses on, bragging about his tan, at the net feeding balls and constantly talking wisdom to whomever would listen.

—Aaron Krickstein

What is amazing to us is that Nick Bollettieri has not lost one ounce of intensity. He is a man who never gives up. We can honestly say he rises as early, drives himself as hard, maintains his global network, tends to his friends and gives of himself to talented athletes as passionately and enthusiastically as he did when we met him 40 years ago.

—Marilyn Nelson

CHAPTER 29

Into the Future

As we were putting the finishing touches on the manuscript, two important things happened. First, IMG Worldwide was sold to William Morris Endeavor and the private equity firm Silver Lake Partners. It will bring new changes and opportunities to all aspects of the company, including IMG Academy, no doubt, and I plan to do what I've always done: put my heart and soul into making the venture a success.

The second thing is that I received notification from the International Tennis Hall of Fame, informing me that I had been selected for induction in ITF's 2014 class. When I received two calls, one from Chairman Chris Clouser and the other from President Stan Smith, I was at a loss for words, something that doesn't happen very often. With tears of joy streaming down my face, I thanked them and my God above for putting this stamp of approval on my 60 plus years in tennis.

Although this award will be presented to me, and I am greatly honored by it, I also know that my family and all the players, parents, friends and coaches who have worked with me for so many years, deserve a moment to revel in this recognition as well. Yes, I had a vision, but it would never have become a reality without their help, dedication and support.

In their separate ways, both events have confirmed for me that there is new ground to be broken, new territory to be explored. I am thrilled with the prospect of the combined forces of IMG and William Morris creating something big and exciting in the sports world. At the same time, being recognized for my work in the tennis industry for the past six decades makes me realize how much the game has changed and continues to change. When I started out, all the balls where still white and tennis belonged to talented, enthusiastic amateurs, mostly from Australia and the United States, with a few Swedes thrown in! Since then, tennis has become a colorful, international sport and the training and preparation required to compete at the elite professional level is unprecedented. As IMG Academy continues to be in the forefront of developing such players from all over the world, there are talented youngsters coming on the scene, and I am as excited as ever about stepping on the tennis court with them. At the same time, I believe that IMG must continue to be a leader in the fields of fitness and nutrition for athletes at all levels.

I have been blessed with an unusual physique and a team of excellent physicians who help me take care of it. My eye doctor, opthalmologist Dr. Dana Weinkle, kiddingly calls me a "freak of nature" because of my 20/20 vision without ever needing glasses. (My students have always wondered how I could see what they were up to many courts away from where I was teaching.) My dermatologist, Dr. Susan Weinkle, keeps my skin baby soft even though I continue to break all her rules regarding suntanning. I appreciate Dr. Terry Alford making sure that my unusually healthy teeth stay white and commend Dr. Larry Lieberman for keeping my heart pumping, so that I can engage in rigorous exercise at 82 that would send many people half my age to the hospital.

I regularly play 18 rounds of golf, often with Judge Farrance, Steve Jonsson, my banker and friend for many years, and Jonnie Williams, a large shareholder in a company now owned by Abbott Laboratories, Inc. His son Frankie attended IMG and went on to play tennis at Penn State. When Jonnie comes to town and the "Famous Foursome" hits the links, it's like a reality TV show. Every time Jonnie misses a shot, he has the caddie go to the pro shop to get him a new club. He is generous to a fault. When you're with him, do not bring your wallet. He insists on treating. He has given me enough new golf shorts, shirts, clubs and balls to outfit a whole team. At the Collegiate School, a famous private K-12 academy in Virginia, he built a tennis center and had it named after me. I can't thank him enough for the many times he has helped me out.

My workday still begins at 4:30 in the morning and I go all day long. For lunch I usually head to South Philly, which has the best cheesesteak in the South. It's about half a mile from IMG, and I have a permanently reserved table there to meet with friends and business associates. I could eat at the Academy dining room, but prefer to get away from the bustle for a brief noontime respite.

For dinner, my favorite place is Gio Fabulous. Owned by four brothers, Anthony, John, Nick and Carmen Hroncich, it has an ambiance that reminds me of my youth and dinners at Grandma DeFillipo's house. Gio's is where I bring my traveling friends when they're in town, including Serena Williams, Tommy Haas, Xavier Malisse and others who appreciate the exquisite food and congenial atmosphere.

Most days I feel as vigorous as a teenager, so when my wife Cindi asked me what arrangements I would want to make for my death and funeral, I was taken aback a bit. Death is not something I dwell on very much. I'm too busy doing things. But then I thought about it and told her that I would like to be cremated and have my ashes strewn in three locations—one third in Capri, a place I have come to love, another in Vermont among the blueberry bushes of Breezy Hill Farm, and the last third at the Academy.

That says as much about me and my life as anything at this point.

There is only one person who can predict what my future will be, and even that person will have to think long and hard before giving an answer. That person is the good Lord. But, before looking forward, I find myself looking backward. One of the big regrets I have is that I didn't spend more time with my father. For the most part. After graduation from college, and for the short period of time that my folks lived in Bradenton, I wish that I had spent more time visiting with them. Our get-togethers became even more infrequent when they moved to the Orlando area and later to Deerfield on the east coast of Florida. I could and should have made a greater effort to see them and to call more frequently.

My son, Jimmy Boy, calls me several times a week and my daughter Nicole speaks to me on a daily basis. I don't hear from Angel very often even though she lives in nearby Sarasota. I'm sure that my many marriages have strained communication as well as affected the frequency of their visits. I realized that my life is the product of my own making. My work and travel schedule would kill the average 82-year-old.

I often wonder why I have such a hard time living a "normal" life. But could I really walk away from tennis and go to our beautiful farm in Craftsbury, Vermont for good? Would skiing in the winter and picking blueberries with my two young sons in the summer fill the void of not being involved with tennis on a daily basis? I would be able to see my four grandchildren more, spend time surfing with my son Jimmy Boy and put on clinics for him at Flamingo Park, and see more of my four daughters and my lifetime friends.

That change sounds like a lovely dream, indeed, but it doesn't make sense for me. One of my close friends with a medical background said that if I were to make such a dramatic change in my life, it could result in various setbacks including the loss of memory. He also told me that at my age, changing my routine could be too much of an adjustment. Being tested each and every day both on and off the tennis court keeps my mind sharp.

I've lived my life moment to moment and I have no plans to make any substantial changes in my routine. I look forward to continuing to be part of IMG Academy and letting the chips fall where they may. I want to continue training players, supporting inner-city programs to help grow the sport of tennis in America, consulting with elite players on their careers, broadcasting at the U.S. Open and tournaments abroad, writing for newspapers and magazines around the world, giving speeches to motivate and encourage others, and more than anything else, working with all kinds of children—from the privileged to the disadvantaged—to open their minds to greater possibilities and the pursuit of their dreams.

In my mind I envision that I have so many more hills to climb on my journey, and I anticipate a soft landing when I fall.

Nick has unbridled passion for everything he does, and his passion as a legendary tennis coach is second to none. He has supported tennis at every level, most recently in his dedicated efforts to help the USTA and American tennis with the 10 and Under initiative. His contributions have been felt, and will continue to be felt, by all of us in the tennis world.

—Patrick McEnroe

APPENDIX

The Status of American Tennis

I am often asked to comment on the status of American tennis: Why are there so few Americans in the top 100, and why have Serbia, Spain, Switzerland, France, Russia and other nations overtaken the U.S. in dominating tennis? I believe that there are many answers to these questions:

- SCOPE: Tennis is now played on a global landscape. Several decades ago, America was one of only a few nations producing top players. Today, the entire world, often with the support of their governments, is our competition.

- COMPETITION: When I started the Nick Bollettieri Tennis Academy, I had the finest players in the world in one location, competing against one another. Agassi, Courier, Wheaton, Sampras, Seles, Kournikova, Majoli, etc. Although I didn't coach Pete Sampras, he and his coach, Tim Gullickson, were welcome at my Academy to train and compete against the best that America had to offer at the time. In the 80s, there were very few top-notch training facilities in the country. Now, with the popularity of training environments, (dozens within a 10-mile radius of IMG Academy alone), there is no single location that brings a critical mass of top players together.

- PLAYERS: America's best athletes are not directed to tennis. Arthur Ashe recognized this problem more than 25 years ago:

Junior high and high school physical education instructors throughout the school system are, for the most part, basketball, football, baseball and track and field coaches who encourage their top athletes to compete in those sports. The USTA created the 10 and Under Program, which is effective at introducing children to tennis, but to the majority of kids in our school system and the public recreational system, this program is not available.

- COST: The cost of becoming a top player is prohibitive. While children can learn to play in local programs (National Junior Tennis & Learning, local not-for-profit programs, etc.) at little or no cost, becoming a highly ranked national tournament player is another matter. Instruction, court rental costs or club membership fees, clothing and equipment, travel, meals, hotels, coaches and other expenses can amount to $80,000 to $150,000 per year. With a median income for American families of just under $52,000, only top earners can afford this without sponsorships.

- SYSTEM: Unlike team sports such as baseball and ice hockey, there are no farm teams in individual sports—minor league environments where coaching and competition is available and the players receive nominal salaries and funds that sustain them while they continue to develop their skills. While the USTA does have "Challenger" and "Futures" tournaments for sub-world-class players, this is not enough. The idea of a minor league team is that the major league team funds it, having a vested interest in developing talented players and grooming them for the "big stage."

- OPTIONS: Let's face it, most parents hope for their kids to go to college. It's also the most practical option, given the miniscule number of talented tennis players who sign professional contracts directly out of high school. Most kids have a better chance of becoming brain surgeons than signing a pro contract. The No. 161 ranked player in the National Football League receives an annual salary of $1.4 million. At the same time, the No. 161 ranked player on the ATP or WTA tour must spend about $100,000 to stay on the circuit. So, with a college scholarship tucked in their back pocket, players question why they endure the pain of injuries, the increasing cost of competing and the frustration of going at it alone.

What measures should be taken to deal with these challenges?

If I were asked what I would do to restore American dominance on the ATP and WTA circuits, I'd say I'd need $50 to $60 million. While some may balk at this figure, in the grand scheme of things, this is not an outrageous sum of money.

I'd have one location at which all of the best American men and women would train. They would feed off one another and, like Agassi and Courier, each would fight the other to be king of the "Grand" mountain. I'd choose coaches and hitting partners that can help these players, and for those who needed financial help, I'd provide stipends.

Back in the 1990s I created a program called "Tennis in a Can." This program was offered to municipal tennis facilities along with elementary, middle and high schools so that their physical education instructors could teach the fundamentals of the sport to children as young as five and six years old. It included 10 one-hour videos, a 350-page teaching manual, on-court teaching tools, and a travel bag with the logos of the USTA and the USPTA, which endorsed the program. I made the entire package available for $295. We sold a few, but the public schools couldn't even afford this meager price. I went to some of my friends and raised enough money to send the "Tennis in a Can" program to nearly 4,000 schools at no cost, and it worked. When learning tennis is made into a fun experience, children love the game and look forward to it every day. I'd have someone on staff to oversee this program on a national level.

To supplement the "Tennis in a Can" program, I'd encourage the growth of the USTA's 10 and Under program and regional National Junior Tennis & Learning networks. This would provide avenues of advancement for those who wanted to take their tennis to the next level.

The USTA's National Junior Tennis & Learning Network (NJTL) is effective at engaging millions of youth through tennis, education and life skills programming. While there are several outstanding NJTL chapters in several metropolitan areas, there are hundreds of major cities without any program at all. We would need to expand this program to make it more widely available.

We also need to understand that the game has changed dramatically over the last few decades. In the 70s, 80s and 90s, most players were making their break into the top 10 while they were still teenagers. The likes of Becker, Evert, Austin and Agassi won major tournaments while still in their teens. Today, the top players in the world are a good decade or more older, and physically more mature and fit. Serena Williams is 32, Venus is 33, Roger Federer is 32, David Ferrer is 31, Maria Sharapova is 26, Li Na is 31. In addition, size is now a factor. The average male on the pro tour is nearly 6' 3" and many of the ladies exceed 6' 0" in height.

Tennis players are now older, taller and more fit than ever before in history and we need to look at American tennis with a new set of eyes.

First, let's take a closer look at the USTA's 10 and Under program. Throughout my 60 years in the business of tennis, I have seen many changes in the sport. In fact, I have been responsible for many changes myself. But the world has changed dramatically. Moms and dads are working two jobs, and recreation centers and school physical education programs have been eliminated due to budget cuts. The popularity of computer games and lack of parental supervision have produced a generation of children sitting in front of the television and dealing with the challenges of drugs, alcohol, bullying and sedentary lifestyles.

I am an innovator and have always been willing to explore different roads to success. I believe that this program deserves our earnest support. I'm well aware of the supporters and critics of innovative thinking. They surfaced when I started my Academy, and they surfaced when the USTA introduced the 10 and Under program. This initiative, designed to attract youngsters to tennis, introduced the following:

- Various sizes of smaller racquets
- Foam and low-compression balls
- Smaller courts
- Lower nets

The USTA came to IMG Academy to demonstrate the program and to solicit my feedback. I told them to review the names that adorn the banners on our stadium court. These names include not only the players who achieved world No. 1 rankings, but dozens who were among the best in the world. At the time, I responded quickly and withheld my endorsement, although it didn't take long for the program to spread. While it received mixed reviews, the positives far outweighed the negatives.

Over time, I gave the program further consideration and came to the following conclusions:

- Young children need to be successful in their early tennis experiences. They need to look forward to their next lesson and above all, they must have fun.

- The motor skills of children in the 10-and-under category are changing dramatically. Increased strength and heart and lung capacity give children the endurance to improve their performance in athletic skills.

It's a daunting experience for a small child to hold a full-size racquet and then have a regular tennis ball come at him from 40 to

60 feet away. It's a wonder how we ever expected our young athletes to deal with a projectile speeding towards them, make the mental calculation as to where the ball would bounce and adjust their bodies to get into the proper position to strike the ball. I now have a new appreciation for the value of the 10 and Under program. I've seen it in action and I know that the kids love tennis as a result.

Not everyone agrees with the 10 and Under program philosophy, the restrictions placed on the children at various levels of competence or the use of balls of varying compression. Many argue that these changes, while designed to make the game easier to enjoy, actually make the transition back to regular court size and ball compression much more difficult.

I urge the USTA to remain open-minded and analyze the program on a continuous basis; it should value the affirmative comments, but give consideration to the negatives, making the appropriate changes so we can continue to increase the number of children being introduced to tennis. I feel certain that this program should continue, and I will provide personal assistance in any way that I can. After all, even if we don't create a pipeline of world-class players, we will be providing kids with opportunities to receive college scholarships, keep their bodies in good health and enjoy tennis for a lifetime.

So, what would I do?

- Develop a questionnaire that would allow us to identify key athletic characteristics, including sports being currently played, winning/losing records, age, height, weight, sports that parents and other relatives played, etc.

- Conduct a talent search throughout America seeking the most gifted 11- to 13-year-old boys and girls.

- Meet with the coaches who have been working with the most talented juniors in America and after an extensive evaluation, enlist them to be part of this development team.

- Ensure that parental involvement—support and potentially negative interference—would be part of the overall evaluation.

- Bring the selected players to IMG Academy.

- Assign IMG Academy experts to oversee the mental and physical development of the athletes.

- Assign the youngsters to dormitories with supervisors that would oversee their studies and provide tutoring when appropriate.

- Keep parents abreast of the progress of their children by providing online video report cards.

- Offer an $800 monthly stipend to families who relocated to Bradenton.

- Discuss the entire program with the NCAA to ensure that the amateur status and eligibility of the students are never put in jeopardy.

- Raise the millions of dollars required to run the program.

I did it before and, with the support of the USTA and others, I am confident that I can do it again!

ACKNOWLEDGMENTS

In a life as full and varied as mine, there are so many people—too numerous to count—who have helped me and made invaluable contributions to my life and career. Some of them I have mentioned and thanked in this book. Others, I want to recognize here. Still others receive acknowledgment on my website, *www.bollettierithebook.com.* If I have left anyone out, it is not intentional—everyone matters to me—and I want them to know that I thank them from the bottom of my heart.

Writing this book has required me to relive the peaks and valleys of my 83 years on this planet and figuring out the complex fabric of my life. I want to thank **Bob Davis** for helping me do that and writing the manuscript with me.

Putting this book together would not have been possible without the tireless support of my manager **Tim Westervelt**, who was 25 when we started the project and ready for Social Security when we finished. Thanks, Tim, for always being there.

The wonderful staff at **New Chapter Publisher** took the initial manuscript and shepherded it to completion. The publisher, **Piero Rivolta**, who has accomplished so many things in his long, creative life, threw his full support behind the project. **Ivana Lucic**, who was a student at the Academy, is now the able president of the company. **Vanessa Houston** made sure all the i's were dotted and all the t's were crossed. Editor **Chris Angermann** brought his experience, invaluable suggestions for rewrites and unwavering vision to bear and made sure all the disparate parts fit together. Gracias to all of them.

A special thanks to **Carolina Murphy** for final name checking and proofing.

I also want to give my appreciation to my son **Jimmy Boy** for his photographs, which do so much to enhance the book.

Since IMG purchased the Nick Bollettieri Tennis Academy, many individuals stepped forward to grow the number and quality of the programs and the reputation of the brand. Key individuals include: **the late Ted Forstmann, Mike Dolan, George Pyne, Knox Millar, Sam Zussman, Greg Phillips, Rohan Goetzke, Chris Ciaccio, Chip McCarthy, Fernando Soler, Mark Tone, Gavin Forbes, Olivier van Lindonk, Max Eisenbud, Tony Godsick, Ben Crandell, Marijn Bal** and **Kevin Callanan;** and there are many others. I wish to thank them all from the bottom of my heart.

Throughout my career, I have worked with many fine coaches from all over the world. Many have been with me for as long as four decades. I want to thank each and every one of them for helping the Academy to become noted for its excellence and for furthering the sport of tennis.

I would like to take this opportunity to thank the many individuals with whom I've had the pleasure to announce or provide color commentary at various events and tournaments across the world. You all know who you are—a fun bunch who cares about tennis and the players and brings the sport closer to its fans.

The USTA is the governing body of tennis in America, and over the years I have had the privilege to work on various projects with them. I would like to recognize the following individuals who made the journey particularly gratifying: **Alan Schwartz, Jon Vegosen, Kurt Kamperman** and **Patrick McEnroe.** I look forward to working with the new president, **John Embree,** and assisting him in any way I can.

Over the years, IMG Academy has been an environment in which students learn not only to play better tennis, but also how to become better coaches. I want to acknowledge the more than 30 players who have gone on to become coaches and share their skills at colleges and universities across the country.

I would like to take this opportunity to thank the local students who were with me at The Colony Beach Resort and the De-Palmer Bollettieri Tennis Club. Your pioneering spirit will never be forgotten: **Rill Baxter, Danielle Bollettieri, Chad and Lisa Glauser, Cayce Connell, Cary Cohenour, Michelle and Mike DePalmer, Jr., Mark and Sarah Dickerson, Mark Dickson, Scott Eversol, Debbie and Renee Giroux, Jay and Michelle Heagerty, Susan Jarrell, Moe Kruger, Mary Jo Landry, Greg Liberman, Dave Marcinko,**

Richie Pierro, Brigitte Platt, Lori Saba, Paula Scheb, Steve Shulla, Mandy Stoll and **Tony Zanoni.**

Sponsors who have been at my side through most of my career include **Adidas, Fila, Polo** and **Nike** with **Phil Knight** and **Ian Hamilton.** Thanks to **Oakley** for protecting my eagle eyes. A special thanks to **Greg Yep** and **Mark Kovacs** of **Pepsico** for selecting me to host inner-city clinics. I started with **Prince** in the late 70s and introduced with my coach Fritz Nau the first oversized racquet. And finally **Under Armour** and its CEO **Kevin Plank:** All of my families and friends are clothed head to toe with Under Armour. You and your team are special.

I want to take the opportunity to recognize **Andy Roddick** and thank him for his many years of playing in Davis Cup tournaments and on the pro circuit. Even though he never trained with me or at IMG, he has always given every ounce of his being on the tennis court. I use him in my speeches and teaching as an example of courage, commitment and determination that is found in all successful people, both on and off the tennis court.

Individuals that I want to especially recognize:

John Donovan and **Keith Callahan:** Thank you for allowing me to offer my recommendations for improvement to the MAC Club. Under your leadership and oversight, it has become one of the top clubs and training centers in the northeast, as well as the home of the Boston Lobsters. I look forward to many more years working with you, along with **Francisco** and **Todd.**

Yoram Ben Israel: I will always be your coach. Cindi and the boys love you.

Andrea Temesvari: Thank you for all that you do for me at Wimbledon. You were one heck of a tennis player, and always the best with me when I was coaching you.

Bill Rompf: You have been at my side for almost 30 years and I will never forget all you try to do for me.

My cousins Cindy and **Kenny,** and **my niece Mary Lou:** Thank you with all my heart for always being at my side.

The Dagostine Family: Andre and I will do all we can for Marshall to reach his dreams to become a top Division 1 college player. My boys and Cindi love spending time with you guys.

The Khanin family: I could write volumes about our relationship, but always know that our friendship will go on. We miss having your son Daniel at the Academy.

The Neel family: Gio and Giacomo love to play with your children, and I love being the coach for your daughter **Ingrid** who brings a different dimension to my teaching: Come to the net, baby!

Mark Verstegen: Thank you for your research to better athletic performance.

Billy Rose, Sammy Aviles, Calvin Cole, Michael Bales, Don Barr, Joe Catabano, Ronnie Robinson, Jeff Russell, Gabriel Trifu, Mike Henderson, Jose DeMata (MuMu), Jose Bernald (Cookie) and **Dennis Pelegrin:** Thank you for your many years of support and friendship, and good luck in the future as fine tennis coaches.

Bill Saba: It sure is a welcome surprise every time you deliver a new car to our family. Many thanks to you and to the **Firkins** dealership.

Christian Harrison: I've never had a student who has had so many injuries and setbacks, and yet keeps fighting to go on. You inspire me with your courage.

David Legge: Thank you for the idea of a Nick Bollettieri life story. The interviews you did were a huge help to my team when writing this book.

David Porter: Many thanks for all your behind-the-scenes support to me, the USPTA and Tim Heckler.

David Portnowitz, John Roberts and **Megan Callaghan:** You all did super jobs keeping me in check when you were my assistants at IMG. Thank you for all your efforts on my behalf.

Peter and **Louise McGraw:** Even though you are back down under in Australia, I will always remember the good old days when we did so much together.

Paul "Killer" Kilderry: You might be small in size, but you have the heart of a lion. I will always look back at your days at IMG with Betsy and Mark McCormack with a smile. Don't ever stop being who you are.

Bunner Smith and **Larry Denyes:** Both of you did whatever I needed and more as students and coaches at NBTA and continue to do so today.

Mark Dalzell: You are a special man with a beautiful family. Many thanks for always being faithful to me and my family.

Ken Merritt: We have argued, fought and called each other names, but never once has our friendship faltered.

Jeff Dillman: You will always be my big man who makes his students get bigger, stronger and always respect their sport.

Peter Bodo and **Ed McGrogan:** It sure is fun doing the wrap-up each day at the U.S. Open. Let's keep going.

Steve Flink, Bill Simons, Jon Wertheim, Brett Haber, Chris Cleary and **Doug Robson:** I appreciate getting to know all of you as outstanding tennis announcers and commentators.

Peg Connor: You will always be my (Prince) girlfriend. You do a super job for Prince Racquet Company. Keep going.

Miguel Rosa: You do a super job whatever you are assigned to do. Let's do more together with Prince.

Greg Yep and **his family:** Being with you and your family, especially staying at your beautiful home, is so special to me.

Luke and Murphy Jensen (and **Mama Pat**): I am so fortunate that you were students at the Academy. You always give your all, including when you won the 1993 French Open Men's Doubles. I appreciate you and Mama Pat always giving a special cheer for me at tournaments.

Jose Lambert, Glen Weiner and **Pat Harrison:** Thank you for working your magic with our top juniors and pros.

Brigadier General John Pray, ret.: Thank you for guiding all the USO tours and centers, which means so much to our armed forces. Thank you for being my friend and a big hug and kiss to your beautiful wife.

Sam Bhada: Thank you for always making sure I have free rooms during the U.S. Open.

Brian Griffin: I hope we always keep our friendship. It is so special and means so much to me.

Pat Dougherty: You have always been at my side helping with my videos, books and articles.

Jason and **Jared Grose:** You started with me in the 80s. You were outstanding players and became outstanding coaches. I appreciate your commitment to our sport and its players.

To Kim Berard, Dan Tierney and **the dedicated staff that are part of Chris Ciaccio's team:** You do a super job.

Bill Dennis: Many thanks for the times at the Grand Slam Cup and for introducing me to Axel Meyer-Wölden.

Tony Driscoll: You do such a super job coordinating the Sarasota Open. Thank you for naming the ladies' tournament in my name.

Todd Morelle: I am still amazed at your dedication—standing next to me on stadium court at 6 a.m. every morning for several months. You had to leave Orlando at 4 a.m. to be with me to enrich your teaching skills.

Tom Perrotta: Tom, I really have so much fun doing our "Ask Nick" questions from the readers of *Tennis Magazine*. We make a great team. Many thanks.

Jimmy Nagelson: Thank you for wanting to help the entire world and expecting nothing in return, as a coach at IMG and now assisting your sister Betsy, who coaches the women's tennis team at the State College of Florida. I only wish there were more people like you.

Chris Kermode: I appreciate that you and your staff have taken the ATP Tour to another level. If you ever need my assistance please get in touch with me. IMG will continue to develop players who, hopefully, will be a part of your tour.

David Brewer: I can still close my eyes and see you as one of my coaches at Beaver Dam and The Colony in the 70s. You have come a long way in your career, being the tournament director of the U.S. Open.

The Gullen family: We will always remember your sons Phillip and Lenny from when they attended IMG as full-time students. Cindi misses Mrs. Gullen's humor; and thanks for the pool table.

Ivo Barbic, Jack Sharpe and **Kevin Kane:** I am sure glad that I didn't have to pay you commissions when you sent your students to the Academy. Ivo, don't give up on Fuzzy and Bouncy!

Toby Foxcroft: Thank you for your time as director of the IMG program in Berlin, for arranging all of the special events I do before Wimbledon and your friendship.

Trevor Moawad: I was honored that upon your departure from IMG, I was the first one you told how you felt. You will always be rememberd by me and my family.

Sandy Klotz: Thanks for being my nurse at Dorado Beach. Nate sends his best.

Art Seitz and **Russ Adams:** When it comes to getting tennis photos on the tour, you are the best of the best. Many thanks.

Stacey Allaster: The WTA has sure come a long way since you became CEO. Under your guidance and with your support team, the women's game has grown in number and in reputation. I hope players from the IMG Academy stand tall for you in promoting tennis throughout the world.

Charles Bricker: Thanks for your supportive articles on The Colony, NBTA and the IMG Academy.

Jim Martz: I have always had fun doing articles with you.

Judge Kahn: Thank you for all the legal advice you have given me and my family.

Melton Little: You were there for all of my divorces, making sure I'd be okay.

Alan Siegel: Your words of wisdom, taking into account all sides of a story, have made a major impact on many of my decisions.

Anthony Gaudio: Thank you for being a tennis fanatic and working up the courage to come up to me and introduce yourself to me; for sending your students to the IMG Academy; and for making it possible for me and my staff to run clinics in New York's Central Park without a fee. I value your friendship beyond words.

Paul Forsyth: Thank you for your humor and ability to tell stories in ways that tie up people in knots for the whole day.

Richie Macey: I appreciate your work as business manager for the IMG tennis program and thank you for always helping me out.

Killeen Mullen: Many thanks for all your work at the very beginning of IMG, even though you abandoned tennis for football when you became director of special events and team operations for the Tampa Bay Buccaneers.

Roger Blackburn: As the spark plug in the adult program for over a decade, your energy and sincere kindness is beyond words.

Steve Shenbaum: Thank you for creating the program that helps prep athletes for interviews. You're an angel to all those you teach.

Bill Galvano: Thank you for your many years of support. We are fortunate to have you represent our district in the state legislature.

Irene Turner: I'm in awe of the way you handle the 50 pros in the tennis program, all their phone messages and emails, and still manage to take care of my extra needs.

Major Dep: Thank you for taking care of logistics for all of my visits to West Point.

And last, but certainly not least, **Steve Sutherland:** You are always ready to help needy students, whether it is with tournaments, tuition or room and board, and ask nothing in return. You also supported Camp Kaizen and honored me by entrusting your daughter Elizabeth to me at the Academy for the past four years. I cannot thank you enough.